Growing Bulbs

ALREADY PUBLISHED

Growing Fuchsias
K. Jennings and V. Miller

Growing Hardy Perennials
Kenneth A. Beckett

Growing Dahlias
Philip Damp

Growing Irises
G.E. Cassidy and S. Linnegar

Growing Cyclamen
Gay Nightingale

Violets
Roy E. Coombs

Plant Hunting in Nepal
Roy Lancaster

The History of Gardens
Christopher Thacker

Slipper Orchids
Robin Graham with Ronald Roy

Growing Chrysanthemums
Harry Randall and Alan Wren

Waterlilies
Philip Swindells

Climbing Plants
Kenneth A. Beckett

1000 Decorative Plants
J.L. Krempin

Better Gardening
Robin Lane Fox

Country Enterprise
Jonathan and Heather Ffrench

The Rock Gardener's Handbook
Alan Titchmarsh

In Preparation

The Pelargonium Species
William J. Webb

Wine Growing in England
J.G. Barrett

Victorians and their Flowers
Nicolette Scourse

The Cottage Garden Year
Roy Genders

Growing Begonias
E. Catterall

Growing Roses
Michael Gibson

Growing Lilies
D.B. Fox

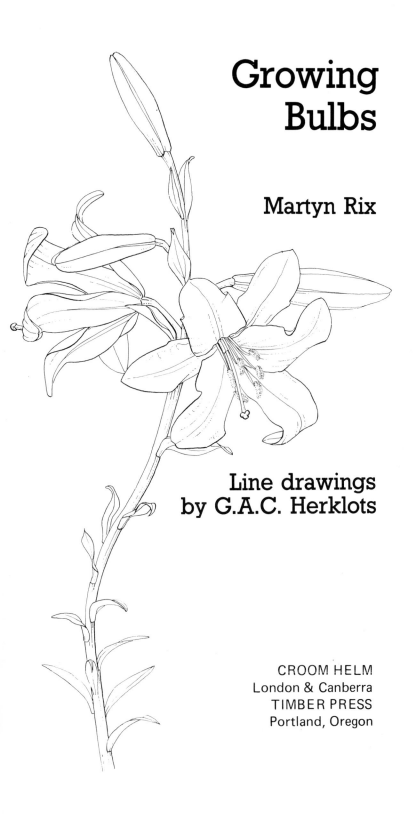

Growing Bulbs

Martyn Rix

Line drawings
by G.A.C. Herklots

CROOM HELM
London & Canberra
TIMBER PRESS
Portland, Oregon

© 1983 E. Martyn Rix
Croom Helm Ltd, Provident House, Burrell Row,
Beckenham, Kent BR3 1AT

British Library Cataloguing in Publication Data

Rix, Martyn
Growing bulbs,
1. Bulbs
I. Title
635.9'44   SB425

ISBN 0-7099-2248-5

First published in the USA in 1983 by
Timber Press,
PO Box 1632
Beaverton, OR 97075
USA
ISBN 0-917304-87-X

Printed and bound in Great Britain by
Biddles Ltd, Guildford and King's Lynn

Contents

List of Figures   vii

List of Tables   ix

Acknowledgements   x

Introduction   1

1   The Evolution of Bulbous Plants   5

2   The Evolution of Flowers   13

3   Seed Dispersal Mechanisms in Bulbous Plants and
     Vegetative Propagation   39

4   Bulb-growing Areas of the World   43

5   A Brief History of Bulb Growing and Collecting   93

6   Cultivation of Hardy Bulbs   125

7   Cultivation of Tender Bulbs   145

8   Propagation of Bulbs   150

9   Pests and Diseases of Bulbs   157

Appendix I: Bulb Genera, Notes and Sources   167

Appendix II: Suppliers and Societies   189

Bibliography   198

Index   203

List of Figures

1.1   *Iris nepalensis*   10

2.1 *Hypoxis rooperi*   14
2.2 *Tigridia meleagris*   18
2.3 *Lilium candidum*   23
2.4 *Gladiolus callianthus*   24
2.5 *Amaryllis solandrifolia* Cutler 19117   25
2.6 *Gloriosa superba*   26
2.7 *Amaryllis evansiae*   27
2.8 *Placea arzae*   30
2.9 *Phaedranassa carmioli*   35
2.10 *Stenomesson variegatum*   37

3.1 *Scadoxus cinnabarinus*   40
3.2 *Eucharis candida*   42

4.1 *Lycoris aurea*   48
4.2 *Lilium nepalense*   50
4.3 *Vagaria parviflora*   62
4.4 *Bloomeria crocea*   71
4.5 *Eustephia coccinea*   76
4.6 *Leucocoryne ixioides*   79
4.7 *Zantedeschia albomaculata*   82
4.8 *Scadoxus nutans*   83
4.9 *Tigridia pavonina*   86
4.10 *Amaryllis calyptrata*   87
4.11 *Stenomesson peruvianum*   89
4.12 *Worsleya rayneri*   90
4.13 *Eurycles cunninghamii*   92

5.1 *Sprekelia formosissima*   96
5.2 Cyclamen: after an engraving from
     Hortus Eystettenis (1613)   98
5.3 *Haemanthus coccineus*: after an engraving
     by Nicolas Robert   100
5.4 *Cypella herbertii*   103

5.5 *Amaryllis machupijchensis* 112
5.6 *Amaryllis advena* B.C.W. 4999 117

6.1 *Galtonia viridiflora* 133

7.1 *Hymenocallis calathina* 146
7.2 *Hymenocallis fragrans* 149

8.1 *Lilium brownii* var *australe* showing hypogeal germination; *Lilium neilgherrense*, showing epigeal germination 153

9.1 *Eurycles amboinensis* 159

List of Tables

2.1   Genera with a Subterranean Ovary   21

Acknowledgements

Many people have contributed much towards this book, by their kindness and enthusiasm, and in telling me how they grow their bulbs. I should particularly like to thank Dr Geoffrey Herklots who has given me the line drawings he has done over many years from plants he has grown himself. Many of them were grown also by Harry Hay, and he has been a continual source of practical advice based on his experience of growing rare bulbs in southern England; I should like to thank both him and Mrs Hay for their kindness. Brian Mathew and Chris Brickell have also been most kind in answering all my questions and giving me the benefit of their experience. I should like to thank also Alison Goatcher for all her help and advice in the preparation of the book, and for the index.

Introduction

This book is intended to make bulb-growing more rewarding and interesting by describing its background in some detail and discussing where and under what conditions bulbs grow in the wild, how they may have evolved, and the circumstances of their introduction into cultivation. The individual species are not described; apart from considerations of space, notes on all the commonly grown bulbs can be found elsewhere, notably in Brian Mathew's excellent books *Dwarf Bulbs* and *Larger Bulbs*, and photographs of most hardy (zone 6) bulbs can be found in *The Bulb Book* by Martyn Rix and Roger Phillips. Further details of rarer species can be found by using Appendix I of this book, which attempts to give the most up-to-date, useful references on each genus.

Most ornamental bulbous plants are covered by this book. The word 'bulb' is used in a wide and inexact sense, to include true bulbs, corms and tubers, as well as some related genera with thickened fleshy roots. The majority of bulbs which are of ornamental value belong to three families: the lily family (Liliaceae), the daffodil family (Amaryllidaceae), and the iris family (Iridaceae). The development of different types of bulbs is. described in Chapter 1.

Orchids have mostly been omitted, although many have tubers or corm-like organs called pseudo-bulbs. This is because they are covered by a great number of books already and because most of them require special cultural methods and conditions, being tropical epiphytes. Temperate orchids will grow in the open garden, as most are terrestrial, but few have been raised successfully from seed; most are short-lived in gardens and rely on repeated importations from the wild. For this reason I believe that their cultivation should not be encouraged until they can be raised commercially in sufficient numbers. There are a few exceptions to this; *Pleione* associates well with other subalpine or woodland plants and is now raised from seed as well as being easy to divide. Similarly some marsh orchids are good garden plants, and increase well in cultivation, notably *Dactylorhiza foliosa*, introduced over 150 years ago.

1

Some interesting generalisations may be made about the distribution of bulbs, corms and tubers between the main families. The iris family with about 70 genera and 1,500 species has a large number of genera and species which are exclusively corm-bearing, though *Iris* itself contains species with all four types of storage organs. One or two genera, e.g. *Sisyrinchium*, are primarily herbaceous, but the family as a whole has a substantial majority of cormous species.

The Amaryllidaceae has about 85 genera and around 800 species, the vast majority of which have simple bulbs. The Liliaceae and the Amaryllidaceae are not clearly distinct, and there is continual disagreement about the position of genera such as *Allium* and *Agapanthus* which have flowers in umbels and a superior ovary.

In any event the family Liliaceae is very heterogeneous with about 200 genera and 3,600 species. Bulbs are common, corms and tubers less so, and many genera are normal herbaceous plants without any modified storage organs, e.g. the lily-of-the-valley (*Convallaria*), hostas and many others. Other important families for the bulb grower are the Araceae, with about 70 genera and 2,000 species, mainly in the tropics and many not tuberous, and those families related to the gingers, the Marantaceae, Zingibera-ceae, Costaceae and Cannaceae, which are almost exclusively tropical. Other mainly tropical families with bulbous members are the Tecophilaeaceae, the Haemodoraceae, and the yam family, the Dioscoreaceae.

Apart from these, bulbous species are scattered throughout the non-woody families of the plant kingdom. Often one or two members of a genus have evolved a root system which enables them to colonise, or survive in a region with a dry climate or prolonged dry season. Examples will be found in Appendix I, but among commonly grown ornamentals the following are especially important: Ranunculaceae (*Ranunculus*, *Anemone*); Fumariaceae (*Corydalis*); Oxalidaceae (*Oxalis*); Geraniaceae (*Geranium*, *Pelargonium*); Gesneriaceae (*Gloxinia*, *Achimenes*, etc.); Primu-laceae (*Cyclamen*), and Begoniaceae.

Bulbs have evolved to enable the plant to survive desiccation during the dry season, so that they grow in areas which have a regular and often prolonged warm, dry season, such as is found in the Mediterranean area or in parts of the tropics. In the mediterranean climate the growing season is cool and wet and in the tropics the growing season is hot and wet. These climates, the areas which experience them, and the different bulbs found there, are described in Chapter 4. Other groups of plants have evolved different ways of surviving the dry season: shrubs and trees, by

2

becoming deciduous or small-leaved evergreens; many grasses, Cruciferae, Leguminosae (vetches) and Compositae (daisies), by becoming short-lived annuals, and Cactaceae, Crassulaceae, Aizoaceae, Asclepiadaceae and Euphorbiaceae, by becoming succulents.

It may seem strange that many bulbs grow in water or at least in moist or shady places where normal herbaceous plants would thrive equally well. Apart from the many water irises, the summer snowflake, *Leucojum aestivum* in Eurasia, and the many *Crinum* species in the tropics are the most familiar examples. It appears that, although bulbs are initially formed in response to a dry season, when a plant migrates to a wetter climate, or when the climate of an area becomes wetter, the bulbous habit is retained, and reversion to a non-bulbous rootstock is relatively slow. The quick growth and flowering necessary for the survival of a bulb in California or in the steppe climate of Central Asia still provides an advantage, to a bluebell or a *Trillium*, for example, in the woodlands of western Europe or North America.

Some water plants which grow in seasonal pools have evolved tuberous rhizomes with which to survive the dry season; examples are many tropical waterlilies (*Nymphaea*) and several *Aponogeton* species. An interesting group of plants are most highly evolved in South Africa; they are semi-aquatic members of primarily terrestrial genera which live in vleis, such as *Romulae aquatica*, *Dipidax triquetra*, and *Oxalis natans*, a beautiful but rare and endangered species in which the leaves and flowers float on the surface of the water.

Bulbs are grown for their large and beautiful flowers or for their weird and unusual ones. These flowers have evolved so as to be attractive to insects and birds which will then pollinate them. Very few bulbs have been observed long enough in the wild for their pollination to be recorded, but probable pollinators can be deduced by comparison with flowers whose natural pollination has been recorded, or by observing pollination in the garden where the range of insects or birds may be similar to those of the natural habitat. Some of the different flower types and their probable pollinators are described in Chapter 2. Travellers can make valuable records of pollinators in the wild, and gardeners can understand some of the possible reasons for the wealth of flower shapes, scents and colours, for the diversity within a single genus, and for the striking parallels between genera.

Changes in the Latin names of plants are the bane of all gardeners and of most botanists. In this book the most up-to-date names are used where possible, but the more familiar ones are also mentioned. The basic problem in many cases is that the earliest

3

name for a species is the correct one, and the researcher often turns up an earlier name than that commonly used, or discovers that a name has become attached to a different species than that originally intended by the author. An unfortunate example which has recently come to light is the belladonna lily from South Africa. When Linnaeus described *Amaryllis belladonna* in 1753 he was not certain of its native habitat, and it was Herbert who attached Linnaeus' name to the South African plant with pale pink flowers. A more critical reading of Linnaeus' account of the name makes it almost certain that he intended to describe not the pale pink South African bulb, but the West Indian red-flowered bulb, usually called *Hippeastrum puniceum*. If this is accepted, all the 75 or so species of *Hippeastrum* from South America must have their names changed to *Amaryllis*! Furthermore, the beautiful belladonna from South Africa becomes *Brunsvigia rosea*.

From the name of a plant the aficionado can often tell a lot about its country of origin and the date and circumstances of its discovery. Chapter 5 describes some of the collectors and growers of bulbs. Many Latin names commemorate explorers, gardeners and scientists, and a knowledge of their lives and careers can make the names more interesting and at the same time easier to remember. At the end of Chapter 5 a list of collectors' names is given, so that the field notes of plants cited under collector's number may be located.

The final chapters of this book give some ideas for bulb-growing in the garden and greenhouse, but they are based only on my own experience of growing bulbs in southern England. Gardeners should above all be prepared to experiment, bearing in mind the conditions in which bulbs survive in the wild and considering how these may be reproduced in the garden.

CHAPTER 1

The Evolution of Bulbous Plants

The essential characteristic of a bulbous plant is that part of it is swollen so that it can store food and pass the unfavourable season underground in a dormant state. At the same time, the stored food enables it to grow up and flower very quickly, as soon as conditions, usually of moisture or warmth, become favourable.

Many different types of storage organ have evolved, depending on exactly which part of the plant becomes modified. For convenience they are often all called bulbs, although there are, strictly speaking, four main types: true bulbs, corms, rhizome tubers and root tubers. It is interesting to compare the different types to see how far they have evolved in different plants and to investigate their distribution among the different plant families. In the next two chapters, flower types and their evolution in the major bulbous families will be examined and different seed dispersal mechanisms will be described. The three parts of the plant have evolved independently: the bulbs in relation to climate and soil moisture, the flowers in response to pollinators, and seed dispersal in relation to habitat.

Many bulbs, corms and rhizomes are familiar as vegetables, the sugars and starch which are stored in them making them valuable as food; onions and Florence fennel are good examples of true bulbs, kohlrabi and celeriac are corms, Jerusalem artichokes and potatoes are different types of rhizome tubers, and carrots and parsnips are rather unspecialised root tubers.

These bulbous vegetables have been selected by gardeners within the last thousand years, for their food value, often from non-bulbous wild plants. The following discussion draws attention to some of the bulbs that have evolved in the wild, by natural selection in response to climate, on a much greater timescale.

Bulbs are formed by the swelling of bases of leaves or leaf stalks. Fennel has already been mentioned as an example of a bulb and the transition from a normal-looking plant to a well-developed bulb can be clearly seen in a poorly grown row in the

Bulbs

5

garden. Leeks and celery show many of the characteristics of primitive poorly developed bulbs; the onion is the most familiar example of a well-developed bulb, made up of concentric rings of swollen leaf bases. Many different types of bulbs have developed in nature and been brought into gardens as ornamentals.

The simplest type of bulb is that shown by an amaryllis or a nerine. All the bulb scales are formed from the bases of old leaves and the flowers appear at the side, from between old leaves or scales. The scales are closely wrapped round one another and are attached to a basal plate, which is all that remains of the main stem of the plant. The new leaves whose bases become scales are formed in the centre of the bulb.

In the daffodil bulb, *Narcissus* species, the flower appears between the current year's youngest leaves and some of the scales have never had leaves at their tips, though they may have formed the sheath which protects the bases of the new leaves. The hyacinth (*Hyacinthus orientalis*) is similar, with some scales formed from the bases of the leaves, while other scales are always enclosed in the bulb. The outermost scales of all these bulbs become dry and papery and form a protective coat or 'tunic' round the bulb. The thickness of the tunic varies greatly between species but, as it protects the bulb from drying, is generally thicker on species from dry climates.

Bulbous irises, such as *I. xiphium* and the pale blue Dutch iris, 'Wedgewood', commonly seen in florists, have few-scaled bulbs and the numerous tunics are formed both by old leaf bases and by dried-up scales. The individual scales are much more swollen than are those of the hyacinth and do not form a complete ring. In the early-flowering dwarf *I. reticulata* the bulb has even fewer scales and the reticulate tunic is formed by the bases of the previous year's leaves. In these and in most of the other few-scaled bulbs, each scale lasts only one year, whereas in many-scaled bulbs the scales tend to last about two years before they dry out and form the tunic.

The tulip is the most familiar garden plant that has a few-scaled bulb. There are no basal leaves in a mature tulip plant so that all the scales are formed inside the bulb, beside the stem. The old scales form the tunic when they dry and in many species they are densely covered inside with silky hairs, a further protection against desiccation. If a bulb which has been growing undisturbed for several years is dug up, there will often be many separate tunics encircling the bulb so that it is very well protected from drying, freezing or even from pests in the surrounding soil.

In lily bulbs (*Lilium* species), and in the bulbs of several other genera, the bulb scales are separate and do not encircle the bulb. No tunic is formed, either by the old scales or by the leaf bases. Lilies are usually found in areas with rainfall in summer and not in the very dry areas favoured by bulbs with thick tunics. Most lilies have leaves only on the stems, unless they are immature, and the bulb scales are formed separately around the base of the stem. When the plants are very young, basal leaves are formed and the bases of these leaves become swollen to form the first scales of the young bulb. *Cardiocrinum giganteum*, often called *Lilium giganteum*, and other *Cardiocrinum* species, differ from *Lilium* in that all the bulb scales are formed from the bases of the previous year's leaves. They remain in the juvenile stage, with basal leaves only, until the huge bulb reaches flowering size. After flowering the bulb dies and several smaller ones are formed around it. These need growing on for several years before they flower. An intermediate stage is seen in the Madonna lily (*L. candidum*), which produces basal leaves which form bulb scales at the same time as the flowering stem. Other lily bulbs have scales of various shapes, from thin, narrow and flat to short and thick. Most are simple, but some are jointed, as if the parts formed from petiole and leaf blade are differentiated. Most bulbs have a short upright axis, but some of the American species, such as *L. pardalinum*, have a bulb with a creeping axis.

Two genera closely related to lilies have rather different bulb types. *Notholirion* has a bulb with a tunic, rather like that of a Dutch iris. *Fritillaria* species have two distinct bulb types: most species have few-scaled bulbs without tunics. In the crown imperial (*Fritillaria imperialis*), the scales are wrapped round each other, making a large, almost spherical bulb. In the snake's head (*F. meleagris*), there are just two or three very fat scales attached only at their bases. They can easily be broken apart – a good method of propagation. Many of the American species have a large number of separate scales, e.g. *F. liliacea*, and are like miniature lily bulbs. This type of bulb reaches its extreme in *Fritillaria camschatcensis* from Japan, eastern Siberia and Alaska. The main bulb of around six scales is surrounded by a hundred or more bulblets, sometimes called 'rice-grains', which either break off to form new bulbs or are absorbed into the parent bulb and replaced every year.

Many-scaled lily-like bulbs are also found as isolated examples in other genera and families. In the South African *Drimia haworthoides*, the bulb scales elongate and swell in their second year, producing a bulb like a very open lily. Also in the

Liliaceae, *Scilla lilio-hyacinthus* from damp places in France and Spain has bulbs with many separate yellowish scales. In the family Gesneriaceae, bulb-like structures are found in several genera. The tropical American *Achimenes*, popular as a greenhouse plant for hanging baskets, produces underground stems which end in small elongated bulbs made up of many thickened overlapping scales. In the related genus, *Isoloma*, these scaly bulbs are formed in the leaf axils. Similar but fewer-scaled bulbs are found also in many temperate and even alpine and arctic plants. Coralroot, *Dentaria bulbifera* (*Cruciferae*), native of woods in southern England and Europe, has elongated underground bulbs and bulbils in the leaf axils. In *Saxifraga*, bulbs are formed by the meadow saxifrage, *S. granulata*, at ground level, by the arctic-alpine, *S. cernua*, in the leaf axils, often at the expense of the flowers, and even by the mossy saxifrage from southern Spain, *S. erioblasta*, at the centre of each rosette.

Corms

As their alternative name 'stem tubers' signifies, corms are the swollen bases of stems. They consist of a single swollen organ, which is replaced every year, and usually consists of a flattened or elongated sphere. In some plants, e.g. the common montbretia, *Tritonia* × *crocosmiflora*, the old corm survives and a new one is added each year. The new shoot emerges from the top (or side) of the corm and roots from the base.

Corms are found in fewer genera than bulbs, but many of these genera are important to gardeners. In the Iridaceae corms are common; they are found in *Crocus* and *Romulea*, in *Gladiolus* and its relatives such as *Watsonia* and *Freesia*, and in the iris-like *Gynandriris* and *Moraea*. In these genera, and in *Crocus* in particular, the corm-tunic is well developed. It is formed by the bases of the previous year's leaves and sheaths and may be either smooth or netted, coarse or fine, papery or fibrous.

In the Liliaceae corms are rarer; they are found in *Erythronium* and *Colchicum* and in the related genus *Androcymbium*, from Africa, Crete and southern Spain. In America they are found in the large genus *Brodiaea* and in the Mexican *Milla*. Other examples are *Tecophilaea* and the genus *Wachendorfia*, a tall iris-like plant in the family Haemodoraceae.

The pseudo-bulbs of many tropical orchids are somewhat akin to corms but they rest on the surface of the substrate or in moss. While some, e.g. *Pleione*, may be almost spherical and of annual duration and so be very corm-like, others, such as those of *Dendrobium nobile*, are merely swollen aerial stems.

The Evolution of Bulbous Plants

It is interesting that, although members of the family Amaryllidaceae have formed different types of bulbs, they have developed neither corms nor root tubers. It is the only family to produce only one type of storage organ.

Tubers are of two kinds, formed from underground stems — rhizome tubers — or from swollen roots — root tubers. In both a continuous gradation can be seen, often in the same genus, between a normal rhizome and a spherical tuber, or between a thickened root and a tuber.

Because they are often relatively unspecialised, it is not surprising that rhizome tubers are found in many different families, both in monocotyledons and dicotyledons. They are common in the Liliaceae, e.g. in Solomon's seal (*Polygonatum*) and in *Paris*, but are not found in the Amaryllidaceae. In the Iridaceae they are found particularly in *Iris*. Most of the 'bulbous' Araceae, such as *Arum* (the cuckoo pint) and the arum lily (*Zantedeschia*), have rhizome tubers. They are common in the gingers (*Zingiberaceae*), and the related Marantaceae, Costaceae and Cannaceae. There are tuberous species too in many Ranunculaceae, such as *Anemone* and *Eranthis*, the winter aconite. In *Anemone* all stages from a thin rhizome to a rounded tuber can be found in one group, well correlated with the dryness of its habitat in summer; the wood anemone which grows in damp woods in northern Europe has a thin creeping rhizome whereas *A. blanda* from dry hillsides in Greece has an almost spherical one. Other genera with well-developed tubers include *Geranium* and *Pelargonium* in the Geraniaceae; *Bongardia*, *Leontice* and *Gymnospermium* in the Berberidaceae.

Several climbing members of otherwise herbaceous genera or perennial members of otherwise annual genera have also developed tubers. Examples are the climbing monkshood, *Aconitum volubile*, the climbing *Codonopsis* species, and the perennial species of *Tropaeolum* most of which are tuberous. In these the presence of stored food reserves probably helps the plant to grow in the shade, until it has reached the light and grown through the shrubs which support it.

Root tubers have also evolved in many completely unrelated families, although they are commonly found in many Liliaceae and Iridaceae. In some cases the plant has several long swollen roots with a single growing point. Commonly grown examples of this type are *Eremurus*, in which the root is long, tapering and fleshy, and *Asphodelus* where the roots are either all fleshy

9

Figure 1.1
Iris nepalensis

or swollen towards their ends. Similar root-types are found in the tropical genus *Costus*. In dahlias the roots are thickened about their middle and a new set is formed each summer. Smaller root tubers are found in many *Ranunculus* species; rounded and fleshy in the celandines (*R. ficaria*), thinner and capable of surviving complete desiccation in *R. asiaticus* from the eastern Mediterranean. Tubers of this type have even evolved in one *Primula*, *P. fedtschenkoi*, which grows on dry hills in Central Asia near Samarkhand, where there is no rain from May until October. See also *Iris nepalensis* (Figure 1.1).

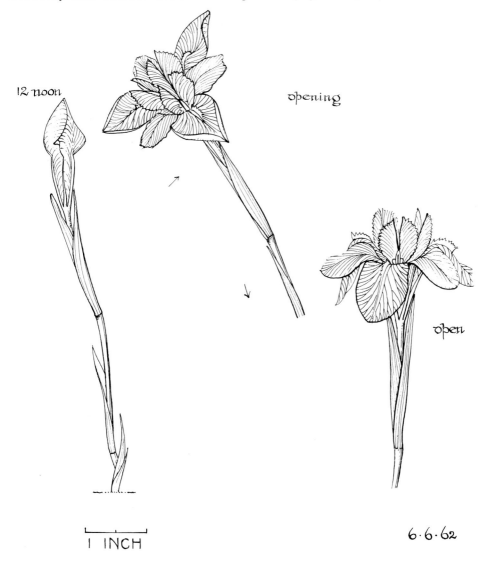

12 noon

opening

open

1 INCH

6.6.62

Single root tubers have evolved in several species, in this case usually from a tap-root. Gradations between a thick tap-root and an almost spherical tuber are found in *Corydalis* in central and western Asia and in *Lewisia* in western North America. Again the thinner-rooted species inhabit areas with relatively moist summers, whereas the tuberous-rooted species inhabit areas with long, dry summers. Orchids provide several particularly good examples of root tubers and again intermediates can be seen between the elongated tubers of *Dactylorhiza*, usually found in wet habitats, and the spherical tubers of *Ophrys* from dry Mediterranean areas.

In some cases it is not clear whether the tuber should be considered a root tuber or a rhizome tuber and, in theory, there is no reason why an organ should not be both at once. In the genus *Cyclamen* some species, e.g. *C. graecum*, root only from the base, giving the impression that the tuber is stem in origin; in others, e.g. *C. purpurascens*, roots emerge from all over the tuber; in the commonest species in gardens, *C. hederifolium*, roots are formed mainly on the upper surface of the tuber, suggesting that it is primarily a swollen root.

Some plants manage to combine bulbs and tubers or bulbs and corms, one storage organ augmenting the other. In the *Scorpiris* (juno) subgenus of *Iris* there is a rather slender bulb with three or four thick tuberous roots emerging from it. Both are necessary for the well-being of the plant, but whereas the bulb by itself will probably not survive, the roots, if they become detached, will often survive and grow a new bulb. In *Eucomis*, a mainly tropical African genus with a few half-hardy species, the rootstock combines both bulb and tuber. The bulb is poorly developed and the basal plate is persistent and swollen, forming a flattened tuber.

CHAPTER 2

The Evolution of Flowers

Since the mid-eighteenth century plants have been classified on the basis of their flowers. This was Linnaeus' great contribution, a standardised nomenclature and a classification based on the number of floral parts, primarily stamens and styles. Although much changed in detail, it has remained until today, and a large number of plants are still called by their Linnaean names.

The main bulbous families are distinguished by their basic flower structure: the Araceae have many small often unisexual flowers crowded onto a spike, the 'spadix', which is subtended by a spathe; the Iridaceae have three stamens and a three-branched style with an inferior ovary; the Liliaceae have six stamens and one or three styles, with a superior ovary; the Amaryllidaceae have six stamens, a three-lobed or entire style and an inferior ovary. Within these limits there has been much evolution in flower shape in response to pollinators and to climate, and in flower colour in response to pollinators. The parallels which have arisen in the different bulbous families are as remarkable as the divergences within the families or within the genera.

Flowers are seldom pollinated exclusively by one species of animal, for instance, bird-pollinated flowers may be commonly visited by bumble-bees, but the pressure towards the evolution of different flower types seems to have been strong, and the main types of pollination syndrome described below can be easily recognised. Both floral biology and pollination syndromes are excellently described by Proctor and Yeo in *The Pollination of Flowers* in the New Naturalist series.

Wind-pollinated Flowers

There seem to be very few species of bulbous plants which are wind-pollinated, and show the combination of large anthers with long filaments, producing large quantities of pollen, together with a brush-like style and reduced nectar-less petals. Those most likely to be wind-pollinated are several species of *Eremurus* from Central Asia. They grow on low hills and steppes, often in large colonies of a single species, flowering at

13

the end of their growth period, after the spring rains have ceased. The petals are reduced and reflexed at maturity, and the large anthers are held horizontal on filaments which elongate as they mature. *Eremurus regelii* and *E. cristatus* from Central Asia are examples of this type of flower, in which the petals are blackish, and another example is *E. spectabilis* from Turkey, which has yellowish petals which curl up before the anthers dehisce.

Insect-pollinated Flowers

The *Scilla* Type

In this group, of which *Scilla bifolia* may be taken as an example, the flowers are very simple, actinomorphic and usually unscented, and are produced many together in a rather loose inflorescence. Although some flower early in the spring, they do not protect themselves from rain by closing in dull weather. Protection may be unnecessary because a number of flowers are produced which open in succession, and therefore if

Figure 2.1
Hypoxis rooperi

some are spoiled, others may open to take their place; a second possibility is that, as in bog asphodel (*Narthecium ossifragum*), transfer of pollen is actually brought about by the raindrops.

Insect pollination is probably more usual, however, by a wide range of flies and bees, attracted mainly by the pollen. Familiar examples of this group are most species of *Scilla*, *Urginea maritima*, most *Eremurus* with showy flowers, such as *E. olgae*, *Asphodelus*, *Ornithogalum*, and many others, especially Liliaceae with spikes or racemes of small flowers. The South African genera *Bulbinella* and *Eucomis* have this type of inflorescence, as does *Wachendorfia thyrsiflora*.

Some genera such as *Chionodoxa* and *Puschkinia* show the beginnings of specialisation, with the filaments swollen and appressed to the ovary to form a tube, and with the tendency towards fewer and larger flowers. In other species of *Scilla*, e.g. *S. verna* and *S. peruviana*, the inflorescence is flat-topped and tends towards that described below, called the 'onion type'.

Few of the Iridaceae have this simple type of inflorescence and flower. In *Gladiolus* a few species such as *G. stellatus* have numerous small flowers, but most have larger, zygomorphic flowers. A few species of other genera close to *Gladiolus*, such as *Lapeirousia erythrantha* from central Africa, do have small simple flowers, though in this case the inflorescence is branched.

The Onion Type

In many species of *Allium* the inflorescence consists of a spherical or flat-topped head, tightly packed with small flowers. They are probably visited by many different types of insects, notably butterflies. In some genera an essentially racemose inflorescence has become umbel-like, providing an easier perch for visiting insects. *Scilla peruviana* and *S. maritima* have been mentioned already, and a similar tendency is found in *Ornithogalum* and *Zigadenus*.

The *Muscari* Type

In *Muscari* the inflorescence is simple with many small actinomorphic flowers, as in *Scilla*, but the individual flowers are bell-shaped and often sweetly scented, producing abundant nectar. The main pollinators are bumble-bees and bee-flies, which can hang upside down on the flowers and get at the nectar with their long tongues. Many genera close to *Scilla* have

15

evolved similar hanging tubular flowers, e.g. the bluebell (*Hyacinthoides non-scripta*), the genera *Bellevalia* and *Hyacinthella*, and in South Africa some species of *Lachenalia*, i.e. *L. orchioides* and *L. mutabilis* with their pale-blue flowers. Some species of *Bellevalia*, e.g. *B. dubia*, and of *Muscari*, e.g. *M. comosum*, have blue or purple sterile flowers at the top of the inflorescence and fertile brownish scentless flowers at the bottom. Knoll (1921, quoted by Proctor and Yeo), found that in *M. comosum* the blue sterile flowers acted as the original attractant, and the bees flew first to these before descending to feed on the fertile flowers. Other experiments carried out by Knoll ruled out scent as the primary attractant.

The tendency towards zygomorphy is seen in the small genus *Alrawia*, with one species, *A. bellii*, which is illustrated in Wendelbo's *Tulips and Irises of Iran*. Its flowers are similar to those of *Bellevalia* but the floral tube is curved downwards.

The *Fritillaria* Type

In many genera the flowers are bell-shaped and hanging, as in *Muscari*, but they are relatively large and produced in small numbers, often only one to each plant. A well-developed and familiar example of this type is the common fritillary, *F. meleagris*. Its main pollinators in England are the large queens of the common bumble-bees (*Bombus* spp.), which can climb right up inside the bell. The nectaries are situated at the angle of each petal, and the stamens and style hang down in the centre of the flower, coming into contact with the back of the large bee.

The hanging bell flower is well adapted to wet cold climates, as the style, pollen and pollinating insect are all protected from any amount of rain and wind. Most of the other fritillaries with large flowers are early-flowering high alpines, e.g. *F. latifolia* from the Caucasus, or from cold windy areas such as *F. affinis* from the north California coastal hills. The large heavy bumble-bees fly early in the year, and can work in windier conditions than lighter insects. Other genera which do not normally have bell flowers have often evolved them, probably in response to wet conditions, either because of their early flowering or because of their flowering during the wet season. In the Himalayas *Lilium nanum* and *L. souliei* have brown pendent flowers, and *L. sherrifiae* also has tessellations, which make it even more like a *Fritillaria*; these, together with several large-flowered *Fritillaria* species, grow at high altitudes and flower during the monsoon.

In *Calochortus*, the early-flowering subgenus *Eucalochortus*, e.g. *C. pulchellus*, has bell-shaped hanging flowers, while the later-flowering subgenus *Mariposa*, e.g. *C. luteus*, has upright tulip-like flowers. In *Scilla* the very early-flowering *S. sibirica* has bell flowers as do a few related species from the cold mountains of northern Turkey. In *Allium*, *A. narcissiflorum* and *A. insubricum* from the Alps and *A. beesianum* from the Himalayas have a few bell-shaped flowers in contrast to the numerous upright flowers of most *Allium* species. Similar bell-shaped flowers are found in the closely related *Nectaroscordum siculum*, a plant of damp shady woods in the Mediterranean region.

Bell-shaped flowers are commonly found in the Amaryllidaceae, for instance, in the daffodil (*Narcissus pseudo-narcissus*). The bell is formed by the corona, a tubular structure distinct from the petals. In the familiar *N. pseudo-narcissus* the flower is held horizontal and slightly nodding, but in the Pyrenean subsp. *moschatus* the flower is even more nodding, and in *N. triandrus* and *N. cyclamineus* it hangs vertically.

In the Iridaceae bell flowers are less common but are found in *Tigridia* from Mexico, which has similarities with *Calochortus* in its range of flower shapes. *T. galanthoides* and *T. meleagris* both have fritillary-like hanging flowers in what is generally an upright-flowered genus. In *Dierama* from South Africa, the flowers are also bell-shaped and hanging and several *Gladiolus* species show the beginnings of campanulate flowers, notably the summer-flowering and almost hardy (zone 6) *G. papilio*.

Bumble-bees have been mentioned as common pollinators of these bell-shaped flowers, but in one group at least, the green- and brown-flowered *Fritillaria*, queen wasps are the most important pollinators. The flowers of these species, e.g. *F. graeca* and *F. pyrenaica*, have a strong spermatic scent, and it is this scent which initially attracts the wasps as well as certain smaller bumble-bees such as *Andrena*. During an experiment some flowering plants of this group in the garden were hidden in muslin cages, and the wasps were seen flying round, trying to enter the cages. In the wild these fritillaries are often found growing hidden inside spiny shrubs which protect them from grazing, so the presence of a strong attractant such as smell would be advantageous to the plant. In other fritillaries the flowers are still bell-shaped, but other pollinators are involved, e.g. blowflies in the black flowers of *F. camschatcensis* and *F. biflora*, and humming-birds in the case of the red *F. recurva*.

Figure 2.2
Tigridia meleagris

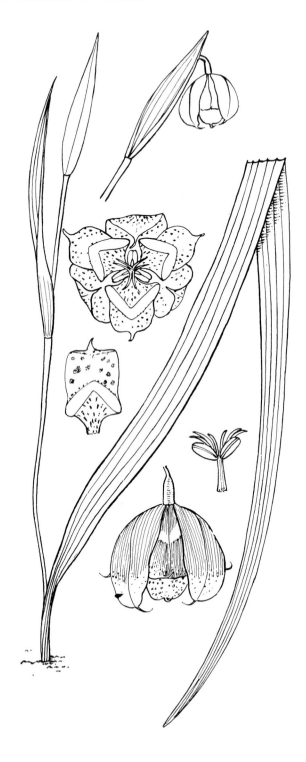

The Tulip Type

The red colour favoured by birds is found in another group of flowers, those with simple petals which open wide in the sun, such as tulips and anemones. Proctor and Yeo take the field poppy (*Papaver rhoeas*) as being typical of this group; there is no nectar but the insects come to collect the pollen which is liberally produced. Poppy flowers last only one day and each plant usually produces many flowers. In tulips only one flower is produced, but the flowers have the ability to stay closed on dull days when visits by insects are in any case less likely, and when the flower might be damaged by rain. Many tulip species have these red flowers, often with a black spot at the base of each petal. This possibly deceives the bees into thinking that there is more pollen to be had than there really is, since the bees see both black pollen and the black basal patch as black. Among other bulbous plants, flowers with this colour scheme are found in *Calochortus kennedyi*. *Ranunculus asiaticus* and *Anemone pavonina* and *coronaria* have no black basal patch but have numerous stamens. It seems likely that yellow and white flowers in these four genera attract a similar range of insects. Similar contrasting centres are found in many South African bulbs, e.g. *Spiloxene capensis*, *Sparaxis tricolor*, *Geissorhiza* and *Ixia*.

The *Crocus* Flower and the Subterranean Ovary

The parallelism shown by the three main bulbous families is particularly striking in this flower type; this is seen in *Crocus* in the Iridaceae, *Colchicum* in the Liliaceae, and *Sternbergia* in the Amaryllidaceae. Other genera in South Africa and in Chile have very similar flowers, and subterranean ovaries are also found in *Iris* in the Middle East.

As far as pollination is concerned the flowers are relatively unspecialised, the insects, probably mainly bees, visiting the flowers primarily for nectar which is exuded at the base of the filaments or seeps up the tube from the ovary. The styles are of various lengths and shapes but are usually rather thin and in a position to intercept incoming insects.

The subterranean ovary is the most unusual feature of this flower type. At flowering the ovary is very little above the corm or bulb, and the only parts above ground are the floral tube which carries the petals and stamens, and the style, which is very long, extending from the ovary up the tube to the flower. The ovary only appears above ground as it ripens in *Crocus*, or is well protected by the developing leaves in *Colchicum*, or emerges in spring on a short stalk in *Sternbergia clusiana*. Having the ovary thus hidden is of benefit to the plant in the protection it gives both against grazing and, in the case of autumn-flowering species, against winter cold. It also enables plants to flower at the end of the dry season, even before their roots have begun to grow after the summer drought. Perfect flowers of all three genera will appear even when the corms are not planted, the necessary water to produce the juicy flowers almost overnight coming from the metabolism of starch inside the corm. The capacity to open and close is well developed in all these flowers, and is regulated by temperature. This provides protection for the pollen and nectar in the unsettled autumn and spring weather.

The stripes and dull colours on the outside of the flowers of most *Crocus* species are probably an added protection against grazing, and the flowers of *Colchicum speciosum* are avoided by grazing cows. The leaves of *Crocus* and *Colchicum* are very different, but both are well adapted to survive, even where grazing is heavy. *Crocus* leaves are narrow and grass-like, and can continue to grow from the base after the tops have been eaten off. *Colchicum* leaves, on the other hand, are often lush and broad, but are very poisonous to cattle, so are not eaten. *Sternbergia* leaves are similar to those of daffodils and are probably eaten only when all the more palatable vegetation has gone.

Where two or more species of *Crocus* grow together, or where members of the three genera grow side by side, the species tend to have differently coloured flowers. I saw this very clearly on the Zigana pass in N. E. Turkey in October 1982. Here *Crocus vallicola* was common, with pure white flowers, growing with masses of *Colchicum speciosum* with crimson to pale pink flowers, but no pure white; mixed with them were a few *Crocus speciosus* with bluish flowers, and nearby were a few *Crocus scharojani* with rich yellow flowers. Further south near Malatya in central Turkey, yellow-flowered *Sternbergia clusiana* grew near mauve *Crocus cancellatus*. *Crocus kotschyanus*, also mauve and flowering at the same time, grows in the same area, but the populations of the two species seemed to be quite separate.

The same colour contrast can be seen in central Asia, where there are two species of *Crocus* and two of *Colchicum*, all of which flower in spring. In the hills south of Samarkhand, flowering in April soon after the snow melts, are the yellow *Crocus korolkowii* and *Colchicum kesselringii*, which is white with mauve stripes. Further east in the mountains near Tashkent two different species flower together: *Crocus alatavicus*, white with blackish stripes outside, and the yellow *Colchicum luteum*.

Different species of different colours flowering together are frequent in *Crocus*, and are found in other genera also, e.g. *Tulipa*, *Fritillaria*. The effect of these colour differences, combined with the flower constancy of bees, is to prevent either hybridisation or pollen wastage by the frequent crossing of incompatible flowers.

Species with crocus-like flowers and subterranean ovaries are found in several other genera and families, in South Africa, California, and Chile, and subterranean ovaries combined with other flower types are found in even more cases. There is strong evidence that these have all evolved independently, so the advantage conferred on plants with this type of flower must be considerable. B.L. Burtt (1970) listed nine independent origins of the subterranean ovary, and his list with additions is shown in Table 2.1. Many species of other genera have the ovary at ground level, and the flowers with a long tube.

Table 2.1 Genera with a Subterranean Ovary (after B.L. Burtt (1970), with additions)

Amaryllidaceae
Anoiganthus
Apodolirion
Crinum
Crocopsis
*Empodium**
*Gethyllis**
Haylockia
*Sternbergia**

Araceae
*Biarum**

Hypoxidaceae
Saniella
Rhodohypoxis rubella

Iridaceae
*Crocus**
Galaxia
Iris persica et al.
Iris reticulata et al.
Lapeirousia oreogena
Romulea (some spp.)
Syringodea

Liliaceae
Bulbocodium
*Colchicum**
*Merendera**
Leucocrinum

The Lily Flower

The flower shape of the typical trumpet lily, such as *L. regale*, is common in the families Liliaceae and Amaryllidaceae, but rare in the Iridaceae. The flower is held more or less horizontal, and the six petals are similar, the three inner somewhat wider than

*species that flower well before the leaves emerge

the three outer petals; the stamens and style are in the centre or towards the base of the trumpet, and are usually longer than the petals. Many of the flowers are white or pale pink in colour and become sweetly scented towards evening. In some the flowers are shallow, but often the tubular base of the trumpet is very long.

Two types of pollinators are common: hawkmoths which hover in the mouth of the flower to suck the nectar secreted at the base of the petals, and come into contact with the protruding stamens and style, and hover-flies which feed on the pollen and also crawl onto the style, attracted by the sticky stigmatic fluid. The smaller trumpet flowers can also be pollinated by bees and flies sucking nectar as well as pollen. (Proctor and Yeo, *The Pollination of Flowers*, p. 193.)

In the genus *Lilium*, white trumpet flowers are particularly common in the warmer parts of eastern Asia, an area where hawkmoths are also present in great numbers and variety. There is only one species, *L. candidum*, the Madonna lily, in the eastern Mediterranean region, and there are two species in western N. America, *L. washingtonianum* and *L. rubescens*. It is interesting to note that, according to most theories on the evolution of lilies, these three are more closely related to the Turk's cap lilies which are found in the same area than to each other, and thus that the white trumpet flower has arisen independently in *Lilium* at least three times. Other genera in the Liliaceae have similar flowers, e.g. the desert lily, *Hesperocallis undulata*, from California, Arizona and Mexico, and the *Notholirion* species from the Himalayas.

The lily flower is common in the Amaryllidaceae, especially in the large genus *Crinum*, and the flowers may have a very long tube, a sure indication of pollination by long-tongued hawk-moths. The common cultivated *Crinum moorei* is an example of this group. In the tropical American genus *Amaryllis* (*Hippeastrum*), the white trumpet flower reaches its extreme form in *A. solandrifolia* in which the tube may be up to 10 cm (4 ins) long. More open, shorter trumpets are found in many genera, notably *Zephyranthes* in America, and in *Brunsvigia rosea*, the belladonna, and in *Cyrtanthus obliquus* in South Africa. In another species of *Cyrtanthus*, *C. mackenii*, the flowers are tubular, white or pale yellow and scented; they are probably moth-pollinated in contrast to the majority of tubular-flowered *Cyrtanthus* species which are red and bird-pollinated.

In some genera of Amaryllidaceae the stamens are attached to a corona which forms the trumpet of the flower, and the petals are almost superfluous. This type of flower is seen in

Figure 2.3
Lilium candidum

Pancratium maritimum, the familiar sea daffodil of Mediterranean beaches. The white flowers are sweetly scented and have
a very long tube and the narrow petals are little longer than the
corona; it is known to be pollinated by hawkmoths. In the south
American genus *Hymenocallis* the flower is very similar.

In the Iridaceae, trumpet lily-shaped flowers are distinctly
rare. One clear, beautiful and familiar example of a hawkmoth-
pollinated flower is the acidanthera (*Gladiolus callianthus*),
found all through east Africa growing on wet rocks. The petals
are white with a dark base and the flower has a curved tube
about 18 cm (7 ins) long. The stamens and style are exserted
from the flower but, as in other Iridaceae, are at the top of the
trumpet. Other long-tubed pale scented flowers are found in
other *Gladiolus* species, e.g. *G. tristis*, and in *Watsonia
ardernei*.

The Turk's Cap Flower

The commonest type of lily flower is not the white trumpet but
the Turk's cap, a downward-pointing flower with reflexed petals

Figure 2.4
Gladiolus callian-
thus (see p. 23)

21 · 10 · 78

5   cms

and style and stamens hanging below the flower. The nectary is located in a groove running down the centre of the basal half of each petal. Each petal forms a separate pollination unit, to be probed separately from a different angle. Proctor and Yeo in *The Pollination of Flowers* give the humming-bird hawkmoth as the pollinator of this type of flower in *Lilium martagon*, and other lilies in all parts of the northern hemisphere have similarly shaped flowers. However, other pollinators must be involved as naturalised populations of *Lilium pyrenaicum*, a yellow Turk's cap, set ample seed in Scotland where hawkmoths are very rare.

The style of most of these lilies is curved to one side to bring the stigma into line with the anthers. An extreme example of this is found in the tropical genus *Gloriosa*. The petals are reflexed or held upright, and the stamens radiate horizontally and end in large versatile anthers; the style, instead of curving, is bent abruptly to the side, so that it is aligned with the anthers as in the normal lily flower (see Figure 2.6).

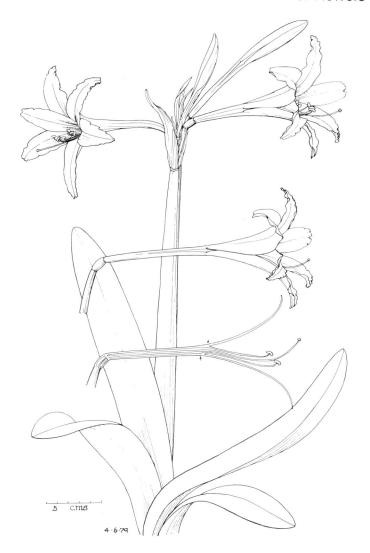

Figure 2.5
Amaryllis solandri-folia Cutler 19117
(see p. 22)

.5 cms

4·6·79

The Cyclamen Type Flower

In several flowers the petals are reflexed like the Turk's cap, but the style and stamens are very short, protruding downwards from the mouth of the flower, the anthers forming a cone around the style. Proctor and Yeo in *The Pollination of Flowers* mention Borage (*Borago officinalis*) as being visited by honey-bees for nectar, and quote Macior (1964) who observed bees visiting the flowers of *Dodecatheon meadia* to collect pollen. The genus *Cyclamen* is closely related to *Dodecatheon* and has a very similar flower structure. The anthers of *Cyclamen* are in a cone, have apical pores, and in some species are almost enclosed in the tube, in others they are exserted. A similar arrangement of stamens and style is found in snowdrops (*Galanthus*), although in this case the outer petals only become reflexed in warm weather and the inner petals remain closed, forming a bell to protect the pollen. Flowers of similar structure to borage are found in the very large genus *Solanum* which has its headquarters in South America, and in Chile a similar flower is found in *Conanthera bifolia* in the Tecophilaeaceae.

The pollinators of the cyclamen-type flowers are honey-bees which take the nectar and extract the pollen from the pores of the stamens by vibrating the flower. Rather similar flowers are found in species in which the stamens do not form a cone, but hang down close to the stigma. *Erythronium*, for example, has flowers of this type, and opens only in warm weather. Similarly shaped flowers are found in *Scilla hohenackeri* and other species in Iran, and in *S. cordifolia* in Africa.

Figure 2.6
Gloriosa superba

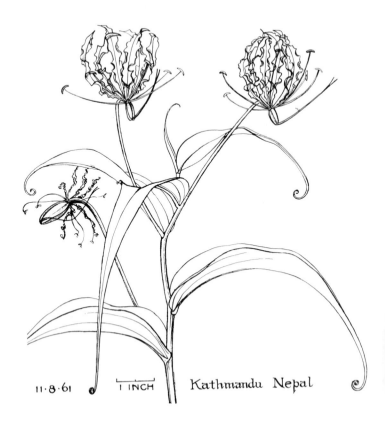

11·8·61   1 INCH   Kathmandu Nepal

The Zygomorphic Flower

Most of the flowers mentioned so far have been radially symmetrical or with two whorls of three more or less equal petals. There is a strong tendency in insect- or sun-bird-pollinated flowers towards a zygomorphic arrangement, in which the flowers are bilaterally symmetrical and the upper and lower parts of the flower are different. This tendency is strongest in those flowers which are held horizontally, so that the lower lip can form a landing platform for the insect or in those flowers in the Iridaceae in which the upper lip can be elongated to reach the head of the sun-bird.

The beginnings of zygomorphic flowers are seen in the asymmetrical position of the stamens and style in trumpet lilies and similar flowers. In a well-developed zygomorphic flower the upper and lower petals are completely different, and are often closely adapted to pollination by a specific insect; other petals may be spurred or otherwise modified to hold nectar.

Figure 2.7
Amaryllis evansiae
coll. P. Herklots,
Bolivia

27

Zygomorphic flowers are relatively rare in the monocotyledons. Only the gingers are exclusively zygomorphic. Most orchids are zygomorphic as are many Iridaceae, notably *Iris*, *Gladiolus*, and those African genera which are bird-pollinated.

There are, however, many examples of zygomorphic flowers among the tuberous dicotyledons. The genus *Corydalis* has many tuberous members in Europe and Asia. The uppermost petal is elongated into a long spur in which nectar collects. The pollination mechanism of *C. cava* from eastern Europe is described in detail by Proctor and Yeo (*The Pollination of Flowers*, p. 203), and shows great similarities to that of many vetches which are pollinated mainly by bumble-bees. In some species, such as the central Asian *C. macrocentra*, the spur is 20 mm (about ³⁄₄ in) long.

Tuberous Scrophulariaceae and Labiateae are common in the dry parts of Central Asia, and most of the genus *Eremostachys* are tuberous. *E. speciosa*, a dwarf species with striking purple and yellow flowers from near Alma Ata, deserves to be more widely cultivated, and many other species have unusual, bi-coloured flowers.

Tuberous *Delphinium* species are common in Turkey, and in the tuberous, climbing *Aconitum volubile* the flowers are typical of an *Aconitum* with the upper petal modified into an S-shaped nectary.

In the Iridaceae, zygomorphic flowers are found mainly in the genus *Gladiolus*, and in red-flowered, bird-pollinated genera such as *Chasmanthe* which are discussed below. In *Gladiolus* every stage can be seen, between a regular, starry flower as in *G. stellatus* and *G. citrinus* and a strongly zygomorphic flower as in *G. orchidiflorus* where the upper petal forms a sharply curving and grooved hood, into which the stamens and style are pressed.

In the Amaryllidaceae, zygomorphy is similarly rare, but the beginnings of it can be seen in *Sprekelia*, mentioned on p. 36 under bird pollination, and in lily-like flowers in which the style and stamens curve downwards towards the base of the flower. This is taken one stage further in the genus *Alstroemeria* from South America, in which two upper petals are usually differently marked and coloured from the others, and the styles and stamens are strongly depressed. Some species are almost actinomorphic, and tubular actinomorphic bird-pollinated flowers are found in the closely related climbing genus *Bomarea*.

On the other hand, in the gingers, and, of course, in the orchids, zygomorphic flowers are usual. The structure of the flowers of the main families is complicated by the reduction in the number of stamens, usually to one (or a half in the *Cannaceae!*) and the petaloid staminodes. The flowers often appear normally zygomorphic with an upper and a lower lip as is seen in the genus *Roscoea* from the Himalayas, one of the few hardy representatives of this primarily tropical order.

In the flowers of the Liliaceae, zygomorphy is also poorly developed. Many trumpet-flowered *Lilium* species, e.g. *L. regale*, have stamens and styles curving upwards from the lower side of the flower. This trend is taken a stage further in *Cardiocrinum* where the lower petal is almost pouched, and the petals are slightly unequal, the lowest becoming longer to form a lip. *C. cordatum* from Japan has more clearly zygomorphic flowers than the other species. A similar trend can be seen in *Camassia* (Stebbins, 1974).

The Iris Flower

The typical iris flower is a very familiar one; the three outer petals curve downwards to form the 'falls', the three inner petals stand up, forming the 'standards', while the three styles are flattened and somewhat petaloid and curve forward over the falls, each covering one of the three stamens. Flowers of this pattern are found in the bearded iris hybrids, and in the species from which they were derived (subgenus *Iris*, section *Iris*), and in the Oncocyclus, Regelia and Pseudo-regelia sections, exotic groups from the semi-deserts of the Middle East and Central Asia.

Within the genus *Iris* in the northern hemisphere several variations have evolved, and similar flower types are found in the related genera *Gynandriris* (*Iris sisyrinchium*), *Hermodactylus* (*I. tuberosa*), and *Pardanthopsis* (*I. dichotoma*). In Southern Africa iris-like flowers are found in several related genera, notably *Moraea* and *Dietes*. The very closely related genus, *Belamcanda*, however, does not have iris-like flowers, but has six equal petals, and slender, not petaloid, styles; it forms hybrids with *Pardanthopsis*.

The iris flower, as far as the pollinator is concerned, consists of three separate zygomorphic flowers, which must be visited separately. Each part is similar in many ways to one complete flower of the snapdragon (*Antirrhinum*). The falls form a lower lip, on which the insect lands, and the petaloid styles form the upper lip. The standards are an extra attractant, especially from side-view, but play no direct part in the pollination mechanism.

Figure 2.8
Placea arzae

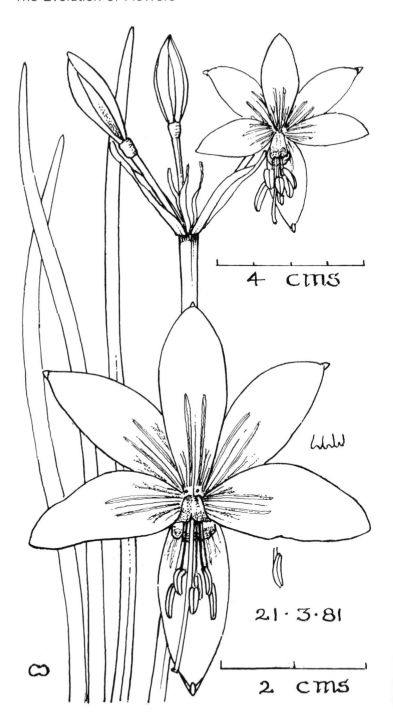

The insect lands on the centre of the falls, attracted in most species by the converging guidelines and by the yellow colour, often augmented by stamen-like hairs, which may indicate the presence of pollen, although the pollen itself is hidden under the styles. The insect pushes up and crawls under the petaloid style, leaving pollen on the style or receiving pollen on its back.

Within this framework, the flowers have evolved in three main ways: towards single, larger flowers, as in the Oncocyclus section, towards more prominent style lobes, often combined with a reduction in standards, as in *Iris danfordiae*, and towards the possession of a subterranean ovary, as in *I. reticulata*. The evolution of single, larger flowers has reached its peak in the Oncocyclus section, where some of the species from the Middle East may have flowers measuring up to 20 cm (8 ins) in diameter, e.g. *I. gatesii*. Most species have a black patch on the centre of the falls, and I have watched large black bee-like flies diving hard at speed onto these patches on falls of *I. elegantissima* on the lower slopes of Mount Ararat and disappearing into the flowers. The Regelia section, from further east, usually have somewhat smaller flowers, and two flowers per stem, without the striking signal patch. However, *Iris afghanica* has single flowers and a clear purplish patch like an Oncocyclus. The Oncocyclus section, and the rather similar Regelia section from further east, also have unusual seeds with a well-developed caruncle, to encourage dispersal (see Chapter 3, page 41).

In most groups, the falls have remained large, but in the Oncocyclus section one or two species have greatly reduced falls, e.g. *Iris paradoxa*, in which the falls are restricted to the area of the beard, and resemble the abdomen of a large, hairy blackish bee, possibly mimicking the pollinator. Pseudo-copulation has been proved in orchids with similar flowers, and patient observation might show it to be the mechanism employed in *I. paradoxa*, and possibly some of the other Oncocyclus species.

The reduction in the size of the standards and a corresponding increase in the upright petaloid part of the styles has occurred, apparently independently, in at least six groups of irises.

In the bulbous reticulata type from the eastern Mediterranean (subgenus *Hermodactyloides*), the largest standards are found in the rare *I. kolpakowskiana* from Central Asia; *Iris reticulata* itself and most other species have only slightly reduced standards, but *I. danfordiae* from central Turkey has tiny standards, about 5 mm (less than ¹⁵ in) long, described by Brian

Mathew as 'bristles'. In the Juno irises (subgenus *Scorpirus*), the standards of most species are reduced in size and are horizontal or pendulous. The largest, about 4 cm (1½ in) long, are found in *I. cycloglossa*, and are held almost horizontal, as are the falls. The smallest standards are found in *I. drepanophylla* which are again almost bristle-like. An unusual intermediate stage is found in *I. fosteriana*, a beautiful plant from the Kopet Dag on the borders of Iran and Turkmenia, in which the styles are large, petaloid and yellow, the standards sharply deflexed and rich purple.

Reduced standards are also found in the Spanish *Xiphium* section in *I. serotina*; the largest standards in this section are found in *I. latifolia*, the 'English Iris', a native of the Pyrenees.

In America the same trend has again happened, this time in a bog iris, *I. setosa*, found from eastern Siberia to eastern Canada.

In the genera close to *Iris*, *Hermodactylus tuberosus* has standards reduced to narrow bristles, whereas in *Gynandriris*, the standards are still large enough to add significantly to the flower.

In the South African genera, *Dietes* and *Moraea*, reduction in the standards is also apparent. In *Dietes bicolor* the yellow flowers have six almost equal petals or perianth segments; the flowers are flat, and the inner segments which would make the standards are unmarked, the outer segments, opposite the styles and stamens, are marked with a shiny, black patch. This patch is even more beautiful in the Peacock Moraea (*M. villosa*), being iridescent blue, ringed with black and yellow, but here the standards are reduced to narrow thread-like petals with a lobed base.

The significance of the subterranean ovary is discussed on page 19 in connection with the crocus flower. Its advantages, especially that of protecting the ovary during winter weather, have ensured that it has arisen at least twice in *Iris*, and several other species have an ovary which, though not subterranean, remains at ground level while the flower is held up on a long tube. As might be expected, these characteristics are especially prevalent in winter or very early-flowering species.

In the reticulata irises, most species have subterranean ovaries, and the seed capsule only emerges as it ripens. The only species with a well-developed stem at flowering is *I. pamphylica*, a rare plant from southern Turkey, with a bicoloured purple and blue flower. It grows in more sheltered places (often in pine forest), and flowers later than the other species.

In the Juno irises the tallest species are found in Central Asia: *I. magnifica* may be up to 1 m (about 3¼ ft) high, with about eight flowers. Again the dwarfer species are early-flowering and several are without a stem or leaves at flowering time. *I. nicolai* from Central Asia is one example, *I. persica* from Turkey a second, and a third, the widespread Mediter-ranean species, *I. planifolia*, can flower as early as December. In this section, intermediates are common, and in some the plant is stemless at flowering time, but a normal stem elongates soon after flowering and before the capsules ripen.

The trend towards stemlessness, a longer tube to the flower, and so to a truly subterranean ovary, can be seen in several species of rhizomatous irises, as well as the bulbous ones described above. *I. attica*, a dwarf bearded species, has the ovaries at ground level at flowering, as does the familiar winter-flowering *I. unguicularis*. In this last, the capsules remain deeply hidden among the leaf bases even after they ripen.

Iris kumaonensis in the Pseudo-regelia section is another which is nearly stemless, as are the forms of the Californian iris, *I. macrosiphon*, in section Limniris.

The Arum Flower

The flowers of the arum family are individually small and insignificant, but are usually surrounded by a showy bract or 'spathe'. The flowers are usually closely packed on a cylindrical inflorescence called a spadix. The simplest flower structures are found in some of the tropical groups of which the common house plants *Monstera* and *Spathyphyllum* are examples. The whole spadix is covered with bisexual flowers.

The familiar 'Lords and Ladies' or cuckoo pint (*Arum maculatum*), has a much more complex inflorescence and a subtle pollination mechanism which is described in detail by C.T. Prime in *Lords and Ladies*.

The inflorescence forms a trap which catches females of a small mosquito, usually *Psychoda phalaenoides* which breeds on dung. They are attracted by the smell given off by the upper part of the spadix, which heats up, in the afternoon, and usually 30 or 40 are caught by each, but occasionally up to 4,000 are caught. The male and female flowers are on separate areas at the base of the spadix. When the insects are caught the stigmas are receptive, so any pollen already on the insect will be utilised. Later the stigmas wither, leaving a tiny drop of nectar which is eaten by the midges. By the following morning the stamens have matured, shedding pollen onto the midges, and the trapping hairs wither, allowing the midges to escape and visit another flower.

Similar traps but with a different mechanism are found in other Araceae. The mouse plant (*Arisarum proboscoideum*), whose flowers remain at ground level, probably attract fungus flies or slugs to the fungus-like apex of the spadix. Many species such as *Dracunculus vulgaris* smell strongly of carrion and attract blowflies. Others, such as *Arisarum vulgare* and many *Arisaema* species, have traps which confuse the insects with windows and translucent guidelines.

What is probably the largest of all geophytes is *Amorphophallus titanum* a member of the arum family from Sumatra. The tubers may be up to 1.5 m (5 ft) across, the spadix 1.8 m (6 ft) high; the spathe is wide and frilly. It smells of rotting fish and burnt sugar, and a press photograph of it flowering at Kew shows an admiring crowd holding their noses. (Prime, 1960).

Similar traps and pollination mechanisms are found in many genera of the Asclepiadaceae, e.g. in the genus *Aristolochia*, which contains several attractive dwarf species with tuberous roots in Greece and Turkey as well as the tall herbaceous birthwort, *A. clematitis*.

Bird-pollinated Flowers

Bird-pollinated flowers are conspicuous and valuable to the gardener because they are almost always bright red or some striking combination of red, green, blue or yellow. They are usually tubular but may be other shapes. They are interesting in that they have often evolved in one or two members of many different genera.

Bulbs with bird-pollinated flowers are found primarily in North and South America, where pollinators are usually humming-birds which hover in front of the flowers while feeding with long tongues, and in Africa south of the Sahara, where the pollinators are sun-birds which perch on the inflorescence and feed with shorter tongues and bills. There are no bird-pollinated flowers in Europe, which has no sun-birds (they range as far north as Israel), and no other birds which have become regular nectar feeders. Bird-pollinated flowers are common in southern Asia and Australasia, but are not significant as far as the bulbous plants of those regions are concerned.

The bird-pollination syndrome contains several features in addition to the colours and the tubular flowers mentioned

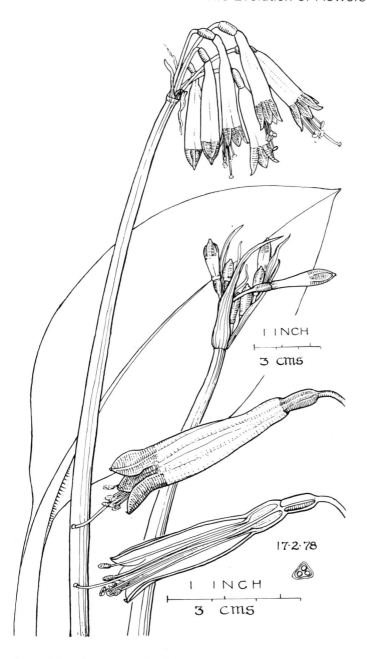

Figure 2.9
Phaedranassa
carmioli

I INCH

3 CMS

17·2·78

I INCH

3 CMS

above. Most flowers are horizontal or pendent or equipped with
a perch from which the bird can reach into the flower.
Alternatively, the flowers may be brush-like, as in the shrubby
callistemons or in *Haemanthus*. The nectar is thick, sweet and
abundant. The anthers and stigma are held out from the flower

35

where they can come into contact with the head or throat of the bird. In zygomorphic flowers such as *Chasmanthe*, the lower lip may be very reduced and the upper lip curved over to protect the anthers.

In North America many familiar bulbous genera have evolved humming-bird-pollinated species. In *Lilium grayi* from North Carolina and Virginia and in *L. maritimum* and *L. bolanderi* from California, the flowers are dark red and tubular; two Californian fritillaries, *F. recurva* and *F. gentneri*, are similar though much smaller. In *Dichelostemma ida-maia* the tubular flowers are crimson with green and white apices, while in other species the flowers are pale pinkish or bluish. In *Iris*, the reddish *I. fulva* from the Mississippi has a long tube with abundant sticky nectar, but all other species are insect-pollinated. Another member of the Iridaceae, *Rigidella* (very close to *Tigridia*) is certainly bird-pollinated. In the Amaryllidaceae there are many examples in America, but the most striking is probably the Mexican *Sprekelia formosissima*, in which the lower three petals are curled at the base to form a tube. The many red-flowered *Amaryllis* species belong to this group, but the most striking are the green and red-flowered *A. calyptrata* from Brazil, and the Sprekelia-like *A. psitaccina* from Peru.

Several other genera have tubular flowers, of shades of orange, red and green. *Stenomesson variegatum* is probably the most beautiful with 12 cm ($4^{3}4$ in) long red tubular flowers, the petals spreading at the mouth, each marked with green on the back (see p. 37). *Phaedranassa* also has red and green tubular flowers, and *Eustephia* is very similar.

Placea arzae from Chile perhaps shows the beginning of specialisation for bird-pollination. It has pale petals and a short apricot-yellow corona with a red zone around the mouth (see Figure 2.8).

Sun-birds are a familiar sight in tropical Africa and bird-pollinated flowers are common. Red tubular flowers of thick substance are usually combined with stiff strong stems so that the plants are not damaged by the perching birds. Aloes and kniphofias are the most frequently occurring genera, although only a few species have bulbs. Many, primarily bulbous Liliaceae, have similar flowers. The familiar red and green *Lachenalia bulbifera (pendula)* and the yellow and red *L. aloides (tricolor)* are two examples, as is *Veltheimia bracteata*, with a spike of narrow pinkish tubes.

In the Amaryllidaceae many *Cyrtanthus* species have thick, waxy, pendulous, tubular flowers; perhaps the finest is *C.*

Figure 2.10
Stenomesson
variegatum

5   cms   1·1·77

obliquus which has between six and twelve funnel-shaped
flowers, each 7.5 cm (3 ins) long, yellow at the base, then
orange, tipped with bright green. *Clivia nobilis* and *C.
caulescens* have rather similar flowers. There are many examples
in the Iridaceae. *Tritonia paniculata* is one of the few hardy in
northern Europe, its stiff horizontal stalks forming a convenient
perch from which the birds can feed from the tubular orange

flowers. In *Antholyza ringens* a bare flowerless extension of the inflorescence provides the perch. *Gladiolus* contains several mainly bird-pollinated species, including the red-flowered *G. natalensis*, found from Abyssinia and Arabia to South Africa, a parent of most of the modern gladioli.

The South African bird flowers already mentioned have all had tubular flowers, but in the genera *Scadoxus*, which is found throughout tropical Africa, and in *Haemanthus*, most species have flat-topped or rounded heads of small flowers. *Scadoxus puniceus*, the royal paint brush, has an upright brush of orange stamens; in *S. multiflorus* ssp. *katherinae* the heads are larger and spherical with masses of long stamens and narrow petals; in a third species, *Haemanthus coccineus*, the heads are umbel-like, and the bracts spreading and bright red to mimic petals.

CHAPTER 3

Seed Dispersal Mechanisms in Bulbous Plants and Vegetative Propagation

While pollination by wind is very rare in bulbous plants, seed dispersal by this method is very common.

In many steppe areas autumn is very dry, and the approach of lower temperatures is accompanied by high winds. Large amounts of dust and dried vegetation can blow long distances in these conditions, and modifications which improve dispersal by wind will be beneficial to the plant. Three different parts of the plant may act as units of dispersal: single seeds, inflated seed capsules or whole plants.

In species where the seed is light, dispersal of single seeds will be efficient. The capsule often acts as a censer, holding the seeds loosely until a sufficiently strong wind can vibrate the capsule, shake out the seeds, and blow them a reasonable distance from the parent. *Tulipa*, *Lilium*, *Fritillaria* and related genera have seeds of this type. Winged seeds are found in *Cardiocrinum* which grows in wooded valleys, but less often in other *Lilium* or *Fritillaria*. Winged capsules are commoner, being found especially in species which grow in forested areas where wind is likely to be lighter. The widest winged capsules in *Fritillaria* are found in species in which the uppermost leaves are modified into tendrils for climbing through shrubs.

Dispersal of whole capsules requires at least some seeds to be retained inside while the capsule is blown along or for the capsule to be inflated and indehiscent, that is, to remain closed until damaged in some way. Examples are found in many genera in the Middle East and in Central Asia. The grape hyacinth-like *Bellevalia* has many species with short-stalked flowers and inflated capsules; *Eremurus lactiflorus* has particularly inflated capsules, up to 3 cm ($1^1\!4$ in) across. In many of the dwarf steppe species of *Fritillaria* such as *F. armena*, the capsule is probably dispersed while some of the seeds are still inside, and they fall out as it is blown along. Inflated capsules with small seeds are found in the *Calochortus* species with nodding flowers (subgenus *Cyclobotrya*), such as *C. pulchellus*, although they are plants of scrub and open woodland rather than steppe. A perfect example of this capsule type is the hellebore,

Figure 3.1
Scadoxus
cinnabarinus

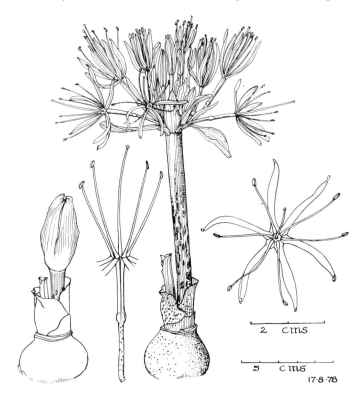

Helleborus vesicarius, from southern Turkey. Its dead stems are very brittle and the large inflated seed pods are completely indehiscent; the few heavy seeds are firmly fixed to the capsule wall.

Dispersal of whole dried inflorescences is also frequent in steppe habitats. Again at least some of the seeds must be retained inside the capsule. The most familiar example of this type of plant is *Gypsophila paniculata*, the common gypsophila or baby's breath. The dried stems break off at ground level and are very effectively dispersed, rolling at high speed across the bare hills. Most of the Juno section (*Scorpiris*) of *Iris* have this type of dispersal, e.g. *I. persica* and *I. caucasica*. The *Bellevalia* species with long stiff pedicels, e.g. *B. longipes*, and *Leontice leontopetalum*, whose fruiting inflorescence is very similar, are also well adapted as tumbleweeds.

Water
Dispersal

As most bulbous plants grow in dry places, dispersal by water is rather rare, but one or two interesting modifications have evolved.

40

Seed Dispersal Mechanisms and Vegetative Propagation

In *Leucojum aestivum*, the summer snowflake, the capsule is large, fleshy, inflated and indehiscent, so that it floats in water and is well adapted to spread along rivers. *Fritillaria meleagris*, the snake's head, is restricted to flood plains though in less wet habitats, and has no such adaptation; the individual seeds are probably the only part likely to be dispersed by the flood water.

In the tropics several *Crinum* species are aquatic. They tend to have very large pulpy seeds which germinate as soon as they fall, but are also capable of floating a short distance. In aquatic irises many species, e.g. *I. pseudacorus*, have fully filled capsules and floating seeds, while others have inflated capsules, e.g. *I. setosa*.

Ant Dispersal

The short growing season to which most bulbs are adapted means that the possession of a large seed with ample food reserves is advantageous for successful establishment of the seedling. The larger the seedling bulb, the more drought it can tolerate during its first summer.

Many of the larger-seeded bulbs have oily or sugary parts on the seed surface which are attractive to ants so that they carry the seeds to their nests, before removing the oily part and discarding the still undamaged seed. In *Iris*, seeds with a large white caruncle are found in the Oncocyclus, Scorpiris and Regelia sections, and in sections Hexapogon from central Asia and Pseudo-regelia from the Himalayas.

In *Colchicum* the whole seed coat is covered with a sweet secretion; in *Puschkinia* the surface of the seed has large cells containing fatty oil. Other ant-dispersed seeds are found in *Crocus* and in *Cyclamen* and in several genera characteristic of damp woodland. *Trillium* is a well-documented example (Berg, 1958) in which the fleshy fruits are often pecked by birds and the seeds further distributed by ants. In some species, e.g. *T. sessile* and *T. grandiflorum*, the capsule remains erect, but in *T. rivale*, for example, the ripening capsules are pushed onto the ground by the elongating and curving flower stalk.

Bird Dispersal

Just as red flowers are attractive to bird pollinators, red fruits and berries are attractive to fruit-eating birds. This phenomenon is common in Europe, and found also in most if not all other parts of the world.

The genus *Arum* is the most familiar example to Europeans among bulbous plants. The fruits are red and fleshy, and, though they are said to be poisonous to children, they are commonly eaten by thrushes. Similarly the Himalayan *Paris polyphylla* has seeds surrounded with a soft red pulp. In South America the tubular red and orange flowers of *Bomarea kalbreyrei* are bird-pollinated, and I have seen the red fleshy fruits being eaten by birds in the garden at Tresco.

Figure 3.2
Eucharis candida

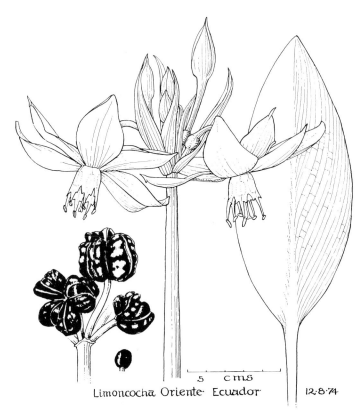

Limoncocha Oriente Ecuador   12·8·74

Some seeds show what Van der Pijl calls 'mimesis' or mimicry. They are red and juicy-looking, but are actually inedible. *Iris foetidissima*, whose open seed pods are so beautiful in winter, is an example of this phenomenon. A similar effect is found where the capsule wall is red but the seeds hard and black, e.g. in *Eucharis candida* from Ecuador, and in *Tritonia aurea* from tropical East Africa.

42

CHAPTER 4

Bulb-growing Areas of the World

As was mentioned in Chapter 1, most bulbs are adapted to a climate in which there is a hot, dry summer and a cool, wet winter. Growth takes place in the autumn, winter and spring, and the bulbs are completely dormant in summer. This is the Mediterranean type of climate found around the Mediterranean Sea, in western Asia, in the Cape region of South Africa, in southern Chile around Santiago, in California and Oregon, and in western and southern Australia.

The other climate which has a high percentage of bulbous plants in its flora is that which produces veldt or savannah country. Here the winters are cool and dry, the summers are hot and wet, and growth takes place in summer. This type of climate is found in central and southern Africa in both tropical and subtropical areas, and in parts of North and South America. Within these general climates there is, of course, every gradation between mediterranean and desert climate towards the equator. There are also many areas intermediate between the tropical savannah and the full equatorial climate with rain all year round.

Bulbs are often found in these humid climates, both temperate and tropical, e.g. bluebells (*Hyacinthoides non-scripta*) in the British Isles, wake-robin (*Trillium grandiflorum*) in the eastern United States, and *Crinum* species in tropical Africa, Asia and America, but there are many fewer species in humid climates than are found in the same or related genera in climates with a pronounced dry season.

In this chapter, we will examine in some detail the main areas of the world in which bulbs are found; we will consider climates, soils and vegetation. By taking these factors into account, the cultivation requirements of the different genera will be better understood, with the result that they can be given water at the right time and grown in the best conditions of soil and shading. First, humid temperate climates such as those of north-western Europe and the north-eastern part of the United States will be described, so that growers in these areas can compare their own climates with bulb-bearing regions in other parts of the world.

Introduction

I Temperate
Climates
(Grower
Areas)

(i) North-western Europe

The climate of north-western Europe is characterised by its lack
of extremes and its variability. Rainfall is more or less evenly
distributed throughout the year, and prolonged summer
drought is rare. In central England about 65 mm (about $2^1\!2$ ins)
of rain falls during the wettest months in autumn and winter.
Summer rainfall is more variable but, on average, June is the
driest month with about 45 mm (about $1^3\!4$ ins). Frost is
common and may be up to -20 °C (-4 °F) or less in the coldest
winters, but the mean daily minimum for each month is above
freezing. On the Atlantic fringe of Europe winters are warmer,
and in exceptional places such as the Scilly Isles the climate is
almost subtropical so that even African plants such as
Agapanthus have become naturalised.

Further east on the continent of Europe the winters are
colder and drier, and the summers warmer, but equally wet. To
the south the climate becomes more mediterranean in character
and the true mediterranean climate is reached in central
Portugal and in southern France around Lyon. There are few
native bulbous plants in north-western Europe but many of
them have been cultivated for centuries and have become
familiar garden plants. Some, such as daffodils and bluebells
(*Hyacinthoides*), are restricted as native plants to the Atlantic
fringe of Europe, others such as summer snowflake (*Leucojum
aestivum*). *Colchicum autumnale* and *Fritillaria meleagris* are
found as far east as Russia.

The climate of the northern side of the Alps and the
Pyrenees is similar to that of continental northern Europe, the
length of winter depending on the altitude. From these areas
come the ancestors of the garden *Crocus* (*C. vernus*), the dog's
tooth violet (*Erythronium dens-canis*), the 'English' iris (*I.
latifolia*) and the lilies *L. martagon* and *L. pyrenaicum*, all of
which can become naturalised in English gardens. Others that
do well come from similar mountain areas: *Lilium monadelphum* and many snowdrops (*Galanthus* spp.) come from the
Caucasus, *Colchicum speciosum* comes from the mountains of
northern Turkey, and trilliums from damp woods in North
America.

Natural soils vary greatly according to site. In alpine
meadows soils are well drained, loamy and often stony with a
high humus content; wild bluebells and daffodils grow in
woodland or in hilly meadows which are also well drained,
though these two are particularly tolerant of heavy soil in the
garden. Fritillaries (*F. meleagris*) grow in flood plains, but also

44

in fields which are dry and chalky on the surface, and it is striking that they avoid the wettest parts of fields. Only the summer snowflake grows in really poorly drained places and will thrive in sodden clay or in shallow water.

Garden soils in many densely populated areas are heavy and poorly drained, with a high percentage of clay. Such soils are basically unsuitable for bulbs as they encourage the bulb grower's worst enemies, slugs and fungal disease. Ways of improving such soils are discussed in Chapter 6. It is not by chance that the main bulb-growing areas in Holland are on well-drained sandy soils, derived from maritime dunes.

(ii) North-eastern America

In north-eastern America the climate is much colder in winter than it is in equivalent latitudes in western Europe, and can be much hotter in summer. For instance, winter temperatures equivalent to those in Nashville, Tenn., 36 °N, are found in Oxford, England, 52 °N. The equivalent summer temperatures at Nashville are at least 17 °F hotter, and the summers are considerably wetter, the rainiest months being June and July. A climate similar to New York is found in Europe in central Yugoslavia. Further inland, e.g. in Ontario, the winters are colder, and the summers drier though still moist with regular rain.

Comparatively few bulbous plants are native to this area. Those that are grown in gardens include several lilies, e.g. *L. canadense* and *L. superbum*, both found in marshy ground, and the various species of *Trillium*. The latter extend from Quebec and Ontario south to Georgia and Arkansas in the Appalachian Ozark Mountains. Many trilliums have the same habit as bluebells in western Europe: they emerge and flower in spring before the leaf canopy has expanded, and the tree cover keeps the tubers somewhat dry and cool in summer.

Soils in this area are as variable as in England. There is no doubt that sandy soils are better for growing bulbs because they are free-draining: if very acid, some limestone should be added to raise the pH to about neutral.

Deep winter freezes in the absence of snow cover are the main difficulties encountered in the growing of European bulbs in eastern North America. Temperatures may be as low as 40 or 50 °F below zero in Saskatchewan, and as low as −20 °C (−4 °F) in New York. Summer-flowering bulbs which are not hardy can be lifted and stored in dry sand or peat away from the frost, but the spring-flowering bulbs which grow through the winter, such as daffodils, must be protected by a deep mulch of leaves or straw. This may have to be up to 60cm (about 24 ins) deep, and should extend well beyond the plants to be protected, so as to keep as much frost as possible out of the soil.

(iii) The Pacific North-west

This area includes coastal Oregon and Washington, and western Canada. It is similar in climate to western Europe, being generally mild and wet throughout the year. In the south it meets the mediterranean climate of California. On the coast at Eureka (41 °N) in northern California there is very little rain in June, July and August, but sea fogs are common. Inland, the summer dry climate extends up the Columbia river valley as far north as the Canadian border.

Summers in the Pacific north-west are generally cool because of the proximity of the sea and cold currents, and winters are generally mild, but occasionally very cold (as in 1972 when $-28\,°C$ ($-18.4\,°F$) was recorded in Oregon) and as wet or wetter than western Europe. There are many different types of soil, but stony acid soils are common in forested hills, and some lilies, e.g. *L. pardalinum*, grow in very wet but freely drained places such as on the banks of rocky streams.

Many bulbs are native to this area and several have become excellent garden plants. The most familiar are the dog's tooth violets, *Erythronium* species (especially the cultivar 'White Beauty' derived from *E. oregonum*, and the pink *E. revolutum*, which is found wild as far north as Vancouver Is.), the black fritillary, *F. camschatcensis*, the camassias, and many lilies. The well-known Bellingham hybrids derived from *L. pardalinum*, *L. parryi* and *L. humboldtii*, were developed at Bellingham, Washington.

(iv) New Zealand

There are very few bulbous plants in the native flora of New Zealand. The main bulbous families, Liliaceae, Amaryllidaceae and Iridaceae, are poorly represented and the mild oceanic climate is not conducive to the evolution of bulbs. In the Liliaceae, *Arthropodium candidum* with starry, white flowers grows in forests and has a poorly developed corm, and some of

46

the yellow-flowered *Bulbinella* have fleshy roots. The small *Iphigenia novae-zelandiae* is interesting in that the few other species of the genus are widely scattered. *I. indica* is found scattered in Africa and India. *Hypoxis pusilla* with small yellow starry flowers is an isolated example of a mainly African genus.

As an area for growing bulbs on the other hand, New Zealand is ideal. Bulbs from areas which receive summer rainfall such as lilies, especially *L. auratum*, and summer-growing South African bulbs, grow very well in North Island, where the temperature never falls below freezing for any length of time and the rain is well distributed throughout the year. Bulbs from drier areas and mediterranean areas do well on the eastern side of both islands, where the rainfall is less and where the summers are somewhat drier.

(v) Japan

Japan consists of a particularly mountainous string of islands and much of the land area has a thick covering of forest or scrub. Many of the soils are volcanic and very free-draining, and the climate is wet at all seasons of the year and especially in summer. Temperatures vary from subalpine (and, of course, alpine in the mountains) in the north of Hokkaido, to tropical in the south, especially in the small Ryukyu islands north-east of Taiwan.

Most of the native bulbs are summer-growing and -flowering. Lilies are particularly well represented and beautiful, with *L. auratum*, *L. speciosum*, *L. japonicum*, *L. rubellum* and *L. lancifolium* (*tigrinum*) being the most familiar of the native species. Other genera which have many species in Japan are *Arisaema*, with no less than 42 species, and *Lycoris* with 5 species. Arisaemas are woodland plants which produce strange arum-like flowers in late spring and summer. *Lycoris aurea* and *L. sanguinea*, the former with flowers like a yellow *Nerine*, grow in more open places and are not satisfactory outdoors in England as they do not get sufficient heat in summer.

Many of the genera of Liliaceae from Japan, e.g. *Hosta* and *Tricyrtis*, are not bulbous or tuberous plants but are herbaceous plants adapted to life in forested areas with summer rainfall. The conditions that suit these are right for most Japanese bulbs. In general, those from the southern islands do better in warmer climates than England (e.g. *Lilium auratum*), while those from the north do well in the moister parts of north-west Europe (e.g. *L. lancifolium*). The most tropical of the Japanese lilies is

Figure 4.1
Lycoris aurea

L. longiflorum, the florist's 'Easter Lily', which is native of the Ryukyu island of Okinawa where it grows in pockets in the coral rock close to the sea. It is not hardy in England but has grown so well in Bermuda that it is sometimes known as the 'Bermuda Lily', and has been grown commercially there in huge numbers.

(vi) China and the Himalayas

Very few of the thousands of wonderful garden plants that have been introduced from China and the Himalayas are bulbs. This huge area of high mountains and deep, often tropical, valleys supports hundreds of species of trees, shrubs and plants, notably rhododendrons, primulas and gentians, but among bulbs only lilies and arisaemas are represented by more than a handful of species.

The whole area has a climate with a dry winter and a wet summer, most of the rain coming in the form of the monsoon. This type of climate extends along the Himalayas as far west as Pakistan, where it meets the essentially mediterranean climate of central Asia. In both Peking and Llasa, for example, the wettest months are June to September, and the spring months, March to May, are rather dry. In the central Himalayas in India there is more rain in spring, e.g. at Gantock in Sikkim where only the mid-winter months are dry, and further west in Simla where there is also significant rain in spring before the monsoon arrives in June.

Soils vary greatly, with limestone and acid rocks both common. In wetter areas most species of bulbs probably grow in loose humus in rock ledges or in alpine meadows among dwarf rhododendrons where the soil will be acid. For all except *Cardiocrinum*, good drainage is essential.

In China and the Himalayas the same bulbous genera which are important in Japan are found. *Lilium* and *Arisaema* both have their centres of diversity here, with more species of this area than in the rest of the world. *Nomocharis*, an offshoot of *Lilium* is confined to this area, and within it, to the Himalayas; *Fritillaria* and *Notholirion* are both represented here by several species. In the tropical area *Crinum*, a mainly African genus, is common, and *Lycoris* has many species in lowland China. Although orchids are largely omitted from this book for reasons given in the Introduction, the genus *Pleione* is included, as it is easy to propagate and suitable for growing with other bulbs. *Pleione* species all originate in this area, from Taiwan where the pink *P. bulbocodioides* is found in the mountains, to Yunnan from where the yellow *P. forrestii* has recently been introduced into England by Roy Lancaster, and to northern India, the home of the white-flowered *P. humilis* and other species.

The white-trumpeted 'Easter Lily' (*Lilium longiflorum*) from Japan was mentioned in the previous section, but all the other white trumpet lilies come from this area. They range from deep in the tropics with such species as *L. philippinense* from Luzon and *L. brownii* from Hong Kong, to the dwarf hardy *L. formosanum* var *pricei* from the mountains of Taiwan: from the cold interior of China where E.H. Wilson found *L. regale*, one of the commonest and easiest garden lilies, growing in thousands on hot, steep slopes in the valley of the Min river in northern Szechuan, to the warm, wet hills of southern India, where the exceptionally elegant *L. neilgherrense* grows on lush, grassy hillsides.

Figure 4.2
Lilium nepalense

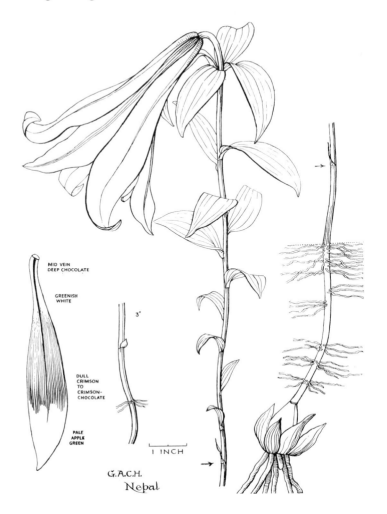

MID VEIN
DEEP CHOCOLATE

GREENISH
WHITE

DULL
CRIMSON
TO
CRIMSON-
CHOCOLATE

PALE
APPLE
GREEN

3"

1 INCH

G.A.C.H.
Nepal

II
Mediterranean
Climates

The coasts and mountains around the Mediterranean Sea provide one of the richest areas of the world for bulbous plants. The mild, wet winters and hot, dry summers which have made this area a tourist's paradise have also favoured the development of bulbs, and the islands, peninsulas and high mountains near the coast have encouraged the evolution of many different species, each suited to its own ecological niche, and separated from its neighbours.

Of all the climates of the world, the mediterranean climate, be it in South Africa, California, Chile, Australia or Europe, encourages the formation of the largest number of different species. Bulbs and annuals are foremost among herbaceous plants, since both are dormant in summer and both can complete their whole season of growth between autumn and the end of spring. Insects, especially bees, have also found the mediterranean climate to their liking, and have evolved many species, again encouraging the evolution of more species of flowering plants.

Because the mediterranean areas are transitional between temperate humid and warm desert areas, they impose stress on plants from each area, and so encourage further evolution. There are many differences between nearby habitats, which will affect the plant communities and species found in each. One side of a hill will catch the prevailing wind, and so be wetter and cooler than the other; a gorge will have one shady side and one sunny. The sides of the hills will be bone-dry in summer but a spring will produce a small marsh or an area of richer soil. Variations in soil depth and fertility will affect the type of tree cover: there will be large trees on deep soils and scrub on dry, rocky slopes. The mountains produce exposures of different rock types, and the thin soils directly reflect the nature of the underlying rock. Limestones, granites, serpentine and gypsum soils all have their characteristic species.

This mosaic of different habitats in one area produces a diverse flora, and has led to the unparalleled richness of the floras of the Cape area of South Africa, of California, of central Chile and of western Australia as well as of the Mediterranean proper in Europe and Asia.

(i) Europe, Asia and North Africa

(a) The Iberian Peninsula

The climate and vegetation of the Iberian Peninsula (and of southern France, Greece, Yugoslavia and Bulgaria), are excellently described in great detail in Oleg Polunin's regional guides to these areas, and there is a general discussion in Polunin and Huxley's *Flowers of the Mediterranean*. The following notes are taken from these sources and from my own observations in these areas.

In north-western Spain the climate is essentially similar to that of western England, with rain falling at all seasons. The Cantabrian mountains run along the coast, and they and the Pyrenees catch the rain coming in from the Bay of Biscay. The northern side of the mountains are forested with oak and beech, and there are heathlands on the drier southern side. These mountains are one of the centres of *Narcissus*, especially the daffodils, with several subspecies of *N. pseudonarcissus*, *N.*

nobilis, *N. asturiensis* and *N. triandrus*, the angel's tears.

South of the mountains the climate changes abruptly and becomes much drier, with greater extremes of temperature; there are hot, dry summers and cold, frosty winters. This is essentially the climate of most of central Spain and of the mountainous areas in the south. Here there is steppe-like flora, similar in many ways to that of the Anatolian part of Turkey. The most interesting bulbous plants are found in the mountains, e.g. *Crocus carpetanus*, *Fritillaria lusitanica*, *Narcissus rupicola*, and *Merendera pyrenaica* all grow together in the Sierra de Guaderrama, north-west of Madrid. Here they flower in autumn after the first rains or in spring as soon as the snow has melted which may be after the summer drought has begun, so that their growth has to be completed in a few weeks. In Madrid itself the autumn rains start in September and reach peaks in October and February before tailing off abruptly in May; June, July and August are almost totally dry. Frost can occur from September to as late as May and, of course, later in the mountains.[1] In the Sierra Nevada *Crocus nevadensis* with greyish striped flowers and the endemic *Ranunculus acetocellifolius* can be found flowering by the snow patches as late as June. At this time the weather is dry, warm and sunny, and at high altitude the sunlight is very intense, so it is not surprising that these species grow poorly in England, flowering as they do in the dark cloudy days of February. Other mountain ranges have their own endemics, notably the Sierra de Cazorla with *Narcissus longispathus* and the dwarf *bulbocodium*-like *N. hedraeanthus*.

The south-west of Spain and Portugal, and the eastern and western coasts, remain very mild throughout the winter, and it is in these areas that the tender crops such as oranges and tangerines are grown. The area between the Algarve and Gibraltar is one of the richest for bulbs, many of which are also found in North Africa. The very mild winters enable plants to flower from the autumn onwards through the winter. For instance, in Gibraltar the average winter temperature is above 10 °C (50 °F), and frosts are rare, the temperature hardly ever falling below 5 °C (23 °F). Autumn rains begin in earnest in October and reach peaks in November and February; January and March are almost equally wet, but April is drier, and from May to September it is dry. In this area *Narcissus papyraceus*, the paper white, is common, and the rarer autumn-flowering *N*.

1 In general temperatures fall by $\frac{1}{2}$ °C for each 100m (328 ft) increase in altitude.

humilis, *N. serotinus* and *N. viridiflorus* are also found. The only member of the Juno group of irises (subgenus *Scorpiris*) to be found in Europe, *I. planifolia*, is common here as it is in North Africa; it flowers from November to February. The region called the Cabo de Gata north of Almeria, between Malaga and Alicante, is particularly interesting in that it is very hot and dry and has many plants with African affinities, for example, *Androcymbium europeum*, a member of the *Liliaceae* related to *Colchicum*. Apart from one species recently discovered on Elaphonisi island off Crete, all other *Androcymbium* species are found in East and southern Africa where they grow in veldt or on wet grassy rocks, their small, pale flowers surrounded by showy white bracts. Also found in this area is the amaryllis *Lapiedra martinesii* which has an umbel of starry white flowers in late summer before the leaves appear. It appears to be an ancient member of the family from which both *Leucojum* and *Galanthus* have evolved.

To sum up, the Iberian Peninsula is the headquarters of the genus *Narcissus* as a whole, the daffodils being found in the north-west, the jonquils in the south, as well as being the centre for *Scilla* in Europe. Compared with Greece and Turkey, *Crocus*, *Fritillaria* and *Tulipa* are poorly represented. Of irises, only the Xiphium group have their centre in Spain, the other groups are centred in Asia.

(b) The Balearic Islands, Corsica and Sardinia

The Balearic Islands are politically part of Spain and were probably at one time connected to the mainland. However, they have been separated long enough to have evolved a high percentage of endemic species. They have also acted as a *refugium* for interesting ancient plants, some of which have also survived in Corsica and Sardinia. As one would expect, the climate is more equable in the Balearic Islands than on the mainland, though because of the mountains the rainfall is very uneven, being high on the north-western coast and lower in the south and inland.

There are several endemic or nearly endemic species in the Balearics. The tiny winter-flowering *Crocus cambessedesii* is closely related to the spring-flowering *C. minimus* from Corsica and Sardinia, and the only autumn-flowering *Arum*, *A. pictum*, with marbled leaves and brown flowers which are said to be sweetly scented, is also found in the other two islands. *Cyclamen balearicum*, a dainty white-flowered member of the spring-flowering repandum group, has also survived in a small area of southern France.

Corsica and Sardinia are also islands of great antiquity, with many endemic species in their flora. The most typical of these are tiny, creeping herbs, some of which are familiar garden plants, e.g. *Arenaria balearica, Mentha requienii* and *Soleirolia* (*Helxine*) *soleirolii*. Much of the rock of central Corsica is granite, and the small, delicate plants survive in shady crevices or under huge boulders in the forests. The climate of both islands is typically mediterranean, the summer drought lasting from late May to late September. The beautiful *Pancratium illyricum*, the hardiest member of a largely tropical genus, is found on both islands as well as on Capri, and there are three species of *Romulea* almost confined to the islands. The miniature *Leucojum roseum, Colchicum corsicum* and *Crocus minimus* are found on both islands, while *Leucojum longiflorum* and *Crocus corsicus* are found only on Corsica.

(c) Southern France

The north-western coasts of the Mediterranean in the south of France and in western and northern Italy have a mild climate as they are protected from the north by the proximity of the Alps and the Appenines. The north-east of Italy is much colder in winter as it is flat and exposed to the north and east. At Marseilles, October is the wettest month, and appreciable rain (50 mm, or almost 2 ins) falls from September until May. Only June, July and August are dry and summer rain continues in the mountains.

The bulbous plants of this area have affinities with Spain and the Mediterranean islands. *Leucojum nicaeense* and *Fritillaria involucrata* are confined to this coast, as are the autumn-flowering *Crocus medius* and the spring-flowering *C. versicolor*, and *Lilium pomponium* has its centre of distribution in the valleys behind the coast. In general, however, the coastal strip is poor in species, compared with the wealth of rare alpines found in the gorges and higher parts of the Alpes-Maritimes. Similarly, the bulb flora is impoverished compared with the warmer areas of southern Spain, Greece and Turkey.

Several interesting bulbs are found in the transition zone between the mountains and the coastal hills. In grassy meadows at about 1,800 m (about 5,900 ft) near Grenoble are found fields of *Fritillaria tubiformis* and *Tulipa australis,* and other fritillaries occur further south and east, especially along the limestone ridges which form the borders of France and Italy.

(d) Italy

Italy contains many different climates. The southern and

western coastal parts have a mediterranean climate. In contrast, the summer rains from central Europe extend southwards along the mountains and down the east coast as far south as the peninsula of Gargano, a mountain of limestone with a good bulbous flora. The whole of Sicily has a typical mediterranean climate and the south coast is particularly dry, similar to the coastal parts of North Africa.

With about 4,800 species, Italy has as large a native flora as Spain, and a larger one than Greece, and so might be expected to harbour as many interesting bulbs, and as many endemics. However, it does not! Only three bulbs appear to be endemic to Italy: these are *Crocus imperati*, *Crocus etruscus* and *Bellevalia webbiana*; only one, an insignificant subspecies of *Allium*, is endemic to Sicily.

The most numerous group of bulbs, with about 40 species, includes those which are found throughout the mediterranean region, e.g. *Sternbergia lutea*, *Fritillaria messanensis*, *Gynandriris sisyrinchium*, and *Anemone coronaria*. The next largest group, with about 25 species, comprises those species found in Italy and the Balkans but not in Spain. This is as might be expected, as less than 50 miles separate the heel of Italy from the coast of Albania. Familiar species in this group are *Galanthus nivalis* subsp. *reginae-olgae* and *Crocus biflorus*.

Similarly it is less than 100 miles from the southern coast of Sicily to Tunisia so connections with the North African flora are also to be expected. *Muscari gussonii* and *Narcissus elegans* are only to be found in Italy and North Africa; the ten other species, such as *Scilla peruviana*, *Leucojum autumnale* and *Iris juncea*, are also to be found in Spain but are absent from Greece. Only one, the mouse plant, *Arisarum proboscoideum*, is to be found only in Spain and Italy.

(e) Greece, the Balkans and Mediterranean Turkey

Greece and the Greek islands, with Aegean Turkey, and the central parts of southern Yugoslavia, Albania and southern Bulgaria, have, in strong contrast to Italy, one of the richest and most interesting bulbous floras in Europe. There are many endemics, both ancient relics and newly evolved species, and many genera have their centres of variation here, e.g. *Crocus*, *Colchicum* and *Fritillaria*. It is an area of isolated high mountain ranges, deep gorges, peninsulas and islands, limestones, granite and volcanic soils, and differing climates. It is also the meeting point of plants migrating from different directions, from Anatolia, from central Europe and from the Mediterranean. All these factors combine to make this area as outstanding for its large number of rare plants as it is for its beautiful and varied scenery.

The climate varies from mediterranean on the coasts and on all the islands, with winter rainfall and long summer drought, to continental inland of the mountains, frozen in winter, wet and hot in summer. The rainfall is greatest along the Dalmatian coast: on the coast in winter, in the coastal mountains in summer. Europe's wettest place, contrary to all expectations, is not Fort William (2,008 mm or 79 ins p.a.) or Valencia Island (1,303 mm or 51 ins p.a.), but Cokvice, some miles inland of Kotor, with a yearly average of 4,640 mm (almost 183 ins) of rain. By contrast, Athens is one of the driest places in the area with 402 mm (16 ins) average; it is almost completely dry from late April to October.

The Dalmation coast to Corfu. The most striking feature of this area is that it is almost entirely composed of limestone rock which produces very characteristic 'karst' topography. The surface is dry and the bulbs grow mainly in soil-filled crevices in the rocks. At higher altitudes and on north-facing slopes these soils are fine and peaty; lower down and on hot slopes they are of the red earth type, the 'terra rossa'. On the coast, e.g. on Corfu, the dry summer lasts from May to September; inland, e.g. at Trikalla, the dry period is a month or two shorter. In the extreme north, e.g. at Trieste, rain falls throughout the summer.

Yugoslavia is an especially good area for *Crocus* species. *C. malyi, C. kosaninii, C. tommasinianus* and *C. thomasii* occur at relatively low altitudes, and *C. veluchensis, dalmaticus, sieberi, olivieri,* and others appear higher up, while three rarities, *C. cvijicii, C. scardicus* and *C. pelistericus,* are found in alpine meadows at high altitudes. Fritillaries are also well represented: *F. messanensis* subsp. *gracilis* around Dubrovnik, *F. graeca* subsp. *thessala* on Corfu and the nearby coast, *F. gussichae* in the gorges and woods, and *F. macedonica* in alpine meadows on the borders of Albania and Yugoslavia.

Another typical bulb is *Lilium carniolicum*, which grows in the mountains in the south (where it is usually yellow), and near the coast in the north above Trieste (where it is orange). It is one of the many Balkan plants with affinities both with the Pyrenees (*L. pyrenaicum*) and with the Pontus mountains in north-eastern Turkey (*L. ponticum*). *Gentiana pyrenaica* also grows in these areas. Other species endemic to this area are *Hyacinthella pallens* (*dalmatica*) and *Scilla litardierei.*

The Peloponnese. The three great peninsulas of the Peloponnese each have their own endemics but the Mani is particularly famous for its profusion of bulbs which grow beneath the garrigue and olive groves. *Fritillaria davisii* was originally found in this area and it was from plants from the area that the first scientific naming and description of the species was made. There is an amazing assemblage of autumn-flowering crocuses, e.g. purple *C. goulimyi*, white *C. niveus*, *C. laevigatus*, *C. hadriaticus*, *C. boryi* and *C. biflorus* subsp. *melantherus* are all recorded from this area.

The eastern peninsula around Neapolis is also very rich with some of the same *Crocus* as the Mani, the endemic red-flowered *Tulipa goulimyi*, and in spring a fine show of crimson *Cyclamen repandum*, in contrast to the pale pink form found in other parts of the Peloponnese. Other interesting plants found here are *Fritillaria messanensis*, white *Romulea bulbocodium*, and colchicums, *C. parlatoris* and *C. boissieri*.

The coasts and islands of the Aegean. To anyone interested in bulbs, the coasts and islands of the southern Aegean, both in Greece and Turkey, are the most interesting places in the whole world. Many of the islands have ancient endemic species, and on the mainland, the peninsulas and promontories – half-drowned mountains sticking out into the sea – harbour their own special plants.

The climate is a typical mediterranean one, with rain starting in late September or October, reaching a peak in mid-winter and ending in April. Soils depend largely on the type of rock which forms them; limestone is common, producing 'terra rossa' in sunny places, and a humus-rich loam is found in shady crevices on north-facing slopes. Crocuses and most other bulbs favour the former whereas fritillaries and snowdrops prefer the latter. Shales are common, as is mica-schist and serpentine, which, though poor in species, has often encouraged the evolution of rare endemics.

Attica is an interesting and well-known area, and good bulbs are found in all the hills around Athens. Mount Parnis rises to 1,400 m (about 4,600 ft) and among the fir forests on the plateau the spring flora is particularly rich. There is the tuberous dwarf *Euphorbia apios*, the purple-flowered *Crocus sieberi* subsp. *atticus*, the blue *Scilla bifolia* and *Anemone blanda*, the purple *Corydalis solida* and a fine form of the chocolate and green *Fritillaria graeca*. Hymettus has many of these and, in addition, *Sternbergia lutea*, *Tulipa australis*, and *Gagea graeca*. Both have the purple form of the autumnal *Crocus laevigatus*.

The island of Euboea, which runs along the north-eastern coast of Attica, is very interesting and rich in endemics. The southern part is mainly schist, the centre limestone. Two interesting fritillaries are found here: on limestone *F. euboeica*, a very rare dwarf yellow species, closely related to *F. carica* from Chios and the Turkish coast; on schist the brownish *F. ehrhartii*, which is common in garrigue. It is also recorded from some of the other islands of the Aegean, including Syros and Andros.

Several Aegean islands have their own endemic bulbs, fritillaries in particular. *Fritillaria tuntasia* is confined to Kythnos and neighbouring Serifos. For such a rare plant it is surprisingly easy to grow, and is well established in cultivation in England, as is the equally rare and very similar *F. obliqua* from Attica. *Fritillaria rhodocanakis* with striking purple and yellow flowers is confined to Hydra, though plants intermediate between this and *F. graeca* have been found on the mainland nearby and on Poros.

The beautiful autumn-flowering *Crocus tournefortii* is confined to the Aegean islands and, although it is found from Rhodes and Crete north-westwards to Kea and Andros, it seems to be absent from both the Greek and Turkish mainlands.

The Greek mountains. The higher Greek mountains, the Pindus, Parnassus, Olympus and the mountains of the Peloponnese, are less rich in bulbous plants than the rocky coastal hills and peninsulas. There is always snow in winter above 1,000 m (about 3,300 ft). As late as April there is still considerable snow on all the higher ranges, and there may be snow patches in sheltered hollows as low as 1,300 m (about 4,260 ft). Often, therefore, the bulbs have to rely on water from the melting snow and water retained in the soil for all their spring growth. They are wet until just after flowering time, and then slowly dry off until the first thunderstorms and showers of early autumn.

Many of the common bulbs, e.g. *Crocus chrysanthus*, *Anemone blanda* and *Fritillaria graeca*, occur above 1,800 m (5,900 ft) as well as lower down, and may be found in flower at higher altitudes in May and June, especially by snow patches. Rather few bulbs are confined to the high mountains; *Fritillaria epirotica* is one example, coming from the serpentine screes at 2,500 m (8,200 ft) on Mount Smolikas. It is a high alpine derivative of the widespread *F. messanensis* which is found near sea level in the Peloponnese and up to 1,000 m (about 3,300 ft) on Mount Olympus. Some of the rare alpine crocuses from Yugoslavia extend into northern Greece, but most of the endemics of the higher Greek mountains are cushion plants or southern relatives of alpine species.

Crete and Rhodes. The flora and vegetation of Crete are well described by Oleg Polunin in *Flowers of Greece and the Balkans.* Like the other large Mediterranean islands of Corsica and Sardinia, Crete is rich in endemic species, especially those which are very distinct and are probably ancient rather than recently evolved. The climate of Crete is typically mediterranean with the rain ceasing in April and beginning again in October; December and January are the wettest months. Most of the mountains are composed of limestone, which makes their surfaces very dry. Endemic bulbs are found both at high and low altitude, the alpine species being hardy in northern Europe, the lowland ones rather inclined to be frost-tender. The small pink and white *Tulipa cretica*, the two endemic Chionodoxas, *C. cretica* and *C. albescens*, and the striking mauve and white *Crocus sieberi* subsp. *sieberi*, all grow in the mountains. The larger *Tulipia saxatilis*, *Arum creticum*, and the fascinating *Biarum davisii* occur at lower altitudes, as does *Cyclamen creticum*, the Cretan equivalent of the widespread *C. repandum*. Most of these may be found round the Omalos plain at around 1,200 m (about 4,000 ft) in central Crete.

The island of Rhodes is in many ways similar to Crete and they have many rare species in common, but Rhodes has fewer endemics, as might be expected from its lack of high mountains and its position so near the Turkish mainland. *Fritillaria rhodia* is one endemic, a small-flowered, narrow-leaved plant which has been found both on limestone in the hills and in sandy soil in garrigue in the lowlands. The Rhodian variety of *Cyclamen repandum* is common in some places, and other interesting bulbs are *Cyclamen persicum*, *Colchicum variegatum* and *C. macrophyllum*, *Romulea tempskyana*, *Ranunculus asiaticus*, and *Crocus tournefortii*, here at the eastern end of its range.

The Turkish mainland and the offshore islands. The islands of Samos, Chois and Lesvos are less interesting than those already mentioned, being botanically extensions of the Turkish mainland. The northern part of this area from Bergama to the Dardanelles and the Bosphorus and into northern Greece has a colder climate than further south, often with much rain in May, and with deciduous oak scrub and beech and pine forests. Typical bulbous species in this area are the large tessellated *Colchicum bivonae*, the one-leaved *Muscari latifolium* and *Fritillaria pontica*, widespread in north-west Turkey, northern

Greece and Thassos, and with a distinct variety on Lesvos.

There are also many *Crocus* species in this area, notably the broad-leaved *Crocus candidus*, and the deep-yellow *C. olivieri* subsp. *balansae*. Both of these are to be commonly found in the pinewoods above Troy, growing with the fritillary which was called *F. schliemannii*, but had earlier been named *F. bithynica*.

It is the mountains along the western edge of the Anatolian plateau which provide the best area for flowers. They are particularly rich in *Crocus* species, *Galanthus* and *Chionodoxa*.

Ulu Dag above Bursa has sheets of the yellow *Crocus gargaricus* in March and April, mixed with the rich purple *C. biflorus* subsp. *pulchricolor*. In the same marshy meadows grows *Gagea bithynica*. Boz Dag is famous for its sheets of *Chionodoxa* described by Sir Colville Barclay and illustrated in the *R.H.S. Journal* in January 1970. Honaz Dag is probably the richest mountain in the area; although it has been visited by botanists over the last three centuries, new species are still being found there, e.g. the ice-blue *Crocus baytopiorum* discovered in 1973. Brian Matthew in *The Crocus* (Batsford, 1982) writes that six other species may also be found here, namely, *C. fleischeri*, *C. biflorus*, *C. cancellatus*, *C. pallasii*, *C. danfordiae* and *C. chrysanthus*. The limestone screes near the summit are also the westernmost localities for *Fritillaria crassifolia* and *F. pinardi*.

The Turkish Mediterranean coast. The Turkish mainland opposite Rhodes is particularly rich in rare bulbs. It has both limestone and serpentine areas, and extensive, still unspoilt wooded hills on the Marmaris peninsula and as far east as Fethiye. The climate of Fethiye is an extreme mediterreanean one, with drought from April to September, and much rain from November to February. Summers are very hot and winters are mild, though kept somewhat cooler than the islands by the proximity of the cold plateau of Anatolia. This area was visited by the early collectors Sibthorp and Forbes (see Chapter 5, pages 97 ff), and fritillaries endemic to Mugla are named after them both. More recently, Oleg Polunin discovered the spring-flowering white *Sternbergia candida* here; it is still known only in this area and has already been decimated by greedy collectors. *Lilium candidum* grows wild in this area on hot, dry cliffs, and *Narcissus serotinus*, *Crocus antalyensis*, *Colchicum macrophyllum* and *Tulipa orphanidea* have also been recorded from the area.

The Mediterranean coast between Fethiye and Antakya is another particularly rich place for bulbs. The Tauros and

Amanus mountains run along the coast, and there are many peaks over two and three thousand metres (between six and ten thousand feet) only 30 miles from the sea. Rocky gorges penetrate deep into the Tauros mountains, forming sheltered valleys so that new species have evolved through isolation and old species have managed to survive. Another factor which adds to the richness of the flora is the limestone which is the dominant rock over large areas. The Amanus mountains run north-east, joining the eastern Tauros near Maras; they form a link between Lebanon and Turkey. Much of the west-facing side is densely wooded, as it catches the rain from the Mediterranean and may even be covered by mist in mid-summer. The climate of Anamur, in the middle of the bulge of Turkey which is opposite Cyprus, is similar to that of Fethiye. Rain starts in October and ends in early April, although there may still be thunderstorms and heavy showers in May.

Crocus and *Fritillaria* are again frequent and diverse in this area, both at sea level and high into the Tauros. *Fritillaria whittallii* and *F. elwesii* are found around Antalya, the new *F. acmopetala* subsp. *wendelboi* and *F. aurea* high in the Tauros; subsp. *acmopetala* itself is found all along the coast. Two rare irises with eastern affinities have survived in the foothills. *I. pamphylica* of the *reticulata* group (subgenus *Hermodactyloides*) is unique in its tall stem, nodding seed capsule and bicoloured flower. Its long leaves climb up through oak scrub. *I. stenophylla* subsp. *allisonii*, a member of the Juno group (subgenus *Scorpiris*) recently described by Brian Mathew, grows in screes in the same area.

(f) The Amanus, Lebanon and Syria

On the inland side of the Amanus, the climate is much drier, but at Gaziantep in the north, the wet months are still October to April. Further south, Palmyra in Syria, east of Homs, is in the desert proper; rain falls in appreciable quantity only in December and January, and from May to October it is totally dry. The high mountains of the Lebanon and Mount Hermon have a climate rather similar to the Tauros, whereas at sea level in Beirut, it is dry from May to September, wettest in December and January, but the amount of winter rainfall is particularly variable.

Bulbous plants are frequent throughout the area. In the north the Amanus mountains west of Gazeantep have endemic species such as *Crocus adanensis*, *Fritillaria alfredae* subsp. *glaucoviridis* and *Cyclamen pseudibericum*, and *Iris histrio* and *Cyclamen coum* are both common. Further south in the

Figure 4.3
Vagaria parviflora
from Syria

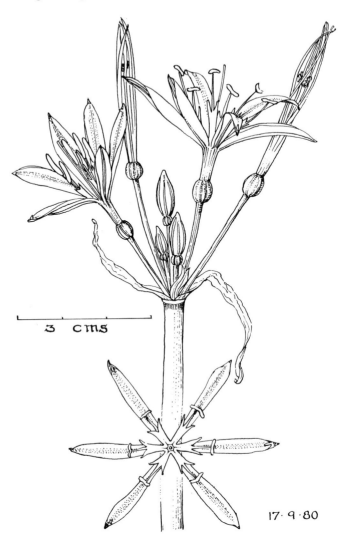

mountains are other crocuses, fritillaries and irises. The dry
hills and deserts of Israel, Lebanon, Syria and Jordan are the
home of the most spectacular of all irises, the southern
members of the *Oncocyclus* subgenus. Their huge, often
blousy, flowers are subtly coloured in shades of black, pink,
grey and gold, and are usually delicately veined. Many of the
species are very rare and in danger of extinction, but are being
preserved in cultivation in Israel and the southern USA.

(g) The Black Sea coast, the Caucasus and the Caspian coast
The Black Sea coastal mountains are quite different from those

of the rest of Turkey. Their lower slopes are densely forested; their upper slopes are covered with subalpine hay meadows and, above the meadows, azalea scrub or grazed alpine turf. Tea is widely grown in the wetter areas on the coast, and in many places hazelnuts are an important crop. Rain falls all the year round at sea level, but the higher slopes are usually rather dry in mid-summer. The same type of vegetation, and many of the same species, are found to the north and east in Soviet Georgia along the southern slopes of the Caucasus, and on the hills between Georgia and Soviet Armenia.

There are fewer species of bulbous plants here than on the dry Anatolian plateau, but they are especially valuable for gardeners in England and northern Europe and America as they can tolerate summer rainfall, which may be heavy and prolonged. June and July are the driest months, and around Samsun, and in one or two inner valleys e.g. near Artvin, there are small pockets of mediterranean vegetation adapted to summer drought.

The bulbs are found either in rocky woods, e.g. *Galanthus rizehensis*, *G. ikariae*, *Cyclamen coum* and *Lilium monadelphum* and related species, or on open grassy slopes, e.g. *Colchicum speciosum*, *Crocus vallicola*, *C. speciosus* and *Cyclamen parviflorum*, where they flower after the hay has been cut and cleared away. Species which are more common in the Caucasus or are only found there include *Crocus autrani* (purple and white); *Crocus scharojani* (golden-yellow); *Fritillaria latifolia* (purple); and *F. collina* (greenish-yellow).

The mountains of northern Iran, from the Talysh to the Kopet Dag, have a similar climate where they lie along the Caspian coast. Rain falls all the year, though it is particularly heavy in winter. There are many species in common between here and the Black Sea coast, but some are distinct, e.g. *Cyclamen coum* subsp. *elegans*, *Muscari chalusicum*, *Fritillaria kotschyana*, *Crocus caspius*, *Allium paradoxum*, and *Lilium ledebourii*, the only lily found in Iran. The southern slopes of these mountains have a normal dry steppe flora, with numerous species of *Iris*, *Tulipa*, *Allium* and *Eremurus*.

(h) Anatolia and northern Iran

The Anatolian plateau which occupies most of Turkey except the coasts, is one of the richest areas in the world for bulbs. This area may be taken to include parts of southern Georgia, Soviet Armenia and Azerbaijan, as well as north-western Iran and north-eastern Iraq. Numerous mountain ranges up to over 3,000 m (9,850 ft), composed of both limestone and volcanic rock and separated by flat plains, produce different habitats, and the meeting of the Caucasian, Mediterranean and Iranian mountains contributes to the remarkable range of species.

The climate of this area is basically a mediterranean one, with rain in autumn and spring, and drought in summer. Winters are very cold and snowy. Only along the Black Sea and the Caspian Sea is summer rain at all regular, and it is confined by the mountains which run parallel to the coast.

Ankara in north-western Anatolia has a climate which is transitional between wet coastal and dry mediterranean types of climate. June to October is invariably dry, although there may be freak storms. The rains come in October; snow comes in November and lies until April. May tends to be rainy. Although the hills are mostly now bare, trees will grow well if protected from grazing. Further north and west the summer becomes steadily wetter; further east and south the summers are longer.

In Erzurum in northeastern Turkey, which is at 1,950 m (6,400 ft), the proximity of high mountains affects the summer climate. Everything is frozen from November to April. May can be very wet and is on average the wettest month; the summer drought starts in mid-June and continues until September, though there may be storms in the mountains. The first heavy rain comes in October and within a week or two changes to snow. On a visit in October 1982 the hills around Erzurum at 2,500 m (8,200 ft) had received their first snow, and the bulbs, when excavated were found to have made two or three weeks' root growth. The pass of Kop Dag to the north-west, more in the rainshadow of the Pontic mountains, was still completely dry and showed no signs of autumn growth.

Further south in Van at 1,800 m (5,900 ft), winters are shorter, the snow lying from December to March. The months of June to September are dry and May can be wet or dry. Further south still in Mosul the rain pattern is similar: May to October is generally dry, the rains starting in October and ceasing in April. The total rainfall of Van itself and of Mosul is very low – 380 mm (almost 15 ins) and 390 mm (about 15^1$_2$ ins) respectively – but the mountains around Lake Van and the northern Zagros mountains receive over 1,000 mm (about 40 ins) of rain, again mainly in winter and spring. Much of the precipitation in the winter falls as snow, and this may lie in the mountains until June, and in isolated patches until August.

The vegetation of this area is either steppe with low bushes or *Artemisia*, cushions of *Astragalus* and *Acantholimon*, often with the grass *Stipa* which has long plumed awns, or a low scrub of oaks interspersed with whitebeams, maples, *Pyrus* and

Prunus species. On the edges of the plateau there may be an open park-like forest of large trees of the same species.

Grazing is very heavy nearly everywhere and strongly influences the reproductive behaviour of the bulbous plants. Soils are chiefly alkaline and very well drained; in general, the bulbs are more frequent on limestone than on volcanic rocks. Most mountain slopes are rocky and scree-like, and have a wide range of bulbs and tuberous plants of all families.

In the west, for instance near Ankara, *Galanthus* species, *Crocus ancyrensis, Corydalis solida, Iris sari, Fritillaria pinardi* and *Muscari armeniacum* are all frequent. In the centre of Turkey near Sivas may be found *Hyacinthus orientalis, Iris stenophylla* and *danfordiae, Crocus kotschyanus, Ranunculus kochii, Scilla sibirica* and *Fritillaria aurea.* Further east between Erzurum and Ağri, *Iris reticulata* and *I. caucasica, Tulipa juliae, Scilla armena, Fritillaria assyriaca* and *F. michailovskyi,* and *Crocus biflorus* subsp. *adami* are among the bulbs to be found. To the south around Van, the commonest species are *Fritillaria crassifolia* subsp. *kurdica, Puschkinia scilloides, Allium akaka, Tulipa humilis, Iris paradoxa, I. pseudocaucasica, I. aucheri* and numerous others.

Two particular habitats are worth a special mention. At altitudes below 1,800 m (5,900 ft) are often found low, rounded hills, apparently bare of vegetation, typical 'badlands'. They are rock-hard in summer, soft and sodden in winter, and composed of glutinous clay. Several beautiful species are characteristic of these hills; *Iris persica* in southern Turkey, *I. elegantissima* in the north-east, and various *Gladiolus, Tulipa* and *Hyacinthella* species. The second habitat is formed by hollows where the snow lies late. These are a characteristic feature of the mountains of Turkey and western Iran and they are particularly good places to look for bulbs. They are best developed on limestone, where shallow solution hollows form, the sides and bottoms being filled with richer and deeper soil than that which forms on the surrounding bare rocky slopes. The greater depth of snow means that the plants growing in these places receive more water during the spring thaw. At high altitudes the spring thaw often comes in May or June after the summer drought has begun, so that melting snow may be the only moisture the plants receive. Many fritillary species are habitually found in this micro-habitat, e.g. *F. crassifolia* subsp. *hakkarensis, F. armena, F. alburyana,* and the dwarfer forms of *F. pinardi.* Other bulbs such as *Hyacinthus orientalis, Puschkinia scilloides,* several *Gagea* species, and *Corydalis rutifolia* are usually found in snow patch hollows.

Plants from drier continental mountains e.g. in Iran, Afghanistan, central Asia and the inner Rocky Mountains in America, have this type of water regime, that is, all their spring moisture comes in one burst at snow melt, while the sunlight is intense, the air dry and warm. The soil starts sodden and, being rather heavy, dries out slowly. Growth is very fast in such ideal conditions. A further probable advantage of this habitat for the plant is connected with grazing. By the time the snow patches have melted, there is plenty of other grass in surrounding areas, so that grazing pressure is less heavy and the leaves of the bulbs are able to survive longer without being eaten off.

In gardens in northern Europe, bulbs from this habitat often present problems for the gardener. They emerge in March or earlier, to gloomy skies, mist and warm rain, and so are liable to fall victim to rot. Because the winters are shorter by at least two months than the winters to which the plants are adapted, their stems do not elongate properly, and the flowers open while they are still at ground level. Thus their emergence must be delayed as long as possible by growing them in a place which is cold and shady at least until April.

(i) Central Asia

The mediterranean climate extends eastwards across Central Asia to the Himalayas in northern Pakistan, and to the southern edge of Siberia north and east of Alma Ata. The mountain ranges of the Kopet Dagh, the Hindu Kush, the Pamir-Alai and the Tien Shan are joined by the Karkoram to the plateau of Tibet, and bounded to the east by the Takla Makan desert and to the north by the deserts east of the Caspian, the Kara Kum (Black sand) and the Kizil Kum (Red sand), and the steppes of Kazakstan. These mountains are particularly rich in bulbous plants, many newly evolved or actively evolving, and many ancient relics. This area is the centre for the genera *Tulipa*, *Gagea*, *Eremurus* and the *Juno* and Regelia groups of *Iris*.

The climate of this area is similar to that of eastern Turkey and plants collected there recently have mostly thrived in the same conditions. In the north-west of the area in Ashkabad, the winter rains last from November to April, and May to October are dry. Further east in Samarkhand, April is the wettest month, June to October are dry, and the rain comes in late October. In Alma Ata the pattern is similar, but the summer drought is shorter, from July to September. Summer rain is found north of the 50 °N latitude, and in the mountains south of Alma Ata. At Przewalsk on Lake Issyk kul, most rain falls from

May to July. On the Salang pass north of Kabul at c. 3,000 m (about 10,000 ft) the snow lies from October to May. It may rain in September but June to September are generally dry. At Kabul the first rain comes in November, often falling as snow, and the wettest months are March and April. Further east in Peshawar, the winter rain falls from December to April, and the remnants of the monsoon often bring rain again in August.

The spring flora of the foothills and mountain slopes of central Asia is most impressive. Of about 60 species of Juno iris (subgenus *Scorpiris*), 44 are found in this area. Some genera have their headquarters in this area: *Eremurus* with 48 species, *Tulipa* with over 60 species, *Allium* with over 200 species, and *Gagea* with about 40 species. In contrast, there are only three *Crocus* species, one *Arum*, two *Colchicum* and one *Iris* in the *reticulata* group (subgenus *Hermodactyloides*), the very distinct *Iris kolpakowskiana*. There are only thirteen species of fritillary but they belong to four different subgenera: *F. raddeana* and related species (subgenus *Petilium*), *F. bucharica* and related species (subgenus *Rhinopetalum*), *F. pallidiflora* and related species (subgenus *Fritillaria*), and *F. severtzovii* (subgenus *Korolkovia*). Bulbous or tuberous members of dicotyledonous families are common, e.g. *Gentiana olivieri*, *Primula fedtschenkoi*, *Anemone* species, *Valeriana* species, *Ostrovskia magnifica* and numerous *Eremostachys*. All these are spring-flowering; it is striking that there are no autumn-flowering bulbs in this area. The easternmost of the autumn-flowering species is *Sternbergia lutea*, which, in this area anyway, is possibly an escape from ancient gardens. The nearest truly native bulbs are the *Ungernia* species which flower here in mid-summer, usually in July.

(j) North Africa

The climate and vegetation of North Africa has many similarities with that of Turkey, but the flora is closer to that of Spain.

The eastern part of North Africa from Egypt to Tunis is very dry, and most of it is desert, but there is one small range of hills which catches the rain in December and January: Jebel el Akdar east of Benghazi in north Cyrenaica. It has one or two interesting relict mediterranean species, such as the very distinct *Cyclamen rohlfsianum* and the newly described *Crocus*, *C. boulosii*. In this area and in the hills above Tripoli, is found the eastern *Ranunculus asiaticus* in all its colour forms, yellow, purple, red, pink and white.

The coast from Tunis west and south to Agadir on the Atlantic coast receives ample rainfall, though it is concentrated on the winter months, producing typical mediterranean vegetation. The mountain ranges of the Atlas and the Rif catch the precipitation, and their southern sides are much drier than their northern sides. For example, Algiers has an average rainfall of 750 mm (29½ ins), while Biskra, only 300 miles to the south, has only 150 mm (about 6 ins).

The rainfall in Algiers is also very variable in quantity from year to year, but June to August is invariably dry and December and January are particularly wet. In Casablanca on the Atlantic coast, the summer drought lasts longer, from May to September.

Limestone soil seems to be the most common type of soil, and most of the interesting bulbs grow on this formation, in well-drained soils in the hills and mountains. Many of the rarer bulbs of Spain are also found in this area, e.g. *Androcymbium graminifolium* and *Lapiedra martenesii*. *Narcissus* is also well represented with a large number of different varieties of *Narcissus bulbocodium*, and two beautiful miniatures close to *N. rupicola*, the white *N. watieri* and pale yellow *N. marvieri*. Stocken records that *Leucojum trichophyllum* is common south of Larache, as is *Iris tingitana*, one of the parents of the common 'Dutch' irises. The rare *Leucojum fontianum* (*L. tingitanum*) is also found in this area. Several bulbs with southern affinities occur on the edge of the Sahara: two species of *Pancratium*, *P. foetidum*, and the dwarf *P. trianthum*, and *Vagaria olivieri*. Another interesting desert bulb is *Urginea noctiflora*, which flowers throughout the summer months; the leaves are very narrow and spirally coiled and the flowers are like minute martagon lilies, with reflexed petals and projecting stamens.

(k) Madeira and the Canaries

These islands which lie off the west coast of Africa are particularly fascinating for the glimpses they provide of an ancient African and mediterranean flora – prehistoric laurels which grew before the ice ages in the south of France, shrubby sow-thistles, foxgloves and chrysanthemums, huge *Echium* and *Geranium* species, and both succulent and woody spurges.

The bulbous flora, however, is poor, and most of the species are related to those found today on the Mediterranean islands. *Dracunculus canariensis* has a greenish or cream spathe and spadix, in contrast to the blackish one of *D. vulgaris*. *Pancratium canariense* is close to *P. illyricum* from Corsica and Sardinia. In the family *Liliaceae*, the only bulbs are two species of *Scilla* and *Androcymbium psammophilum*, a plant of sand dunes related to *A. graminifolium* as its name suggests. Tubers are equally rare in other families. The beautiful *Canarina canariensis* has fleshy tuberous roots with annual stems and rootlets, and can be treated like a bulb. Its only relatives are *C. eminii* and *C. abyssinica* from the mountains of tropical east Africa.

(ii) California

Although the mediterranean areas of western and central Asia and of California are so widely separated geographically, their floras have many genera, and even one species (*Styrax officinalis*), in common. The question of whether there was in the past some connecting zone of mediterranean climate between the two areas has been the subject of much thought and several papers, but the most recent view, that of D.I. Axelrod (formerly of the University of California at Davis), is that there has been no such connection, and that, in response to similar climatic factors, the plants have evolved similar growth forms, from different, or possibly the same, temperate and tropical ancestors.

It is also interesting that there are relatively few connections between the floras of Chile and of California. Most of the bulbous plants of Chile belong to southern hemisphere genera, most of those of California to primarily northern genera.

The climatic similarities between California and western Asia are produced by the world weather patterns; the main differences are produced as a result of the direction of the mountain ranges, north–south in the case of the Californian Sierras and the Rockies, confining the mediterranean climate to a narrow coastal band, and east–west in the case of Europe and Asia, allowing the mediterranean climate to penetrate deep into continental Asia. The greater latitudinal range of California means that absolute altitudes are of less significance there than they are in Turkey, for instance; the same plants occur at 1,800 m in the Cascades in northern California and Oregon and at 3,000 m in the Sierra Nevada of southern California.

To the north of California the summer drought becomes progressively shorter until at Vancouver only July and August are generally dry. To the south both winter and summer become progressively drier up to the Mohave and Colorado deserts of southern California, Arizona and New Mexico. Further south, in Mexico, the rainfall increases again, but occurs in both summer and winter.

In central California, e.g. at San Francisco, the summer drought lasts from May to September; there is little rain in October, and most of it falls between December and February. The coast ranges receive much fog during the summer, and it is this which feeds the giant Redwood forests, with their often subtropical luxuriance. Further south, in San Diego, the dry season lasts longer, from April to October, and the rain that there is comes in the winter months. In the mountains nearby, nearly all the precipitation falls as snow. Inland, in the foothills of the Sierra Nevada, Yosemite (1,216 m, or 4,000 ft) also experiences summer drought, with rain in October, followed by snow and spring rain, which ceases in May.

The mediterranean climate extends inland in Washington up the Columbia river valley. At Spokane, near the eastern border with Montana, the summer drought lasts from June to October; rain comes in October and snow from November to March. April and May are rather dry. Further east still in the Yellowstone National Park, Wyoming, the summer rainfall is beginning; May and June are the wettest months, whilst July and August are almost dry.

Frost is common in California, especially in the northern part of the state, and in the mountains, but really low temperatures are rare. Deep freezes such as occurred in 1972 mean that the native species are hardier than is often imagined, even many of the constituents of the hot, dry chaparral scrub. Only those plants which are strictly coastal, or lowland, such as many *Ceanothus* and *Cupressus macrocarpa*, seem to be tender in cold winters in England, and here also they seem to survive best on the coast. Most bulbs, however, will probably survive freezing, even if the leaves, which emerge in winter, are damaged.

The flora of California is comparatively well known, and twenty-nine plant communities have been recognised by P.A. Munz and D.D. Keck. These are described briefly in the introduction to their *A California Flora*, and the community or communities in which each species occurs is given in the Flora. Members of the bulbous genera are found most frequently in seven or eight of these communities, and a striking preponderance of these are found in four. Within each community there is a range of different habitats, so that related species may be kept apart even though they grow near one another.

In the coast ranges from Southern Oregon to Monterey the Redwood forests have survived in deep valleys facing the coast and on more open slopes there is dense scrub in which *Ceanothus thyrsiflorus* var. *repens* and *Mimulus aurantiacus* (*glutinosus*) are prominent by the roadsides. In even more

70

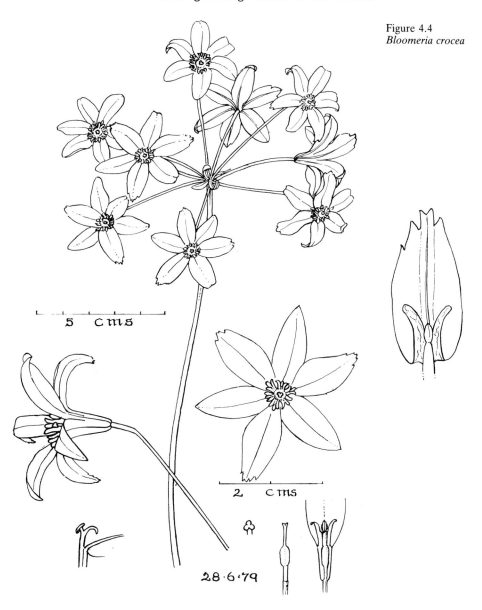

Figure 4.4
Bloomeria crocea

28·6·79

exposed places, such as cliff tops, a low scrub has developed
with *Gaultheria shallon* and shrubby lupins as well as extensive
grassy areas. Both these types of vegetation are rich in bulbs,
e.g. coastal type *Fritillaria affinis*, *F. liliacea*, *Zigadenus
racemosus*, *Lilium maritimum* and *L. columbianum*, *Calochortus uniflorus*, *Trillium chloropetalum*, *Brodiaea stellaris* and
B. douglasii.

Of the more inland plant communities, the valley grasslands and the mixed evergreen forest are both very rich in bulbs. This evergreen forest occurs along the inland edge of the Redwood forest in the coast ranges. Douglas fir, *Arbutus menziesii*, and *Cornus nuttallii* are familiar constituents of this community, and are mixed with various oaks, *Lithocarpus* and *Castanopsis*. Typical bulbous species, many of which are also found in the Redwood forest, are *Erythronium revolutum*, *Fritillaria affinis* (*F. lanceolata*), *Lilium rubescens*, *L. kelloggii* and *L. pardalinum*, the last especially by streams, *Calochortus tolmei*, *C. vestae* and *C. luteus*, *Camassia quamash* in marshes, *Trillium chloropetalum* and *T. ovatum*, and several *Brodiaea* species such as *B. laxa* and *B. ida-maia*, the bird-pollinated fire cracker flower.

The characteristic bulbs of the valley grassland belong to fewer genera than those of more montane plant communities, but are often particularly rare and beautiful. Soils here are often the very heavy 'Adobe' clay; the bulbs may be very deep and so protected from the intense heat of summer, when the ground has dried out and become rock-hard. Typical bulbs in this habitat are the fritillaries *F. striata*, *F. agrestis*, *F. biflora* and *F. pluriflora*, the mariposa tulip *Calochortus*, *C. splendens*, *C. venustus*, *C. superbus* and *C. luteus*, the brodiaeas *B. hyacinthina*, *B. elegans*, *B. coronaria*, *B. minor* and *B. pulchella*, *Muilla maritima*, the night-flowering *Chlorogalum pomeridianum*, *Bloomeria crocea* and several *Allium* species.

In these lowland communities, by early June, the grasses are dead and brown and the soil surface more or less dry. The early spring bulbs such as fritillaries, trilliums and erythroniums are in seed, but the later-flowering ones, the mariposa *Calochortus* and *Brodiaea* species, are in flower and often very conspicuous against the dead, brown grass. No more rain will be expected in this area until late autumn when the leaves emerge. This gives a guide to the cultivation of these plants: watering should cease gradually when the leaves die, as the bulbs become dormant at that stage, and should not be started up again until flowering has finished.

Above the grasslands and evergreen forest, more deciduous trees appear, and higher still or on drier slopes, these give way to low evergreen scrub, the chaparral. These communities are found both on the inner side of the coast ranges and in the foothills of the Sierra Nevada. Both are very rich in bulbous plants.

The 'Foothill Woodland' consists of evergreen oaks, *Pinus sabiniana* and *P. coulteri*, *Aesculus californica*, and *Umbel-*

lularia californica, and the evergreen *Ceanothus cuneatus*. The oaks are usually found on the flatter land, forming park-like scenery with grassy areas in between; the conifers occur on the sides of the valleys. Many of the species which are found in the valley grasslands are found here too. The tall yellow-flowered *Erythronium tuolumnense* occurs in open woods in this community, as do *E. helenae* and *E. californicum*, which are commonest in the chaparral, but also found higher up. It is the *Calochortus* and the brodiaeas which are especially well represented here, both the hanging-flowered *C. albus*, *C. pulchellus* and *C. amoenus*, and the mariposa tulip *C. superbus*, *C. venustus* and *C. clavatus*, and the brodiaeas, the loose-headed *B. peduncularis*, *B. laxa* and *B. hyacinthina*, the yellow *B. lutea* and the compact-headed *B. pulchella* and *B. multiflora*.

The chaparral is usually found on the steeper hills and more stocky slopes. It is similar in general appearance to the maquis and garrigue in Europe, and the Fynbos in South Africa. Apart from the numerous *Arctostaphylos* species, *Fremontodendron californicum* and *Rhamnus californica*, several evergreen *Ceanothus* species and the superb *Yucca whipplei* are typical of this community. Most of the bulbs typical of chaparral grow in other communities as well, but a few, e.g. *Fritillaria viridea*, *Calochortus weedii*, and the weird *C. obispoensis* (all from southern California), are confined to it, while the lilies, *L. washingtonianum*, *L. rubescens* and *L. bolanderi*, are more common here than elsewhere.

Above the chaparral is the community which contains the largest number of bulbous species, the yellow pine forest. Coniferous trees are dominant here, especially *Pinus ponderosa*, called yellow pine because of its yellowish bark. Other common trees are *Libocedrus decurrens*, *Abies concolor* and *Pseudotsuga menziesii*, the Douglas fir. The shrubs beneath are *Arctostaphylos* and the deciduous white, pink or blue-flowered *Ceanothus integerrimus*, the deer bush.

This type of vegetation is found especially on rocky slopes, and covers huge areas of Oregon and California. In the north it is found from 400 to 1,700 m (1,300 to 5,500 ft) above sea level, and progressively higher to the south and on the coast, until in southern California it is at up to 2,700 m (8,850 ft). The giant Sequoiadendrons, now restricted to 32 groves in the southern Sierra Nevada, are found in this zone and in some places the vegetation may be reduced to an oak scrub. Above the yellow pine forest, the range of conifers changes until the highest and driest of all is the famous bristle-cone pine forest, found at above 3,000 m (about 10,000 ft) in eastern California and Nevada.

73

Several species of most bulbous genera are found in the yellow pine forest and their numbers decline in the other montane coniferous forests above it. The erythroniums are confined to Oregon and northern California at altitudes of between 500 and 1,500 m (1,600 and 5,000 ft); *E. hendersoni* and *E. californicum* are both found in this zone. The scarlet, bird-pollinated fritillary, *F. recurva*, is commonest here, though it extends into subalpine meadows at about 2,000 m (6,500 ft); *F. purdyi* and *F. glauca* are both found mostly on screes. Most lilies are found at lower altitudes, but *L. humboldtii*, *L. parvum*, *L. pardalinum* and *L. parryi* are all found in different habitats within these montane forests. *Calochortus* are also common, notably the small, bluish, hairy *C. caeruleus* called 'Pussy's Ears', and the beautiful tulip-flowered white *C. leichtlinii* which is found on the floor of the Yosemite valley. *Allium* species are also common, but there are fewer brodiaeas than at low altitudes. Bulbous or tuberous members of other families are also frequent, e.g. in *Dentaria* (Cruciferae), and in *Delphinium* and *Aconitum* (Ranunculaceae).

Above the subalpine pine forests bulbous plants become fewer, and the climate more extreme. By the time the snow melts, the summer drought has often begun, and so the plants have to make all their growth in a few weeks. Many tend to be found below or beside snow patches where more water is available. Erythroniums in particular are found in these habitats in Oregon and northern California, the glacier lily, *E. montanum*, covers large areas in the Mt. Rainier National Park in Washington State, and *E. purpurascens* is found in similar places through the Sierra Nevada south to Tulare Co. Two Claytonia species with globose corms, *C. umbellata* and *C. lanceolata*, are found in the higher forest levels from 1,600 to 3,000 m (5,250 to about 10,000 ft), where they grow in bare soil near snow patches; two other species from alpine meadows which do not have to survive such drought have long tap-roots instead, and similar pairs of species have evolved in *Lewisia*. Subalpine bulbous species are also found in *Dentaria* and in the dwarf *Dicentra uniflora*, aptly called 'Steer's Head' because of the shape of its flowers. This and the similar *D. pauciflora* have a bundle of tuberous roots, and flower by late snow patches throughout the Sierras at up to 4,000 m (about 13,000 ft).

On the eastern side of the Sierra Nevada the climate is very dry. The Sierras form a barrier to winter rain from the Pacific, the Rockies to summer rain from the Prairies. The low-lying areas in the south are mostly desert, the Mojave, Death Valley and the Arizona deserts, where cactus and tree yuccas, the

Joshua trees, are common. The more elevated areas in the north are in Nevada and Oregon and are semi-desert with sagebrush, a carpet of blue-grey *Artemisia* bushes up to 1 m (3 ft 3 ins) tall. Most of this area has winter moisture which falls as snow, but in the far south the rainfall is irregular and may come at any time of the year.

The bulbs in this area are few, but interesting. The beautiful orange-red *Calochortus kennedyi* is found in many areas from low-lying salt flats to high mountains, e.g. around Death Valley; at higher elevations and in the south of its range it is often yellow. The large *C. macrocarpus* with purple flowers is primarily northern, and the white *C. nuttallii*, the state flower of Utah, often grows among the prickly pears. The sand lily, *Leucocrinum montanum*, is like a large-flowered stemless *Ornithogalum* and is sometimes called 'Star of Bethlehem'. It grows in sandy places among sagebrush and in open pine woods. The desert lily, *Hesperocallis undulata*, is a true desert plant of sandy flats in south-east California and Arizona. It is reminiscent of a *Paradisea*, with wavy leaves and white flowers about 6 cm (about 24 ins) long. Other desert bulbs in this area are the white-flowered *Anemone tuberosa*, also southern in distribution, and *Iris missouriensis*, which colours large areas of wet soils with its pale-blue flowers.

In Arizona the rains, such as they are, come in winter from California, and in summer both from the Gulf of Mexico and the Gulf of California. The winter rains are gentle and often prolonged; the summer rains are short and violent. It is interesting to note that the winter-growing annuals have northern affinities; they germinate in autumn and winter and flower in spring. On the other hand, the summer-growing annuals, such as zinnias, which germinate after heavy summer rain, have southern and tropical affinities. As far as the bulbs are concerned, some have northern, some Mexican origins; *Anthericum torreyi, Hypoxis mexicana, Milla biflora, Nemastylis tenuis* and *Zephyranthes longifolia* are all at the northern end of the range.

(iii) Chile

Central Chile is the third of the areas of mediterranean climate encountered in our world tour. Like the others it boasts a wide range of bulbous genera which have evolved relatively recently in response to the winter rainfall climate found between the Andes and the Pacific.

Figure 4.5
Eustephia coccinea

The Atacama desert along the coast in northern Chile is one of the driest in the world. At Coquimbo (30 °S) some rain falls in winter, and at Valparaiso on the coast near Santiago, the winter rain comes in April and lasts until August. From September to March is dry. Further south the summer drought becomes shorter until, at Valdivia, there is rain throughout the year, although there is less in the summer. In the foothills of the Andes, the climate is wetter and in the desert area an interesting zone of 'fog oasis' is found in the hills back from the coast, between 400 and 1,000 m (1,300 and 3,300 ft). The lower fog zone has a good growth of annuals and bulbs, which makes leaves in winter: many flower in summer after the foliage has died down. Grazing is heavy here, as in the Mediterranean, and much of the natural tree cover, which helped to trap the fog, has been destroyed.

Much of this area is volcanic, and poor, sandy, pumice-like soils appear to be common, as are bare, rocky slopes, composed of richer lavas. In wetter areas, soils are usually acid.

The alpine species flower in spring or summer at the same time as the leaves emerge. As in California and Turkey, many do not emerge from the snow until the summer drought has begun, so they complete their growth in a few weeks. In the mountains in the south, above the monkey puzzle forest, are extensive areas of tussock grass and *Pernettya* heath. *Habranthus andicola* and small *Amaryllis* species are found in this area. Chilean bulbs belong to only a few genera, but some of these contain many species (often closely related), and possibly still actively diverging. *Amaryllis* (*Hippeastrum*), *Alstroemeria*, and *Tropaeolum* are three of the largest genera, *Tropaeolum* being especially diverse. The delicate *T. azureum* and *T. tricolorum* grow in the Mediterranean mist belt north of Santiago. *T. polyphyllum*, creeping and with yellow flowers, is common on volcanic screes in the foothills. The familiar *T. speciosum* (Perth weed) with rich, red flowers and long swollen roots, grows in the far south and so is happier in cool maritime climates such as Scotland.

The richest area for bulbous plants is around Santiago and in the foothills of the Andes nearby. Light frost is common in winter, but very low temperatures, less than −5 °C (23 °F) are unknown, and for this reason most of the Chilean bulbs are not reliably hardy in northern Europe. The famous *Tecophilaea cyanocrocus*, with its gentian-like blue flowers, came from the Santiago area. It is said to have been exterminated by collectors and overgrazing, but fortunately it has been preserved in cultivation so it may one day be re-established in the wild.

77

Other beautiful but unfamiliar genera from this area are *Calydorea speciosa* (Iridaceae), with violet flowers shaped like *Gentiana verna*, *Alphia lahue* (Iridaceae), rather similar to *Tigridia*, and *Conanthera campanulata* (Tecophileaceae), with bell-shaped purplish or white flowers. The unusual *Conanthera bifolia* has reflexed petals like a cyclamen, and like the cyclamen, has a *Solanum*-like stamen cone (see Chapter 2, page 26). As with many of the Californian bulbs, the flowers are produced in early summer after the leaves have died off.

Of the Liliaceae, *Leucocoryne* is the most familiar genus. Green-flowered *Tristagma* species were recently introduced by the Beckett, Cheese and Watson expedition, and they also found the winter Aconite-like *Barneoudia major* (Ranunculaceae), flowering by snow patches. It has a cyclamen-like corm, yellowish or bluish many-petalled flowers, and silky-awned seeds.

In the Valdivia area and southwards, rain falls in summer as well as winter and the climate is cool, rather similar to that of the west of Ireland. Many slightly tender (zone 7) garden shrubs, such as *Fuchsia magellanica* and *Embothrium* originate here, and there are a few, almost hardy, bulbs. *Amaryllis pratensis* (*Hippeastrum*), with scarlet flowers in early summer, originated near Valdivia, and other species of *Amaryllis* in shades of yellow and red have recently been introduced to cultivation in Europe by Beckett, Cheese and Watson (see p. 117).

(iv) South Africa

The Cape Province of South Africa is the richest area for bulbs, and possibly for all flowering plants, for its size, in the whole world.

One corner of the Cape Province, from Cape Town to near Port Elizabeth, has rainfall in winter, a dry summer, and mediterranean-type vegetation. The remainder, which includes large areas of desert and semi-desert, has rainfall mainly in spring and summer. Near Cape Town, the total annual rainfall can vary from 500 to 1,270 mm a year (1916-1933). The midsummer months of December and January are totally dry, November to March are drier, and May to September are the wettest months. On Table Mountain nearby, summer mist has an important moderating effect on the vegetation, rather as it does in California, and the winters, from April to October, are wetter. At Port Elizabeth only December and January are dry, rain being distributed throughout the other months.

Figure 4.6
Leucocoryne ixioides

3   cms

Evenly distributed rainfall is confined to some areas along the coast. At East London no month is totally dry but there is more rain in summer, from October to March. Inland and north of the Mediterranean zone, the rainfall is erratic and unreliable, forming the deserts and semi-deserts of the Karroo and Namibia. At Middleberg in the Karroo, most rain falls from October to March, primarily in autumn, and it is dry from June to September. Summer rain tends to come in heavy thunderstorms, winter rain in light showers.

The South African climate is also characterised by a large amount of sunshine; in most places, two days without sun are exceptional. Lack of winter sunlight in northern Europe, and especially in England, is one of the factors which makes Cape winter-flowering bulbs difficlt to grow; they tend to become etiolated and both lose much of their beauty and become susceptible to botrytis.

Frosts are unknown on the coast but common inland, especially in the summer rainfall area, but rarely very hard or long-lasting. On Table Mountain the mean winter minimum temperature is only 7 °C (44 °F); inland in the arid mountains at Sutherland the mean winter minimum is 1–6 °C (34–43 °F), and almost as much rain falls in summer as in winter. The total rainfall, however, averages only 25 cm (about 10 ins), and at the same time is particularly unreliable, especially in the drier regions. Snow is rare and seldom lasts more than a day or two in the mountains.

In great contrast to Chile, the soils of South Africa are derived from ancient rocks. Granite is found over large areas in the north. Hard sandstones form most of the hills of Cape Province. The Karroo is largely sandstone with areas of basaltic lava, and only rarely with deposits of volcanic ash. Limestones are rare, and accumulations of lime are hardly ever found, even in the desert areas. Most soils are poor in lime and acid (pH .5), and are also very stable due to the absence of earthworms. In the Mediterranean part of the Cape, soils are also acid and sandy, and limey sands of marine origin are confined to the coast. In the lowland savannah areas the soils are rather heavy with a high percentage of clay; in the upland savannah and grassland they are somewhat lighter, and in wet places in the mountains there are accumulations of peat.

The main bulb areas are the Cape (winter rainfall), the eastern Cape and Natal (summer rainfall); the Karroo semi-deserts (erratic rainfall, mostly in spring); the mountains, especially the Drakensberg (summer rainfall, winter snow); and the northern subtropical savannah and bushveldt (summer rainfall). The last area is discussed below under 'Tropical Climates' (see page 90); the remainder are, for convenience, discussed here.

(a) The Cape Peninsula

The richness of the flora of the Cape Peninsula is hard to visualise. In the area between Cape Town and Cape Maclear, less than 40 miles long by 10 miles wide, a great wealth of bulbs is found, belonging to all the main bulbous families. There are 23 genera of Liliaceae, including 18 species of *Anthericum*, 15 of *Urginea*, 10 of *Ornithogalum* and 14 of *Lachenalia*, including the familiar cultivated species *L. aloides* (*tricolor*), *L. bulbifera* (*pendula*), and *L. orchioides* (*glaucina*). There are 12 genera of Amaryllidaceae, including 4 species of the *Colchicum*-like *Gethyllis*, 10 *Spiloxene*, and such familiar plants as *Nerine sarniensis* and the belladonna (*Brunsvigia rosea*). In Iridaceae there are 31 genera including over 20 *Gladiolus* species, 9 *Romulea*, 16 *Moraea* and 7 *Watsonia*, as well as fewer species of such familiar genera as *Freesia*, *Tritonia* and *Ixia*. In other families, there are over 32 species of *Oxalis*, all bulbous, and over 27 *Pelargonium*, of which 11 are tuberous.

The majority of these bulbs flower in spring and summer. The vegetation of the area consists of evergreen scrub, similar in general appearance to the Mediterranean but with a much larger range of species, especially of heathers and Compositae.

The figures above refer to the Cape Peninsula only and are compiled from Adamson and Salter's excellent Flora (1950). The Cape Mediterranean flora extends along the coast as far east as Port Elizabeth. The mountains which lie parallel to the coast keep the rain from the semi-desert areas of the Karroo.

(b) The Karroo

The Great Karroo south of Middleburg and the little Karroo between the Swatberg and the coast are particularly rich in both bulbs and succulents. Rainfall is irregular and the wonderful carpets of annuals develop after good spring rains.

Many of the genera are the same as are found on the Cape but the species are different. The semi-desert area of the north-western cape, Namaqualand, has a wealth of unusual bulbs, often with adaptation against drought. Rainfall is usually in winter so the plants are winter-growing but require even more sun than those from the Cape itself. Flat ground-hugging leaves are found in *Massonia*, which has a stemless tuft of long-stamened flowers between its leaves, and in *Whiteheadia*, in which the inflorescence is like a small *Eucomis*, with green

Figure 4.7
Zantedeschia
albomaculata

starry flowers and overlapping bracts. *Trachyandra falcata* has flattened fleshy upright leaves and an aloe-like inflorescence.

(c) The Drakensberg

The Drakensberg mountains stretch for nearly 400 miles along the borders of Natal and Lesotho, extending to Cape Province in the south-west and to the Transvaal in the north-east. The peaks rise to over 3,000 m (about 10,000 ft). The main vegetation is grassland with forests in sheltered valleys below about 1,500 m (5,000 ft). The grasses generally grow in tussocks, with other plants growing between. Many of the most interesting bulbs grow in rock crevices, in bogs or in damp seepage channels where the soil is very shallow.

The higher mountains are snow-covered in winter, but most of the rain falls in summer, so many of the plants can tolerate north European weather. Several of the bulbs are frost-hardy in southern England (zone 6–7), and in places further north where

Figure 4.8
Scadoxus nutans

5 cms

prolonged, deeply penetrating frosts are rare or snow cover is reliable.

Nerine bowdenii, the most reliable of autumn-flowering bulbs, grows among rocks, making its growth in summer in contrast to the winter-growing *N. sarniensis*. The high alpine var *wellsii* was collected at over 3,000 m (9,000 ft), and should be especially hardy. *Rhodohypoxis* species grow on wet rocks and in small bogs. Moraeas also like wet areas and the tall, yellow-flowered *M. spathulata* requires plenty of moisture when in growth. Also primarily a marsh plant is *Gladiolus papilio*, one of the few South African species hardy in England. It was used in the production of the Butterfly hybrid Gladioli. Its flowers are variable from yellow to purple but the commonest form in cultivation in England has greyish hooded flowers, and increases by long stolons.

Dieramas are also commonest in the mountains. The inflorescences curve over gracefully and the pinkish, bell-shaped flowers hang down on their wiry pedicels. They usually grow in deep peaty soil in nature which is moist at most seasons of the year. They do especially well in cool, mild climates such as Ireland, but *D. pendulum* and *D. pulcherrimum* at least seem hardy down to zone 5.

(v) Western and Southern Australia

The fifth area of mediterranean climate in the world is in western and southern Australia. The winter rainfall climate extends along the south coast east to Wilson's promontory near Melbourne. Northern Australia is wet and tropical on the coast, and, as in other parts of the world, the area between the mediterranean climate and the tropical is largely desert.

Western Australia, especially the area around Perth and Albany, has a flora almost as fascinating and rich as that of South Africa, but it has many fewer bulbs. The great families in which there is such a tendency towards the bulbous or cormous habit, Liliaceae and Iridaceae, are largely absent, and the species that are found in Australia mostly form tough herbaceous rootstocks rather than bulbs. Some other families, however, have developed interesting tuberous species. The insectivorous genus *Drosera*, Sundew, has many tuberous species with small leaves and relatively large flowers.

Bulb-growing Areas of the World

III Tropical
Climates and
Subtropical
Climates with
Summer
Rainfall

(i) Mexico

The Californian climate with its long summer drought extends as far as the southern deserts and New Mexico, and in Texas and in Mexico itself rain falls in summer as well as in winter. For instance, in Fort Worth near Dallas most rain falls in April and May, and June to August is rather dry. In northern Mexico in the Chihuahua area, there is a period of heavy rain in summer, from late May to late September in the mountains, and a period of gentle rain in winter. Further south, in Mexico City, the summer is wet, from May to October, and the winter, November to April, dry. Southwards towards the equator, the wet summer season becomes longer, and the dry winter becomes shorter.

Mexico is very rich in bulbs; some of the genera, e.g. *Calochortus* and *Zigadenus*, are common to California and Mexico, but most are of different genera altogether, and have tropical or even southern hemisphere affinities. *Tigridia* species are frequent, as are *Hymenocallis* which are similar to old-world *Pancratium*, and *Zephyranthes*. The ancestors of the cultivated dahlias originated in Mexico, being brought to Europe by the Spaniards in the sixteenth century. Of the species which are still grown, the beautiful scarlet *D. coccinea* is found in canyons in the mountains; it is almost hardy in England, and can tolerate some frost if kept rather dry. The giant *D. imperialis*, with nodding silvery lilac flowers, is too tender for cultivation outside in northern Europe because of its late flowering, but is a fine sight in the mediterranean areas and in the hill stations of southern India. Another almost hardy species from this area is *D. merkii* (*D. scapigera f. merkii*), with delicate pink flowers on tall elegant stalks. Tigridias are particularly diverse in Mexico, both in flower shape and in colour. *T. galanthoides* is like a brown-veined snowdrop, and *T. meleagris* like a pink-spotted fritillary. Other species have the usual three-petalled flat flowers, in shades of white, blue and yellow as well as red, which is the usual colour of *T. pavonina* in the wild. Their habitats are varied, from dry, wooded hills to seasonal pools and marshes.

(ii) Tropical South America

The bulbous riches of South America are still poorly known, especially to gardeners in Europe. New species and even new genera are described every year, notably in the families Amaryllidaceae and Iridaceae which are very diverse in this area.

85

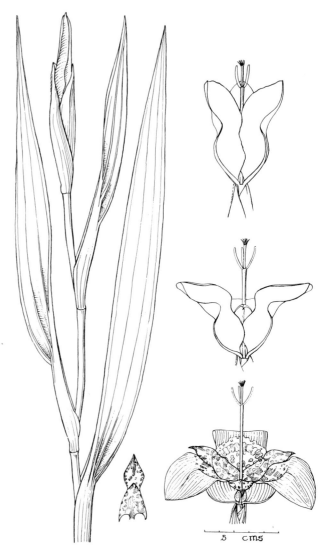

Figure 4.9
Tigridia pavonina
(see p. 85)

.5   cms

It is in the mountainous and subtropical areas that most of the bulbs are found, since bulbs are not well adapted to life in the wet forests of the Amazon. Only one or two, such as *Amaryllis calyptrata* and *Pamianthe cardenasii*, have been able to evolve to become epiphytic, the former growing low down, the latter high on forest trees. The climate around the equator is continually wet, e.g. in Bogota in Columbia (c.5°N), there is rain all the year, with peaks from September to November and March to May. Further south and east the winter rain becoms less, and the general climate over much of South America is a cool, dry winter and a wet summer of variable length.

Plate 1 *(right). Lachenalia aloides* *(L. tricolor)*, native of South Africa, flowering in a cool greenhouse in January.

Plate 2 *(below). Cyclamen cilicium* in October near the Cilician gates in Turkey.

Plate 3 *(above). Impatiens acaulis* in Kerala, Southern India, in November. A tuberous species growing on wet rocks in forest.

Plate 4 *(above). Fritillaria recurva*, a humming-bird pollinated species, in scrub in Mendocino Co., California, in June.

Plate 5 *(below). Lilium pyrenaicum*, naturalised in Aberdeenshire, Scotland.

Plate 6 *(above)*. *Gloriosa superba* near Monkey Bay in Malawi, flowering in January.

Plate 7 *(above)*. *Crocosmia aurea*, one of the parents of the Montbretia, on Zomba mountain, Malawi, in a *Widdringtonia* plantation.

Plate 8 *(below)*. *Watsonia* hybrids in the garden at Tresco, Isles of Scilly. In the background can be seen the yellow *Wachendorfia thyrsiflora*.

Plate 9 *(above)*. *Iris elegantissima*, near Mount Ararat, Turkey, in May.

Plate 10 *(below)*. *Iris histrioides* in the 'Caucasian herb field' in early spring.

Figure 4.10
Amaryllis calyptrata
(see pp. 36 and 86)

5   c m s   30·12·77

At Recife, the period from September to December tends to be dry, and in southern Brazil at Petropolis just north of Rio, there is rain from November to April and only August is dry. On the borders of the Matto Grosso and the savannah areas, June to August are dry, and in the eastern foothills of the Andes at Mendosa in western Argentina (33°S), the driest months are April to December.

In the Andes themselves at Muchuchies (8° 50′N) at 3,000 m (about 10,000 ft), June to September is dry and frosty, and summer is wet. At Las Pas (3,658 m or 12,000 ft) in Bolivia, there is also a short three-month winter, whereas at S. Antonio

87

de los Cobres (3,777 m or 12,400 ft) near the Argentina-Chile border just south of the Tropic of Capricorn, the dry winter lasts in effect for 9 months, and frost may occur from October to April: only in the three warmest months is there any appreciable rain.

In southern Argentina the climate becomes drier even on the coast. At Buenos Aires rain falls throughout the year, but June, July and August are the driest. South of this is the cold dry Patagonian desert which extends as far south as Tierra del Fuego.

The most important bulbous plants from South America are undoubtedly the potatoes, but many other familiar garden bulbs or tubers originated here, e.g. tuberous begonias, gloxinias and other gesneriads and hippeastrums (*Amaryllis* spp.).

The American Amaryllis Society has been responsible for publishing many of the recent discoveries in the Amaryllidaceae in South America in their journal *Herbertia*, or *Plant Life*. There is a wonderful range of exotic, beautiful and little-known plants. The genus *Hippeastrum*, now correctly called *Amaryllis*, is one of the largest, with plants of all sizes and flowers ranging from open red, through green and tessellated, to long white or blue trumpets, indicating adaptations to a wide range of pollinators. The famous blue amaryllis, *Worsleya procera* (or *A. rayneri*) grows at c. 1,200 m (about 4,000 ft) in the mountains near Petropolis, on moist cliff ledges, alternatively bathed in mist and baked in the sun. Other important and beautiful genera are *Stenomesson* with tubular hanging flowers of red and green, and *Pamianthe* with white, sweetly-scented flowers.

The iris family has also evolved many genera (about 25) related to *Tigridia*. Their leaves are 'plicate', folded lengthwise when in the sheath; their flowers come in all shapes, sizes and colours. *Tigridia* itself has some species in the Andes and others as far south as Chile. *Cypella* is strictly South American, with about 30 species. The yellow *C. herbertii* from Argentina and Uruguay is almost hardy (zone 7), but other more tropical species have blue, pink, and white and orange flowers. There is even one species, *C. aquatilis*, whose flowers float on the water like yellow waterlilies.

Apart from the potatoes (*Solanum tuberosum*, etc.), other tubers are cultivated in the Andes for food. *Oxalis tuberosa*, the oca, is much grown in the high Andes around Lake Titicaca, has orange-yellow flowers and variously coloured tubers like small elongated potatoes. *Tropaeolum tuberosum*, the anu, is a climber, with orange flowers; the tubers are more pointed at one end, blunter at the other, and are said to taste like

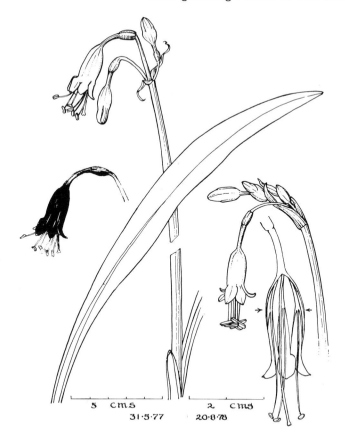

Figure 4.11
*Stenomesson
peruvianum*

Jerusalem artichokes. It is very decorative but most forms are short-day plants, so do not flower in higher altitudes until late autumn. The day-neutral form called 'Ken Aslet' will flower earlier and is to be preferred for ornament. (G.A.C. Herklots, *Vegetables of South East Asia.*) The fourth Andean tuber plant is the ulluco, *Ullucus tuberosa* (Basellaceae). The flowers are insignificant; the tubers are small, tasting rather like potatoes.

(iii) Tropical Africa

Africa south of the Sahara and north of the Limpopo has a bulbous flora which is a feeble shadow of the richness of South Africa. Rainfall is seasonal over most of the continent except on the Equator in the Cameroon and the lower Congo basin, where the dry season is very short.

In Nairobi just south of the Equator, it is dry from June to

Figure 4.12
Worsleya rayneri

September, wet from October to December, rather dry again in January, and very wet from February to May. This pattern of two rainy seasons ceases southwards; in Lusaka (Zambia), the summer rain lasts from November to March and the winter months, from June to September, are dry.

A savannah type of vegetation covers much of this area, from Kenya southwards to the northern part of South Africa and Mozambique. Many different vegetation types have been recognised within this, but over much of it is found the

90

essentially African landscape of rather flat grassland with scattered low trees, often of *Acacia* species.

Bulbs are common in this vegetation, flowering usually near the beginning of the rainy season. The commonest bulbous genus throughout tropical Africa is *Crinum*; many of the species grow in low-lying places which are seasonally flooded, and some, e.g. *C. natans* from Liberia, grow in streams. The leaves are submerged and ribbon-like; the flowers emerge above water. *Gloriosa superba* and related species or varieties grow in grassland or scrub, using their tendrils to climb, with exotic reflexed flowers in shades of red, orange or yellow. Other common genera, the red-flowered *Scadoxus* (*Haemanthus*), the yellow starry *Hypoxis*, *Scilla* species often with mottled leaves, and numerous gingers, notably the tuberous *Costus* and *Kaempferia*, make up the bulbous flora. Many primarily South African genera, e.g. *Tulbaghia*, *Moraea*, *Tritonia*, *Gladiolus* and *Drimia*, have one or two species in tropical Africa compared with dozens south of the Tropic.

(iv) Tropical Asia

The bulbous flora of tropical Asia is again less rich than the temperate, and less rich than that of America or Africa.

Summer rainfall, usually of the monsoon type with regular heavy rain during the wet season, is usual.

As in tropical Africa and America *Crinum* is an important genus. *Pancratium* with white flowers has several species and *Eurycles* with broad, lanceolate leaves has three species in Malaysia and northern Australia. Other common tropical genera are *Gloriosa*, common in southern India and Ceylon, and many gingers, of which the best garden plants are the hedychiums. The sweet-scented, white *H. coronarium* is used for garlands in India. The magnificent torch-ginger, *Phaeomeria magnifica*, is native of Indonesia. Edible ginger, *Zingiber officinale*, with its tuberous rhizome, is the most useful of the family.

Araceae are common, and the largest of all tubers in the world comes from this area, species of *Amorphophallus*. The leaves are compound and raised up on a tall stalk; the flowers are stemless; the tuber of the edible species, *A. campanulatus*, can be up to 13.6 kg (30 lb) in weight. It is soft and good to eat when cooked, with a rather nutty flavour and a consistency somewhat coarser than potato. Other Araceae are commonly eaten, notably *Colocasia antiquorum*, the taro, which probably originated in northern India.

91

Figure 4.13
Eurycles
cunninghamii

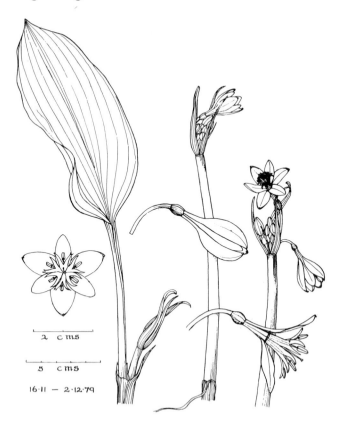

2 cms

5 cms

16·11 — 2·12·79

CHAPTER 5

A Brief History of Bulb Growing and Collecting

Bulbs were probably amongst the earliest of ornamental plants to be cultivated.

Madonna lilies were grown by the Minoans in Crete, and are depicted on their vases and frescoes. They also grew saffron (*Crocus sativus*), which was an important article of trade; it is clearly shown on a vase painting which dates from around 1550 BC. In classical times gardening methods reached considerable sophistication, but were mainly directed towards the production of vegetables and fruit. Nonetheless, the sea squill (now *Urginea maritima*), called *Scilla* in Greek and Latin, is often mentioned as being used as a medicine and is still used in Easter ceremonies in Greece. *Hyacinthus* is also commonly mentioned, probably for several different species, with a spike of flowers, either an asphodel or a *Muscari* (grape hyacinth) rather than the scented *Hyacinthus orientalis*. Lilies and *Crocus* are also frequently mentioned.

During the Dark Ages in Europe, science continued to thrive amongst the Arabs and it was through them that many of the most ornamental bulbs were introduced to western Europe. Both Mohammed II, who conquered Constantinople in 1453, and Suleiman the Magnificent (reigned 1520–1566), who enlarged the Topkapi seray and built the Suleymaniye mosque in Istanbul, were lovers of gardens, and tulips and other bulbs were widely grown.

It was during the reign of Suleiman, when the Turks were extending their power into Europe, that Ogier Ghiselin de Busbecq was sent as ambassador to the Sultan from the Emperor Ferdinand I in Vienna. He sent back huge quantities of classical and Byzantine manuscripts, and, at the same time, tulips and other bulbs which he saw in gardens in Edirne and Istanbul. In *Tulips and Tulipomania*, Wilfred Blunt quotes one of Busbecq's letters, 'on his way from Adrianople [Edirne] to Constantinople he observed "an abundance of flowers everywhere – narcissus, hyacinths, and those which the Turks call tulipam – much to our astonishment, because it was almost midwinter, a season unfriendly to flowers. The Turks pay great attention to the cultivation of flowers, and do not hesitate, although they are far from extravagant, to pay several aspers for one that is beautiful." ' Ferdinand also employed a botanist from the Netherlands, Clusius, who arrived in Vienna in 1573, perhaps particularly to look after these introductions.

It is with Clusius that serious cultivation of bulbs in western Europe began, and through him that the Netherlands became the centre of commercial bulb-growing in the world. He was born in Arras in 1526, of a well-to-do family, and destined for the Law, but his parents' confession of Protestantism led to the confiscation of their property, and Clusius was forced to leave home, and to study at various universities throughout Europe, as was the custom at that time. In 1551 he arrived at Montpellier and lodged with Professor Rondelet, among whose students were such famous early botanists as Rauolf, P. Pena, M. de l'Obel and Caspar Bauhin. Clusius' interest in botany began in Montpellier, which he did not leave until 1554. His first botanical work dates from 1557 when he published a French translation of Dodoneus' *Cruydeboeck*. He seems to have been in Paris during this period for in 1562 he was forced to flee from Paris to Antwerp; in Antwerp he complained that he found himself *'inter mercatores qui perpetuo de suis mercibus confabulantur'* (among tradesmen who only talk shop). In 1565 Clusius made a long plant-collecting expedition to Spain and Portugal, going as far south as Seville and Andalusia, and collected seeds and bulbs as well as herbarium specimens. It was while he was living in Bruges, and for a time in Mechelen nearby, working on his collections from Spain, that he became interested in garden plants, and especially in bulbs. At this time he received his first tulip bulbs from a Dr Jean Craton, who had had them from Busbecq. In 1573 he went to Vienna to the court of Maximilian II, but his exact position is doubtful and his income seems to have come to an end with the death of Maximilian in 1576. However, he continued to live in Vienna, at least until 1580, before returning to Holland where he became Director of Leyden Botanic Garden in 1609.

Clusius' works were published by the house of Plantin in Antwerp, the foremost scientific publisher at this time. The first work, published in 1576, was *Rariorum aliquot stirpium per Hispanias observatorum historia*, the result of his Spanish expedition. It describes many bulbs, notably jonquils which he found near Toledo, Seville and Cadiz, *Narcissus tazetta* which came from Portugal and Gibraltar, and *Romulea clusiana* from 'southern Spain'. His greatest work was published in 1601, the *Rariorum Plantarum Historia*. One whole volume is devoted to bulbs, from fritillaries and tulips to anemones, cyclamen and *Corydalis*. Over 80 well-known horticultural species are covered, from Europe, the Middle East, and a few from Mexico. Clusius gives some of their histories: for example, *Iris susiana*, first brought by Busbecq from the Turkish Sultan to the Emperor in 1573; *Galanthus elwesii*, from Byzantium, mixed with narcissus bulbs; *Colchicum autumnale* f. *album*, from near Bristol in Avon. He even mentions that he has heard a report of a yellow spring-flowering colchicum, but the bulb of it which he had died before flowering. This *Colchicum luteum* is found only in Central Asia and the western Himalayas. He writes of *Fritillaria imperialis* which 'I grew it in my little garden in Vienna in 1580'; *Sprekelia formosissima*, 'sent by the learned Dr. Simon D. Torvar, Spanish Physician, which flowered in June, 1594'; *Fritillaria persica*, brought from Constantinople by Ulrich de Königsburg in 1582; tulips – 'I received a large quantity of seeds and other bulbs from Busbecq on the year I arrived in Vienna [1573]. Many tulips of all colours were produced'. This was not, however, the earliest introduction of garden tulips; one had been illustrated by the Swiss zoologist and botanist, Conrad Gessner, in 1561 in *De Hortis Germaniae Liber*, from a plant he saw which had been grown from seed from Turkey. It was from this that Linnaeus took the name *Tulipa gesnerana*, the species from which the modern cultivated tulips are derived.

Although the introductions to Vienna and the Netherlands recorded by Clusius are the best known, many ornamental bulbs were grown during the latter part of the sixteenth century in Italy, where the first botanic garden had been set up at Padua in 1545. In the 1580s Jacobo Ligozzi had produced wonderfully realistic paintings of *Iris susiana*, *I. xiphium*, *Muscari macrocarpum*, and *Tulipa gesnerana*, as well as of *Narcissus tazetta*, *Pancratium maritimum*, and numerous anemones: they are preserved in the Uffizi, where he was Director, and at the University of Bologna.

Clusius is remembered by the numerous species named after him, mostly by Linnaeus, e.g. *Tulipa clusiana* (from Iran), *Sternbergia clusiana* (from Turkey and Iran), *Crocus clusii* (from Spain).

Clusius himself did not visit Turkey or the east, and it is not known whether any of the early-seventeenth-century botanists who travelled in that area introduced living plants. The early Florelegia give a record of the bulbs which were in cultivation at the time. Such books as *Le Jardin du Trés Chrétian Henry IV, Roi de France et de Navarre* (1608) by Pierre Vallet described

Figure 5.1
Sprekelia
formosissima
(see p. 95)

22·4·78   5   cms

plants in the garden of the Louvre set up by Jean Robin. Another was *Hortus Eystettensis* (1613), an account of the flowers grown in the garden of the Bishop of Eichstatt in central Germany. One which shows many bulbs is the beautiful little *Hortus Floridus* (1614) by Crispin de Passe. The frontispiece shows a Dutch formal garden, with a parterre of beds edged with box, and a grand display of tulips, crown imperials, *Fritillaria persica*, lilies, crocuses, irises, narcissus, and so on. In 1629 came Parkinson's *Paradisi in Sole or A Garden of all sorts of pleasant Flowers which our English ayre will permitt to be noursed up.* In its frontispiece Adam and Eve tend a garden with lilies, cyclamen, broken tulips, anemones, colchicums and dog's tooth violets, as well as prickly pears, pineapples, bananas and other exotica.

One of the first major botanical expeditions to the east was that made by J.P. de Tournefort and D.A. Gundelscheimer, with the painter Aubriet, to Greece and Turkey in 1700. They spent the first year in Crete and the Aegean and the second in Turkey, going from Trabzon through Erzurum to Tblisi, before returning across Anatolia in autumn. Tournfort was not especially interested in bulbs, though several that he collected were named after him, e.g. *Crocus tournefortii* from the Aegean islands.

Similar expeditions were made in 1786 and 1794 by J. Sibthorp, Professor of Botany at Oxford, John Hawkins, his friend, and Francis Bauer, the botanical artist. They were chiefly interested in medicinal plants and hoped to rediscover some of those mentioned by Dioscorides in *De Materia Medica* in the first century AD. They spent most of the time in Greece and the Aegean and only visited the western part of the Turkish mainland. Their collection and Bauer's wonderful paintings cover plants of all kinds. After Sibthorp's death in 1796, probably of tuberculosis contracted in Greece, J.E. Smith continued to publish the results of the expedition and named several plants in Sibthorp's memory, e.g. *Fritillaria sibthorpiana*, which came from near Marmaris and was not re-collected till 1972. *Colchicum sibthorpii*, however, was named by J.G. Baker (see page 109).

Another collector who discovered new bulbs from the east was P.S. Pallas (1741–1811), a German born in Berlin who became professor of Natural Science at St Petersburg under Catherine the Great. He travelled in Siberia from 1771–1773 and found many new plants, three of which were named after him – *Ixiolirion pallasii*, *Crocus pallasii* from the Crimea, and *Iris pallasii*, a synonym of his own *I. lactea*, an eastern species found from Kazakhstan to Tibet.

It was about this time that a few plants were beginning to appear from Japan. The earliest western botanist to penetrate the islands was Engelbert Kaempfer (1651–1751). He went as a physician to the Dutch East India Company, which was allowed to maintain a trading post on Deshima island, and arrived in 1690. Kaempfer's drawings were acquired and published by Sir Joseph Banks in 1791 and include the first glimpses of Japanese lilies, *Lilium lancifolium*, *L. speciosum*, *L. concolor* and

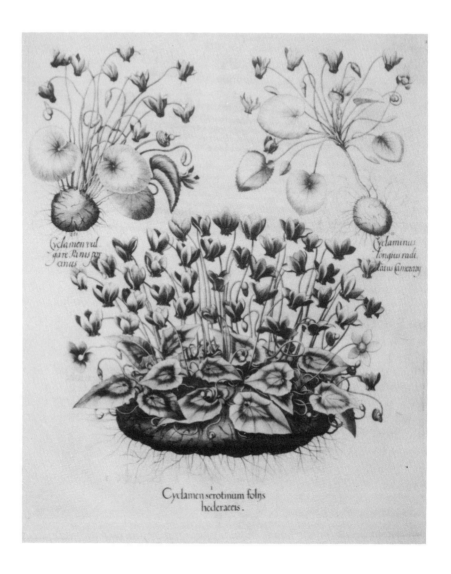

Cyclamen serotinum folijs
hederaceis.

Figure 5.2
Cyclamen: after an
engraving from
Hortus Eystettensis
(1613)

Cardiocrinum cordatum. The next botanist of note to visit
Japan was Carl Thunberg who also arrived in 1775. Thunberg
was a good botanist, had studied under Linnaeus and had also
qualified as a medical doctor. Among the bulbs he collected and
probably introduced were *Fritillaria thunbergii* and several
hostas.

On his way to Japan, Thunberg had spent two years
botanising at the Cape where he met Francis Masson (1741–

1805) and the two men made long trips into the African interior together.

Before Masson's sojourn at the Cape, only a small sample of the wonderfully rich flora of the Cape had appeared in Europe. The Dutch had set up a trading station there, and a small garden had been made, mainly to supply passing ships with fresh vegetables.

A few bulbs such as *Boophane disticha*, *Haemanthus coccineus*, and one or two *Gladiolus* were included in Sweert's *Florilegium* of 1612 and, in the 150 years following that, a trickle of plants continued to arrive in Europe, mainly in Holland.

Francis Masson was born in Aberdeen but moved to Kew where he served under William Aiton. It was at Sir Joseph Banks' suggestion that a collector was sent to the Cape and Masson was chosen. He sailed in 1772 and remained there for two and a half years. After an expedition in 1776 to Madeira, the Canaries, the Azores, and the West Indies, during which he was taken prisoner, Masson visited South Africa again in 1786, where he remained for another ten years, sending back a regular supply of seeds, specimens and bulbs.

Thunberg was primarily a botanist, Masson a gardener and plant collector, but the two seem to have got on well and made two journeys together. Thunberg's collections were published in his *Flora Capensis*, which includes 24 species of both *Gladiolus* and *Ixia* and an equally representative number of other genera. Masson's collections were grown at Kew, and many were described in Aiton's *Hortus Kewensis* and illustrated in the early volumes of the *Botanical Magazine*, from 1787 onwards, and in Andrews' *Botanists Repository* (1797–1812). The great popularity of the Cape flora in Europe led to many other collectors being sent to collect heathers and succulents as well as bulbs; notable among these were Boos and Schroll who collected plants for Jacquin who was based in Vienna, Niven collecting for the nurseryman, George Hibbert, and Ecklon, Zeyher and Drege, who collected vast numbers of specimens for European herbaria. Other famous nurserymen such as Lee and Kennedy at Hammersmith kept a collector at the Cape, and for a time they shared one with the Empress Josephine who was building up a fine collection at Malmaison (Hadfield, p. 287). This collection was the source for many of the plant illustrations in Redouté's *Les Liliacés*. The period of keen interest in Cape bulbs lasted until about 1830 when the fashionable areas became Pacific North America, from where David Douglas was sending back numerous new species, and China, which was

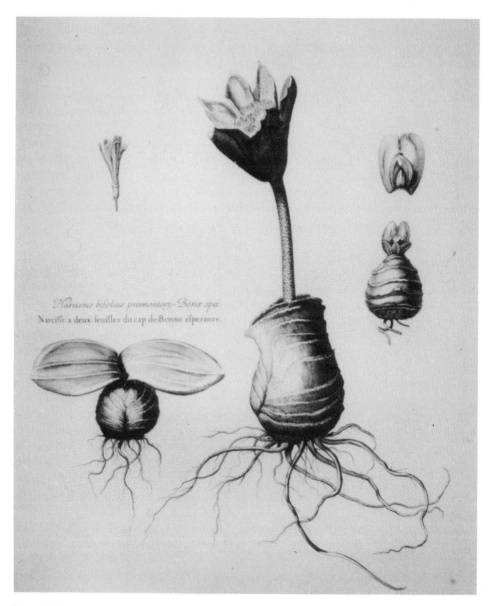

Narcissus bifolius promontory-Bona spa.
Narciffe a deux feuilles du cap de-Bonne efperance.

Figure 5.3
Haemanthus
coccineus: after an
engraving by N.
Robert

opened up after the Treaty of Nanking in 1842. The interest of
fashionable gardeners then turned from the semi-hardy bulbs
and heathers to hardy trees and tropical orchids, ferns, and so
on.

David Douglas (1799–1834) is well known as a plant
collector, primarily for his introduction of conifers and other
trees from California and Oregon. Douglas was sent out by the
Horticultural Society in 1823 with instructions to collect seeds

100

and herbarium material of new plants suitable for cultivation. Trees such as the Monterey pine (*Pinus radiata*) and the Douglas fir (*Pseudotsuga menziesii*) were introduced by Douglas, as were shrubs such as *Mahonia aquifolium* and *Garrya elliptica* and flowering currant (*Ribes sanguineum*), and annuals such as *Clarkia elegans*, *Nemophila insignis*, and *Limnanthes douglasii*. He was particularly taken with *Calochortus*, and sent back *C. luteus*, *pulchellus*, *albus*, *splendens* and *venustus*, as well as bulbs of *Camassia* and *Brodiea*. His paper *An account of the species of Calochortus, a genus of American plants* was published in the *Transactions of the Horticultural Society* in 1828, along with a beautiful illustration of *C. macrocarpus*.

There were several other collectors in this area, for example, Thomas Nuttall (1786–1859), who travelled widely in north-eastern America between 1809 and 1841. In 1834 he joined a transcontinental expedition and spent the spring of 1836 on the Californian coast. He is remembered by many plants, notably *Calochortus nuttallii*. Thomas Drummond was in California at the same time, and he also collected in Mexico where he found *Cooperia drummondii*.

Gardeners in England were also becoming aware at this time of the great richness of the flora of Chile. The Italian lawyer, L.A. Colla (1766–1848), who described a collection made by M.D. Bertero in the 1830s, grew many of the new plants in his private botanic garden. The beautiful *Tecophilaea*, which means lover of children, is named after his daughter Tecophila, who drew most of the plates.

The great nursery firm of Veitch was then in the ascendant, and they sent one of their collectors, William Lobb, to Chile in 1840 and again in 1845. Most of the plants Lobb sent back were from the wet temperate areas of the south where there are few bulbs, but he did introduce the Perthweed, *Tropaeolum speciosum*, and the very rare blue-flowered *T. azureum*, as well as *Alstroemeria* and *Amaryllis* species. His more important intro-ductions were large quantities of monkey puzzle seed, as well as *Lapageria*, *Desfontainea*, and *Escallonia rubra* var *macrantha*.

While the travels of Masson, Douglas and others who were collecting new plants are reasonably well documented, the gardeners for whom the plants were collected have left little account of their labours. Most of the bulbous plants probably did not live more than a few years, and it is only those which became the parents of popular cultivated flowers that have survived to the present day in their descendents.

The most eminent of the gardeners and hybridists of the time was undoubtedly the Honourable William Herbert (1778–1847), son of the first Earl of Caernarvon. He was a scholar and linguist as well as a botanist and accomplished botanical draughtsman. While still at Eton he edited a book of his fellow scholars' poetry, and he published an important book on the Norse sagas in 1804. Most of his life was spent as Rector of Spofforth in Yorkshire, and it was while he was here (1837) that he published his major work, *The Amaryllidaceae*, the first systematic account of a very complex family, illustrated by his own drawings. Paintings by him of bulbs, notably crocuses, were used in both the *Botanical Magazine* and in *Lindley's Botanical Register*. He visited Greece in 1845, no doubt collecting material for the monograph on *Crocus* which was completed on the day he died. His careful work on hybridisation was very important at the time, and he worked on several genera. He passed on his daffodil work to Edward Leeds whose hybrids are among the parents of present-day large-flowered narcissuus.

Herbert conducted careful experiments on hybridisation with many different plants, both carefully emasculating the unopened flowers and checking the pollen under a microscope to see if it was fertile. Some illustrations of his early winter-flowering *Gladiolus* and *Crinum* hybrids are to be found in the *Transactions of the Horticultural Society*. He was surprised to find that hybrids between many South African gladioli were fertile and not sterile as he would have expected crosses between different species to be; furthermore, he failed to make crosses between South African and European gladioli.

The nurserymen, Colvilles of Chelsea, also worked on *Gladiolus* hybrids, and *G. × colvillei* was raised by them from *G. tristis* and *G. cardinalis*. The forerunners of the large-flowered summer-flowering gladioli were bred at this time in Belgium and were sold by Messrs Van Houtte of Ghent as *G. gandavensis*. The parentage was probably *G. natalensis* × *G. opposotifolius*.

Interest in the flora of the Mediterranean and Middle East was centred in Geneva in this period under the influence of Edmund Boissier (1816–1883). Boissier visited southern Spain in 1837 and published the results of the trip between 1838 and 1845 in *Relations de Voyages en Orient de 1830–38* (Paris, 1843). In 1843 he began his *Diagnoses* of new eastern plants which culminated in the monumental *Flora Orientalis* (1867–1884), which is only now being superseded by the combined efforts of *Flora of Turkey* (published in Edinburgh), *Flora Europaea* (published in Cambridge), *Flora Iranica* (published in Vienna),

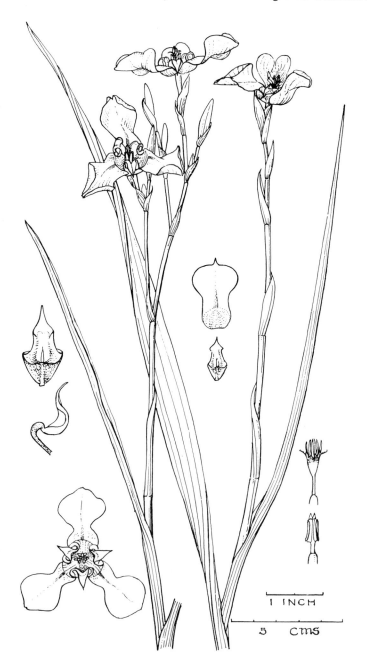

Figure 5.4
Cypella herbertii

and *Conspectus Florae Asiae Mediae* (published in Tashkent).
Many collectors who worked for Boissier or whose plants he
studied are remembered in his plant names.

The most industrious of the Greek collectors was Theodore de Heldreich who was persuaded as a young man by Boissier to live in Greece. He lived there from 1844 until his death in 1902. He travelled all over the mainland and visited many of the islands, including Crete. He is remembered by many species of bulbous plants, notably *Anemone heldreichii* and *Lilium held-reichii*. For many years he was Director of the Botanic Garden in Athens; at the same time, Orphanides was Professor of Botany at the University of Athens. Both men sent large numbers of specimens to European herbaria.

The journeys of Tournfort and Sibthorp to Turkey have already been mentioned. A man who is of much more importance as far as discoveries of bulbs are concerned is P.M.R. Aucher-Eloy (1793–1838), who settled with his family in Constantinople in 1830. He travelled many times through Turkey to Egypt, and as far as the foot of Mount Demavend and the Persian Gulf in 1838. It is not known whether he brought back living bulbs, but he collected at least 4,000 species, and his specimens are to be found in herbaria all over Europe. Among his discoveries were *Fritillaria reuteri* from near Isphahan and *F. acmopetala* in the Amanus. He is remembered in the pink-flowered *Tulipa aucheriana* and in *Allium aucheri, Muscari aucheri* and *Iris aucheri*.

Contemporary with Aucher-Eloy was Theodore Kotschy, an Austrian botanist and explorer. He concentrated on the very rich area of southern Turkey and also visited Iran, succeeding in climbing the Demavend where Aucher-Eloy had failed. There he discovered *Fritillaria kotschyana*, named by Herbert, and *Colchicum kotschyi*; in south-eastern Turkey he discovered the very rare *Crocus karduchorum*, and is commemorated by *C. kotschyanus* Boiss.

Other collectors in this area were B. Balansa, who lived in Izmir from 1857 to 1866 and was involved in the liquorice trade. He collected mainly in western Turkey and along the Black Sea and is commemorated in a *Crocus* and an *Ornithogalum*. The rather mysterious Pinard, described by Boissier as 'drogman intelligent', is commemorated by a very common *Fritillaria*.

The period from 1860 until the beginning of the First World War was probably the heyday of bulb-growing and bulb-importation in western Europe. Great Dutch bulb companies such as de Graaf, W. Blom & Son, E.H. Krelage, Th. Hoog and C.G. van Tubergen, Kelway, and Barr & Sugden in England offered a greater variety of plants than ever before, both of their own breeding and selection and through their agents in such places as Smyrna, Tiflis, Port Elizabeth, Yokama and California. Gardeners such as Max Leichtlen of Baden Baden, H.J. Elwes and Ellen Willmott could still afford large numbers of skilled gardeners to look after their collections, and standards of horticulture were never higher. Botanists such as E. Regel, Director of the Botanic Gardens at St Petersburg from 1855 to 1892, and J.G. Baker at Kew, specialised in bulbous plants in general, and amateurs such as George Maw, W.R. Dykes and Sir Michael Foster described new species of plants grown in their gardens.

Botanical exploration was concentrated on the inaccessible interiors of continents, with A. Regel and A. Fedtschenko and N.M. Przewalski visiting Turkestan, Maximowicz collecting in Siberia, and David and Delavay collecting in western China, followed by A. Henry and E.H. Wilson.

N.M. Przewalski (1839–1888) was one of the most important of Russian biologists to collect in central Asia and Mongolia. Apart from his famous primitive horse, *Equus przewalskii*, he discovered a new species of *Fritillaria* which was named after him. He continued to collect until his untimely death at Karakol on Lake Issikkul, now re-named Przewalsk, in Turkestan.

Przewalski's specimens were studied in St Petersburg by Carl Maximowicz (1827–1891), who had been botanist on a Russian expedition to the Far East in 1854–5. Maximowicz concentrated on the valleys of the Amur and Ussuri rivers and produced an important flora of the region *Primitivae Florae Amurensis*. He is remembered by *Fritillaria maximoviczii*.

The most important botanists and collectors in Russian Central Asia were the Regels, father and son. Eduard von Regel (1815–1892), a German, became Director of the Imperial Botanic Garden in St Petersburg in 1855, and remained there for 37 years. His son, Albert, was the collector: he was appointed district physician in Kuldja near Bokhara in 1875, and spent the next ten years collecting and sending back the plants for his father to grow and describe. He stayed mostly within the Russian empire, but made one daring journey into China, reaching the ancient city of Turfan. From 1885–1916, E. Regel and J. Kesselring were in partnership in a general nursery business. They sent bulbs to growers in western Europe and their catalogue includes *Tulipa greigi* Regel, *T. praestans* Regel, *Colchicum kesselringii*, *Fritillaria pallidiflora*, and other central Asian specialities. Both Regels are commemorated by numerous bulbs: Eduard by *Eduardoregelia* (now reunited with *Tulipa*), and *Fritillaria eduardii*; Albert by *Eminium albertii*, *Gymnospermium alberti*, and others, and also by the epithet *regelii* used by other Russian botanists.

Another botanical family which was active at the same time was the Fedchenkos. The father, Alexei, was born in Irkutsk on Lake Baikal in 1844 and made a three-year collecting expedition with his wife Olga in 1869–71. In 1873 he was killed climbing in the Alps. In 1898 Olga began publishing botanical works again with her son, Boris Alexeivitch, then aged 25, and together they concentrated on the flora of the Pamirs and central Asia. Olga is best known for her monograph of *Eremurus*, and is commemorated in one of the most beautiful species *E. olgae* Regel; her husband is remembered by *Primula fedtschenkoi*, the remarkable red-flowered species from near Samarkhand which becomes completely dry and dormant in summer.

The Russian empire did not then include Afghanistan, and the rich flora of Afghanistan remained almost entirely unknown* until 1884 when Surgeon-Major Aitchison visited the country with a commission which was to survey the border between Afghanistan and the Russian and Persian territory to the north and west. Judging by the beautiful specimens of *Fritillaria gibbosa* which Aitchison collected, the spring flora around Merat and Meshed was particularly fine. He discovered many new bulbous species e.g. the yellow *Corydalis aitchisoni* and *Iris aitchisoni*. Many of these were not cultivated in western Europe until they were introduced by the expeditions in the 1970s.

In the last decade of the nineteenth century, the interests of gardeners in western Europe, and especially in France and England, were directed towards the discoveries that were coming from the borders of Tibet and China. This area is not rich in bulbous plants, except for lilies, and the subscribers who contributed to the expeditions were mainly interested in rhododendrons and other trees and shrubs which occur there in incomparable variety.

The earliest collectors in western China were French priests who belonged to the Societé des Missions Étrangères. The first and most famous was Père Armand David, who collected both in Mongolia and in the border area between Tibet and China in 1866–1870. The area between Tibet and China is particularly rich in ancient and unusual plants and animals, and David discovered the giant panda, as well as the handkerchief tree, *Davidi involucrata*. *Lilium davidii*, a delicate red Turk's cap, is named after him, as is *Fritillaria davidii*, a most unusual plant with a single large flower on an almost leafless stem and a basal

* Bunge had reached Herat from the west in 1858 with a Russian expedition. Griffith had visited Kabul in 1841, and ten years later Dr Stocks collected around the North-west Frontier.

leaf like an erythronium. This species does not seem to have been collected since.

David was followed by Père Delavay who collected for several years in the Yunnan, sending back huge numbers of herbarium specimens and seeds to Paris. Delavay is remembered by *Lilium delavayi* and *Fritillaria delavayi*, as well as new species of almost every other major genus in the area.

Contemporary with Delavay were two other missionaries, Père Soulie and Père Farges, both of whom collected new lilies, which were named in their honour.

One of the most famous collectors in China was Augustine Henry (1857–1930), who lived in the centre of the country for several years from 1881 and later collaborated with Elwes on *The Trees of Great Britain and Ireland*. He is commemorated by *Lilium henryi*, a fine species with orange flowers and, for a lily, an unusually strong constitution. He collected it on limestone cliffs in the Ichang gorges of the Yangtze river in 1888, and it first flowered at Kew the following year. The white trumpet-flowered *L. leucanthum* was introduced at the same time.

Henry's collections and those of the French priests persuaded the nursery firm of Veitch to send out E.H. Wilson to China. Wilson's brief was to concentrate his search on the *Davidia* and to introduce it into cultivation. In this he succeeded and at the same time collected other plants, notably lilies in which he became an expert. His greatest find was *Lilium regale* which he sent back to Veitch in 1903. Details of the habitat of this and the many other species that he collected both in China and Japan are found in his *Lilies of Eastern Asia*, published in 1925. Wilson ended his life as Director of the Arnold Arboretum, a post he held for only a short time before he was killed in a car accident.

Botanical exploration in China and the Himalayas continued until the Second World War. The collectors George Forrest and Joseph Rock concentrated on China, Frank Kingdon-Ward and R. Farrer collected both in China and the eastern Himalayas, and Frank Ludlow and George Sherriff collected mostly in Bhutan and Tibet. Among the plants they collected were new lilies, *Nomocharis*, *Fritillaria* and *Arisaema*, but most of these, sadly, are no longer in cultivation. Of the few that are, *Arisaema candidissimum* was introduced by Forrest. Kingdon-Ward found *Lilium arboricola* from Upper Burma, but it soon died out in cultivation. Farrer is remembered by the pale pink *Nomocharis farreri* which he found growing in thousands in Burma. The more spectacular *N. basilissa* (the colour of *Papaver orientalis*), which he found in the same area just before his death, is known only from his painting. Ludlow and Sherriff introduced several species, the most interesting of which is *L. sherrifiae*, named after Mrs Sherriff who first saw it in Bhutan; the flower is like a fritillary, dark purple, bell-shaped and tessellated inside; sadly, it is very difficult to grow, and, as far as I know, only survives at Keillour Castle, Perthshire.

H.J. Elwes (1846–1922) had a profound and lasting influence on bulb-growing in England in the late nineteenth and early twentieth centuries. He was a traveller, sportsman, collector and gardener in the grand style. As he says in his *Memoire of Travel, Sport and Natural History* (1930), his interests slowly changed from killing game to collecting and growing plants, and bulbs were his favourite; he is said to have remarked to E.A. Bowles, the foremost bulb grower of the next generation: 'to think that I spent 20 of the best years of my life catching butterflies!' Elwes' travels took him all over the world and wherever he went he collected new plants, for example, in Chile he found *Oxalis adenophylla* and *Hippeastrum elwesii*, and in Turkey he found *Galanthus* and *Fritillaria elwesii* and several *Tulipa* and *Crocus* species. Trips with his brother-in-law, F.J. Godman, produced *Lilium wallichianum* in India and *L. humboldtii* in California. He also visited Formosa with W.R. Price and brought back the dwarf *Lilium formosanum* var *pricei* and *Pleione pricei*. Elwes' interest in lilies led to the finest plant monograph ever devoted to a single genus, *Monograph of the genus Lilium*, which was published in 1877–1880. Many new species were introduced by Elwes himself and others in the early years of the twentieth century, and a large supplement appeared in 1933, followed by seven other parts, the last coming out in 1962.

Another fine monograph, this time devoted to *Crocus*, was produced by George Maw. Maw grew and illustrated the plants himself, receiving them from correspondents and collectors abroad and visiting Turkey himself in 1877. He named new *Crocus* species after Mrs Danford and A. Biliotti, British Consul at Trebizond. Mrs Danford sent herbarium specimens and bulbs to J.G. Baker at Kew and to George Maw who dedicated his monograph of *Crocus* to her. She drew many of the vignettes of wild places in Turkey which appear in the book, and both *Iris danfordiae* Baker and the miniature *Crocus danfordiae* Maw are named after her. Maw's book is one of the most beautiful of all monographs and has only just been superseded by *The Crocus* by Brian Mathew.

A great gardener whose name often appears was the redoubtable Ellen Ann Willmott (1858–1934). In its heyday, her garden at Warley Place in Essex was tended by no less than 85 gardeners! Her own collecting was done mainly in southern France where she had another house, but she is remembered by several plants which were described from her garden *Iris willmottiana* Foster, *I. warleyensis* Foster, from near Samarkhand, *Lilium davidii* var *willmottiae*, collected by Wilson in Hupeh, as well as paeonies and roses.

James Allen of Shepton Mallett, who died in 1906, was a less flamboyant character, but he seems to have had a penchant for spotting unusual hybrids in his garden. He is remembered by *Galanthus allenii*, which appeared among a batch of snowdrops imported from the Caucasus, and × *Chionoscilla allenii*, which appeared in about 1891. This is a hybrid between *Scilla bifolia* and a *Chionodoxa*. Allen also named the snowdrop hybrid *Galanthus* 'Atkinsii', which is intermediate between *G. nivalis* and *G. plicatus*, after James Atkins of Painswick in Gloucestershire.

Equally famous in his own country as H.J. Elwes, but less well known in England, was the German nurseryman Max Leichtlin of Baden Baden who died in 1910. At first he intended to specialise in lilies, but they did not grow well in his garden, so he grew more alpine bulbs such as *Iris*, *Tulip* and *Eremurus*, and hybridised *Aubrieta* and *Gladiolus*. His catalogues are simple printed sheets of mixed bulbs and herbaceous plants, many of which are unnamed or new species which he may have collected himself on his annual collecting trips. At the end of his life he commissioned Paul Sintenis to collect for him in Turkey and this visit produced *I. bakeriana*. One list included the unusual *Leichtlinia protuberans*, a genus intermediate between *Agave* and *Polianthes*. *Crocus*, *Lilium*, *Camassia* and *Kniphofia* are other genera which include species named after Leichtlin.

During the late nineteenth century, most of the scientific work on bulbous plants and descriptions of new species in cultivation was carried out at Kew by J.G. Baker (1834–1920) and Otto Stapf (1857–1933). Baker became assistant at the Kew herbarium in 1866 and Keeper of the herbarium from 1890 to 1899. His most important publications on bulbous plants were *The Handbook of the Amaryllidaceae* (1888), *Handbook of the Iridaceae* (1892), and an account of the Liliaceae in the Journal of the Linnean Society (Vol. XIV) 1874. Baker is remembered by *Tulipa bakeri* Hall and many other species. Otto Stapf was an Austrian who came to Kew in 1891 and was Keeper of the herbarium from 1909 to 1922. Stapf travelled to Persia in 1885 and thereafter took a particular interest in bulbous plants, describing many new species in the *Botanical Magazine*. His botanical eye seems to have been unerring and his remarks on species and their variations are particularly valuable.

During the later years of the nineteenth century there arose a considerable trade in bulbs collected in the wild. In response to the brisk demand for new species, particularly from the American and English public, some of these were sent back by wholesalers who were based abroad, others by collectors working for specific large nurseries. Their activities were not well publicised, probably for commercial reasons, and some of the species described from cultivated plants have still to be re-collected in the wild.

Some of the collectors sent by the English nursery of Veitch have been mentioned. In 1947 the Dutch firm of Van Tubergen, which is still one of the largest dealers in unusual bulbs, published an account of their collectors and of the bulbs they introduced in cultivation. Their most successful collector was P.L. Graeber who travelled every spring from 1897 to 1914 in the environs of Tashkent and Bokhara. He introduced many new species, most of which had been found by Albert Regel but not introduced into general cultivation. *I. graeberiana* was named after him, and among those he introduced were *I. warleyensis*, *I. tubergeniana*, *Crocus alatavicus*, *Tulipa kaufmanniana*, *T. greigei* and *T. hoogiana*.

A. Kronenburg began by collecting for European herbaria but from 1897 collected exclusively for Van Tubergen. For his first two years he was based in Beirut, from where he introduced *Iris histrio*, *I. vartani* and *I. sofarana* among others. He was then instructed to visit the area between Lake Van and Lake Urmia, made difficult at this time by obstructive Turkish bureaucracy and pillaging bands of Kurds, so had to keep to the major roads. However, he managed to introduce quantities of *I. barnumae*, *I. urmiensis* and various colchicums and fritillaries. Later he visited the Caucasus specifically to obtain *Crocus scharojani*: he found it after much searching, and at the same time introduced *Tulipa eichleri*, *Crocus caspius*, and a number of the fine colour forms of *Crocus speciosus*, of which the white form and 'Cassiope', 'Artabair' and 'Pollux' are still in commerce. In 1903 Van Tubergen sent Kronenburg to Bokhara where he found and introduced *I. rosenbachiana* and *Fritillaria eduardii* as well as several tulips. Later from this area Van Tubergen also received *Fritillaria raddeana* and *Allium christophii* from Paul Sintenis, and *Tulipa fosteriana* and *T. praestans*

110

from Joseph Haberbauer who ran the hotel in Samarkhand where Kronenburg had stayed.

One of Van Tubergen's collectors whose introductions have done well in English gardens was J.J. Manissadjian, an Armenian teacher in an American mission school at Mersifon in northern Turkey. He sent back *Iris danfordiae, I. histrioides major, I. gatesii, Galanthus fosteri,* and *Tulipa sprengeri* (an excellent garden plant not yet re-collected in the wild). When the Armenians were driven out of Turkey, Mannissadjian emigrated to North America.

One plant which has not fulfilled the promise expected of it, is *Amaryllis (Hippeastrum) candida* which was found by Van Tubergen's collector Harry Blomfeld in the Salta province of Argentina 'at the blooming period' covering 'the slopes with a snow white cloth' and filling 'the atmosphere with a delightful fragrance'. It proved almost hardy, growing well for many years in an unheated greenhouse in Haarlem, but is now no longer in general cultivation in Europe. Blomfeld is still living and collecting in this area.

Another large nursery firm was that of Dammann and Sprenger based near Naples. Their list of 1891 makes amazing reading in 1983. They offered no less than 61 *Crocus* species, 59 *Tulipa* species, 53 fritillaries, 14 Oncocyclus iris, 11 each of *Romulea* and *Watsonia*, and 20 cultivars of montbretia. Their introductions include *Arum creticum, Gladiolus byzantinus* × *cardinalis* (new for 1893), *Arum pictum* 'Album' (new for 1891), and *Tulipa sprengeri* (new for 1895, and presumably sent to them by Manissadjian). Many of their other new introductions were sent from Ethiopia by the botanist Terraciano.

Many of the plants in Damman's catalogue and in the catalogues of other bulb nurseries at this time were imported from dealers who arranged the collection of bulbs in the wild. One of the best known of these dealers was Edward Whittall (1851–1917) of Smyrna, now Izmir, in Turkey. The Whittall family had settled in Smyrna in 1809 and were engaged in the fig and currant trade. Edward Whittall was a keen sportsman and it was on his sporting trips into the hinterland that he became aware of the wealth of the native flora. Soon he had made extensive gardens in the suburb of Bornova, erected large greenhouses, and opened a flower shop. He sent out villagers to collect bulbs and sold some of the excess to Europe to defray the expenses. Between 1890 and 1907, he sent large numbers of bulbs and herbarium specimens to Kew, free of charge. Others – several million of them – he planted in a garden on Nif Dagh above Izmir. Whittall was the first to send back *Fritillaria*

Figure 5.5
*Amaryllis
machupijchensis*

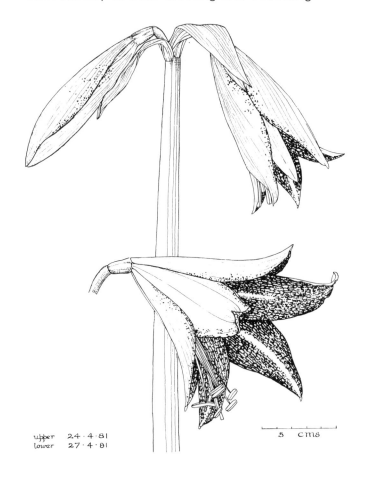

upper 24·4·81
lower 27·4·81

5   cms

whittallii. Several other species were named from plants he introduced, e.g. *Chionodoxa gigantea, C. tmoli* and *Tulipa whittallii.*

Other dealers based in the Middle East were Schlosser of Smyrna (from 1893 onwards), W. Siehe of Mersin (1896–1913), and W.C. Mountain of Istanbul (1890–1914), as well as Egger in Jaffa (1893–1914), and Kvees & Larche of Tiflis (1895–1910). Kvees & Larche specialised in the Caucasus and were probably responsible for the importation of large numbers of Caucasian snowdrops. This trade still continues. Some idea of the quantities and prices of the bulbs offered can be had from Mountain's catalogue of 1909. Some were grown at Mountain's nursery at Floria outside Istanbul, some were sold direct from the wild.

112

Chionodoxa luciliae – cultivated	9 to 15 shilling per thousand	
– collected	7/6 to 14 ” ” ”	
Cyclamen 'rhodium' (?= *repandum*)	£2 – 10 ” ” ”	
Fritillaria whittallii	£2 – 00 ” ” ”	
F. aurea	£1 – 10 ” ” ”	
Galanthus elwesii	£45	per 100,000
G. ikariae (first size)	£1.10/- per thousand	
Sternbergia clusiana	£2 ” ”	
S. fischeriana	£2 ” ”	

It is difficult to assess the effect that collections on this scale had on the wild populations and how long the trade could have lasted if most of the collecting had not stopped by the time of the First World War. Snowdrops and *Chionodoxa* were probably seriously depleted in western Turkey, other genera less so.

Although Turkey was the centre of the trade in the Middle East, there were other dealers in most parts of the world where desirable bulbs are found. There was W. Vivien in Porto in Portugal, Kramer & Co. and K. Wada in Japan, Roth & Cullingbourne in Port Elizabeth in South Africa, and Carl Purdy in California. Purdy's business started in Ukiah, California in 1893, and continued until c. 1950. During this time he and his family sold several million native bulbs from California to Europe, as well as seeds of Californian annuals. His list of 1929–30 includes 17 *Erythronium* species and varieties, 10 Californian fritillaries, and 13 lilies, as well as numerous *Calochortus*, *Brodiaea*, *Camassia* and other bulbous genera: interestingly, four *Delphinium* species were also sold, e.g. *D. californicum*, *D. nudicaule* and *D. cardinale*. In a letter in *Pacific Horticulture* in the fall of 1981, one of Purdy's grandchildren defended their collecting methods. The same patches of wild bulbs were sometimes harvested for many years, the small non-saleable bulbs being replanted in the ground, and an attempt made to improve the habitat. He also made the point that while collecting may reduce the size of a population in a particular habitat, it is rarely totally destroyed as it is when the habitat is built on, ploughed or converted into a road. Purdy is commemorated by many species, notably *Fritillaria purdyi* and *Iris purdyi*.

In the last sixty years bulb-growing has probably held its popularity, but the range of bulbs grown, both cultivars and species, has contracted greatly. New areas to explore have become fewer, and many are politically more unstable than

1914–1980

they were in the early years of the twentieth century. At the same time, the purely physical barriers have been much reduced and air travel has made short visits to see bulbs growing in the wild much easier.

Professional bulb collectors have become fewer and their activities more secretive as the need for conservation of wild populations has come to be recognised by governments throughout the world. Botanical exploration has continued as before, and this has led to new species being discovered and introduced into cultivation. A few of these botanists, some professional, some amateur, have made great contributions to our knowledge of bulbous plants, and their names have become well known, especially through the activities of societies such as the Royal Horticultural Society and the Alpine Garden Society in England, and the Amaryllis Society in N. America.

In the inter-war years bulb-growing in England was greatly encouraged by the enthusiasm of E.A. Bowles, a gentleman–gardener of great eminence, and by Sir Daniel Hall, Director of the John Innes Horticultural Institution. Bowles collected bulbs all over Europe and grew them in his garden in Enfield in Middlesex. He wrote books on *Crocus* (1924), *Narcissus* (1934), and *Colchicum* (1952), and his influence as a populariser of spring bulbs was extended by his other writings, e.g. *My Garden in Spring*. Sir Daniel Hall published *The Tulip* in 1929. During the inter-war years, Turkey and the Middle East were in turmoil and Russia was closed to travellers, so horticultural exploration was almost confined to the Himalayas. However, one or two expeditions did visit the Middle East and had lasting effects.

E.K. Balls was born in England, and made several journeys of great significance before he emigrated to California. In 1932 he visited Iran, entering the country in the south from Baghdad, and found several bulbs including *Fritillaria olivieri* and *Allium akaka* on Mount Elwend. In 1933 and 1934, Balls visited Turkey with W. Balfour Gourlay of Cambridge. They discovered *Fritillaria glaucoviridis* Turrill and the beautiful form of *Fritillaria hermonis* ssp. *amana* EKB 1034, which is still in cultivaton as it reproduces freely by bulbils. Also still grown, is Balls' original collection of *Cyclamen cilicium* var *intaminatum* from near the Cilician gates, which reproduces freely from seed.

On 20 February 1935, Balls set off on a collecting trip to the area west of Lake Van. The *Gardener's Chronicle* reported that 'the friendly relations he has already established with the Turkish authorities will permit Mr. Balls to explore districts generally closed to foreign travellers'. But by 15 June he reported little progress due to continual obstruction by police and the difficulty in getting permission to go into the mountains. Finally, the expedition was abandoned, and in the *Chronicle* the following notice appeared: 'A widespread rumour is that Mr. Balls has been regarded as a secret service agent and, indeed, as no less a person than Lawrence of Arabia, whose decease, apparently, is not admitted by the Turkish authorities.'

In 1936 Balls spent some months in Morocco and in 1937, again with Balfour Gourlay, Balls visited northern Greece and found a new fritillary, *F. epirotica* Turrill, on the high serpentine screes of Mount Smolika. This collection has also survived in cultivation (EKB 3434) and the plant has only been re-collected in the last few years.

It was not until after the Second World War that botanists again began to visit Turkey. Peter Davis had been to Greece, had climbed Honaz Da in western Turkey (in 1938 and 1939) before the war, and had managed to collect while in the forces, e.g. in Cyprus, Egypt, Lebanon, Syria and Jordan. After the war he decided to concentrate on Turkey, and has been Editor, in Edinburgh of *Flora of Turkey*, the last volumes of which are about to be published (1983).

Davis and his co-collectors, notably Oleg Polunin, both discovered and introduced numerous new bulbs from Turkey, and Polunin made important collections in northern Iraq. New species or introductions include *Biarum davisii* from Crete, *Fritillaria davisii* from the Peloponnese, and several other fritillaries and *Sternbergia candida* from south-west Turkey. Bulbs from Davis' collection of *Fritillaria elwesii* and *forbesii*, in 1947, are still in cultivation.

Patrick Synge (1907–1982) was a keen grower of bulbs, especially lilies, all his life, and had great influence as editor of the Royal Horticultural Society. His *Lilies, together with Notholirion and Nomocharis* was published in 1981. In 1960 he went with Admiral and Mrs Paul Furse to north-east Turkey and northern Iran, thus initiating one of the most remarkable series of bulb-collecting expeditions made since the war. They visited Trabzon, Erzurum, Tabriz, Tehran and Meshed, finding and reintroducing to cultivation many plants that had not been seen in England since before 1914. This expedition also discovered a new lily, *L. ciliatum*. Admiral and Mrs Furse followed this up with four other journeys between 1962 and 1966, each overlapping the last and extending further east. They visited much of eastern Turkey, most of Iran and northern and central Afghanistan, reaching deep into the mountains and valleys of the Hindu Kush. Their journeys are described in detail in the R.H.S. journals of the period. It is difficult to imagine the richness of the flora they encountered or to select, from the many new species they brought back, a few to mention. Sadly, only a small percentage have remained in cultivation: *Fritillaria raddeana* was found in great profusion, pounds of seed collected, and is now in commerce, as is *F. uva-vulpis* (which was at first misidentified as *F. assyriaca*) from the Zagros Mountains; there is the graceful *Muscari chalusican* from the mountains north of Tehran and *Iris afghanica* from the Salang Pass; and the Furses are commemorated by *Scilla furseorum*, *Eremurus furseorum*, and others.

Another collector who specialised in Afghanistan was the Norwegian botanist, Per Wendelbo, for some years Director of the Botanical Garden at Göteburg and in Tehran. His main introduction is the beautiful *Iris cycloglossa* which should become a familiar garden plant. Wendelbo prepared the accounts of *Dionysia*, *Allium*, *Eremurus* and Iridaceae with Brian Mathew for *Flora Iranica*. He is remembered by *Iris wendelboi* from Afghanistan and *Fritillaria acmopetala* subsp. *wendelboi* which he discovered in southern Turkey.

A third important collection from Afghanistan is that of the botanist Chris Grey-Wilson, of the Royal Botanic Garden, Kew, with Tom Hewer, a medical professor of Bristol University. Their expedition produced, among other new species, *Iris heweri*, *I. hymenospatha* and *I. kuschkensis*.

The large and beautiful genera *Crocus* and *Iris* have recently been the subject of monographs by Brian Mathew of the Royal Botanic Garden, Kew, and his earlier books, *Dwarf Bulbs* and *Larger Bulbs*, are excellent examples of good advice based on personal experience coupled with scientific knowledge. As a collector, he has been active mainly in Turkey where he has collaborated with A. and T. Baytop of Istanbul University in the study of *Crocus*; other specialists who have collected recently in Turkey are C.D. Brickell of the R.H.S. gardens at Wisley who has studied *Colchicum* and other bulbs, and the present writer, who has concentrated on *Fritillaria* and *Gagea*.

The days of the professional collector are not, however, entirely over. A series of expeditions, first to Lebanon in 1962, then to Turkey and Iran, and most recently to Chile by John Watson and co-collectors found interesting species, including the new and striking pink fritillary, *F. alburyana*, from north-eastern Turkey (ACW 1664). This was named in memory of Sydney Albury, a member of Watson's first expedition to Turkey in 1966, who died while plant-collecting in the Himalayas in 1970. Watson's expedition to Chile in 1971–2 produced hardy but small-flowered *Amaryllis* species, and reintroduced several beautiful tuberous alstroemerias and tropaeolums.

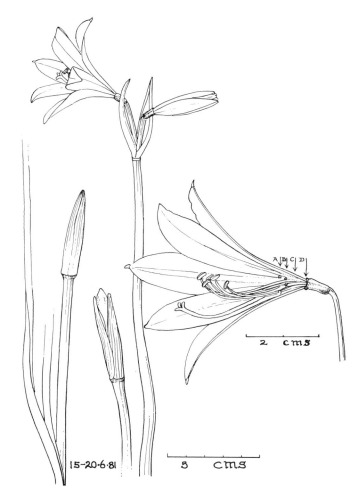

Figure 5.6
Amaryllis advena
B.C.W. 4999

There are very few new bulbs being introduced into Europe at present from either California or South Africa, and the study of them is conducted on the spot. Sima Eliovson has done much to popularise bulbs in South Africa, both cultivars from the northern hemisphere and native South African species. Her books *Spring Flowers of Namaqualand* and *Wild Flowers of Southern Africa, How to grow and identify them* have long sections on bulbs with careful instructions for their treatment. Wayne Roderick has sent many seeds and bulbs of Californian plants to England, and others have come from South African botanic gardens, and from Dr Weynanki in Santiago, Chile. These have been seen, occasionally, at flower shows, having been grown by specialist amateurs and botanic gardens.

Conservation and Collecting Today

The expansion of civilisation has put most forms of wild life under increasing pressure, and bulbs are no exception. Their survival is threatened by three major factors: destruction of the habitat, collecting, and grazing by domestic animals.

Destruction of the habitat is probably the most dangerous of these three factors because it is so final. I do not know of any European bulbs that have become extinct through building, and, as most of them grow on rocky hills, they are probably in no danger. However, in California, and possibly in South Africa, some species are in very real danger as they may be endemic to very small areas, often on low hills. Some of the few remaining habitats of *Fritillaria liliacea* near San Francisco are threatened by development, and can be seen protected in the midst of a sea of houses and gardens. Other species in North America have probably been destroyed by agriculture, especially in the semi-desert areas where whole valleys can be irrigated and cultivated. Inadequate protection from forest fire can also adversely affect bulbous species which depend on it to keep their communities open and to prevent the establishment of a dense shrub layer. Fortunately, the mediterranean eco-system is not so complex and the species are not so interdependent as in tropical forests, with the result that far fewer species are threatened.

There is a double threat from human collecting, for food and for horticulture. Some species were, in the past, an important food for the local population. *Camassia* and *Fritillaria camschatcensis* were both used as winter staple by the American Indians, and Purdy found that one of his Indian workers had become very fond of *Calochortus* bulbs! In the eastern Mediterranean, a porridge-like gruel called 'salep' is made from orchid tubers; owing to the similarity of these tubers to testicles, salep is thought to have aphrodisiac properties. Many different orchid species are used and this type of collecting probably keeps overall numbers down without threatening rare species in particular. The same type of danger probably affects *Fritillaria* species in China where they are still used in cough medicine under the name of Pei-mu. Stephen Haw in the *Bulletin of the Alpine Garden Society* reports that many species are also

Plate 11 *(above).* A ginger, *Kaempferia rosea*, in central Malawi in December.

Plate 12 *(below).* *Lycoris squamigera* flowering in the bulb house, growing with *Alstroemeria* sp., *Zigadenus*, *Amaryllis advena* and *Allium christophii*.

Plate 13 *(left)*. *Hedychium flavescens* by a stream in the forest in Kerala, Southern India.

Plate 14 *(right)*. *Bomarea* species climbing in the forest near Bogota, Colombia. *Photograph: G.A.C. Herklots.*

Plate 15 *(below)*. *Calochortus* and *Brodiaea* flowering in early June in Mendocino Co., California.

Plate 16 *(right). Erythronium californicum* in open woods in Mendocino Co., California, in June.

Plate 17 *(left). Calochortus tolmiei*, 'Pussy ears', in open pine forest in Mendocino Co., California, in June.

Plate 18 *(below). Corydalis popovii*, a tuberous species in Central Asia near Dushanbe, in April.

Plate 19 *(left). Lapeirousia grandiflora* growing in savannah grassland near Blantyre, Malawi, in December.

Plate 20 *(below). Crinum distichum* flowering in December in a flooded field near Lilongwe, Malawi.

cultivated for this purpose, e.g. *F. thunbergii*, which has been grown in Japan for many centuries. In the Amanus mountains in Lebanon, Syria and Turkey, crocuses are widely collected for food: the favourite species seem to be *Crocus cancellatus*, which I have bought and sampled near Gaziantep, in the north, and *C. aleppicus* in the south.

Horticultural collecting is more dangerous because it is selective and threatens rare species more than common ones. However, a distinction must be made between the commercial collector who visits the same area regularly and the botanical tourist who is unlikely to visit exactly the same place more than once. Bulbs are particularly vulnerable because they are so easy to collect and keep alive during the transfer from the wild to the garden.

While there are few examples of bulbs known or believed to have been made extinct by overcollecting, many are in potential danger of extinction by collectors. The huge numbers of snowdrops and chionodoxas imported from western Turkey have made these plants rare in Turkey today. A more recent example of the type of decimation that can occur is that of *Sternbergia candida*, recently discovered and described in 1978 as being rare and very restricted in distribution. Within two years, hundreds of bulbs appeared on the market. Cyclamen, especially those of limited distribution such as *C. libanoticum*, are also in great danger, and the importation of collected corms into this country is supposed to be banned. All the species are, however, available from home-raised plants, either through specialist nurseries or through the Cyclamen Society (see page 196 for the address). Seeds or bulbs of many other rare species can also be had through the specialist societies listed on the same page.

Grazing is less of a threat to bulbous plants than it is to most other forms of vegetation. It has been very heavy in southern Europe and western Asia for many centuries and bulbs have either adapted to it or disappeared. Many bulbs survive by being unpalatable to sheep and goats or else very poisonous. *Eremurus* leaves are full of a slimy, sticky juice and seem to be left alone by livestock; a large population of *Eremurus* is often a sign of overgrazing. *Colchicum* leaves are very poisonous, containing the alkaloid colchicine which prevents the formation of cell walls and produces chromosomal abnormalities. They are not eaten, nor are the flowers. The finest display of wild bulbs I have seen was in Turkey, above Trabzon, in an area close to some cowsheds. The ground was eaten bare of grass, and well fertilised. The *Colchicum speciosum* had thrived to form a carpet of flowers of all shades from palest pink to rich crimson-purple.

The *Crocus* adaptation is more subtle. The leaves can continue to grow up from the base even when the tops have been grazed off: the flowers spring up quickly and are short-lived and the ovary remains safely underground until the seeds are ripe in summer. By this time the herds have probably moved elsewhere.

Fritillaries and many other bulbs do not have any adaptations to grazing but can only survive on cliffs or among rocks, out of the reach of goats, or inside spiny bushes. *Quercus coccifera*, the dwarf holly-leaved mediterranean oak, forms a safe refuge for most mediterranean species, and spiny *Astragalus* plays the same role on the steppe. If no cover is available and the seed capsules are eaten every year, plants have to rely on vegetative propagation and many species from heavily grazed areas do produce large numbers of bulbils.

The twining *Brodiaea*, *B. volubilis*, from California is especially subtle as it always seems to choose to grow up through bushes of the poison oak. However, in California, the main predators of bulbs are gophers and deer, and the deer were never kept in large domesticated herds as were sheep and goats in western Asia, so grazing pressure seems to have played a smaller part in the evolution of bulbous plants. *Fritillaria affinis* (*lanceolata*), however, seems to owe some of its variability to the palatability of its seed capsules to deer, and the ease with which it can spread by bulbils.

The day of the commercial collector who regularly sends large numbers of collected corms to the trade should be over. However, this is easily said by the urban gardener and less easily accepted by the peasant who sees hundreds of bulbs growing in the fields and can make much-needed extra cash by selling them. The onus of stopping this trade rests with the buyer who should resist buying cheap imported bulb species and be prepared to spend more on ones which have been commercially propagated.

The amateur collector should be prepared to exercise restraint when collecting, and many different factors may be taken into account.

The first of these is the accessibility of the habitat, either to people who go to look at flowers, or to other collectors, either local or foreign. It is obviously wrong to collect plants in places where tourists go regularly, such as around sites in Greece and Turkey or near resorts. If every visitor took only a few, the plant would soon be extinct in that area. The same applies to places close to large towns such as San Francisco or Cape Town where wild plants are under increased pressure already. The only exception to this rule is when the habitat is about to be destroyed anyway, either by housing or road-building.

If the habitat is not readily accessible, that is, it is in a place remote from civilisation, the other factors should be taken into account.

Is the species known to be rare or endangered? If so, it should be left alone. Many countries publish *Red Data Books* of protected species, and bulbous plants often make up a significant proportion of them. In Central Asia, many of the tulip species are restricted to only a few localities, and they are threatened not only by the few collectors who go in from the west, but by the eastern Europeans as well, for whom access is easier and who can earn valuable hard currency by exporting them to non-communist countries.

If the species is not very rare, it may be in cultivation already, in which case it is probably better to buy some large bulbs than to collect it from the wild. However, it may be that variations are found in large wild populations which are not in cultivation, and these are probably worth collecting.

If you have decided to collect the bulb of a particular species, there are several things to remember. Bulbs of medium size, that is, about 2–3 cm (1 in) across travel best: if they are smaller than this, they are likely to dry out; if they are larger, they are more difficult to move without damaging them. If the species is spreading by bulbils, choose good forms, surrounded by healthy young. If the species is spreading by seed only, the forms chosen are less important. It is never necessary to collect more than about three bulbs of each plant, especially if it is not present in thousands. Three bulbs of different clones will be enough to establish a breeding population from which the plant can be established in cultivation, and distributed.

The safest type of collecting is to take only the seed. This only marginally affects the chance of survival, even of those particular seeds, as, if a species increases only by seed, the survival to maturity of one seed, during the whole life of the individual, will ensure that the species does not decline. Plants raised from seed generally grow better than collected plants.

In bulbs which normally reproduce from seed, there is great benefit to be had by introducing in cultivation a clone which increases vegetatively. This is well illustrated by the following example. In August 1965, I collected two corms of *Crocus vallicola* on the Zigana pass above Trabzon. One soon died without flowering; the other has flowered almost every year in

121

the open garden, without increasing or setting seed, as, like the majority of wild showy-flowered plants, it is not self-fertile. In 1983 I was on the Zigana pass when *Crocus vallicola* was flowering in thousands in the meadows. The plants were evenly scattered and every one had only one flower, showing the species to be propagated by seed. After an exhaustive search, two plants were found which appeared to increase vegetatively (there was a clump of several identical flowering plants), and these were brought into cultivation; if they prove to increase and grow well, the species could soon become as common in gardens as are *C. speciosus* and other species which are grown commercially in large numbers. Almost without exception, the bulbs which are in commercial production belong to clones which can be easily reproduced vegetatively in large numbers.

Treatment of Collected Bulbs

An ice axe or small pickaxe is the best tool for the collection of bulbs. In peaty turf an old knife is more effective. If the bulbs are in active growth when collected, keep as much soil as possible around the root, and tie the roots and soil tightly into a polythene bag leaving the green bulbs protruding. Allow them to dry slowly. If the bulbs are dormant when collected, they may be wrapped in soft paper (tissue paper or newspaper), and put into a perforated polythene bag. They must then be kept as cool as possible so that condensation does not cause them to rot. Strong linen bags would also work well, but polythene is adequate if used with care.

On arriving at home, dormant bulbs should be stored in a cool place to await planting at the normal time. Any still growing can be planted in sand, watered once, then kept cool, and dried slowly before being replanted in autumn.

Names and Main Areas of Activity of Post-war Collectors of Bulbs

A. Ala	Iran
S. Albury	Turkey, Himalaya.
J.C. Archibald	Iran, Lebanon, Turkey, North Africa.
W.K. Aslet	Greece, Lebanon.
E.K. Balls	Turkey, South America.
F. Baxter	Greece, Iran, etc.
A. and **T. Baytop**	Turkey.
K.A. Beckett	Chile, etc.

122

C.D. Brickell	Greece, Turkey, South Africa, California etc.
P. Christian	Southern France, Greece.
P. Cox of Glendoick	Turkey, Himalaya, China.
P.A. and **M.J. C**ox	Turkey, Greece, Yugoslavia (with J. Marr).
H. and **M. C**rook	Greece, Turkey etc.
P.H. Davis	Turkey, North Africa, Syria, Lebanon, etc.
C. Ecker	California, Mexico.
G. Forrest	Himalaya.
C.R. Fraser-**J**enkins	Turkey, etc. (mainly ferns).
P. Furse	Turkey, Iran, Afghanistan.
E. Gabrielian	Soviet Armenia.
C. Grey-**W**ilson	Iran, Afghanistan, East Africa, Himalaya, etc.
I. Hedge	Afghanistan etc.
T.F. Hewer	Iran, Afghanistan.
M. and **A.H**oog	Greece, Central Asia.
S.V. Horton	Turkey, Greece, Spain.
R. Lancaster	China, Turkey, Caucasus, Iran, etc.
H.J. Leep	Turkey.
R. and **S. L**inzee Gordon	Greece, Turkey, Himalaya.
W. Marais	Turkey, etc.
J.R. Marr	Greece, Yugoslavia, Turkey.
B. Mathew	Turkey, Greece, East Africa, etc.
L. Maurice Mason	Tropics *passim*.
R.D. Nutt	Turkey, etc.
V. Pilous	Soviet territories.
O. Polunin	Himalaya, Turkey, Iraq, Greece, etc.
C. Quest-**R**itson	Spain, Caucasus, etc.
E.M. Rix	Turkey, Greece, Caucasus, Central Asia, etc.
W. Roderick	California.
O. Sonderhousen	Turkey, Greece, etc.
N.J. Stevens	Turkey etc.
P.M. Synge	Greece, Turkey, etc.
S. Walker	Southern USA, Mexico.
J.M. Watson	Turkey, Chile, etc.
M. Young	Greece.

Initials of
Groups and
Expeditions

ACW	Albury, Cheese and Watson.
BCW	Beckett, Cheese and Watson.
B & M	Brickell and Mathew.
BSBE	Bowles Scholarship Botanical Expedition (with B. Mathew).
BSSA	Botanical Society of South Africa.
CMW	Cheese, Mitchell and Watson.
F & S	Furse and Synge.
G-W/H	Grey-Wilson and Hewer.
H & S	Horton and Stevens.
L & P	Leep and Pascher.
M & T	Mathew and Tomlinson.
PAC/M	P.A. Cox and Marr.
PF/PS	Furse and Synge.

CHAPTER 6

Cultivation of Hardy Bulbs

(i) Bulbs Naturalised in Grass

Bulbs in the
Open Garden

Bulbs look best surrounded by grass or growing up through it as many of them do in nature. Unfortunately, it often happens in gardens that the grass is too thick for small bulbs to grow through, or the root competition is too much for them to survive.

Daffodils cope best with thick grass, especially on heavy soils. They emerge and flower before the grass has grown up and are large enough to hold their own and increase. For a natural look, it is best to get the wild yellow *Narcissus pseudonarcissus* and the white *Narcissus poeticus*, the pheasant eye, or at least the more old-fashioned hybrids with smaller flowers. The leaves can be cut off six weeks after the last flowers have faded, usually about mid-June in southern England, without harming the bulbs. Any earlier removal will result in the number of flowers diminishing year after year. Planting should be as early as possible in autumn and the bulbs should be placed in informal groups, not evenly spaced but with a few in tight groups, some further apart and a few at a distance. This gives the impression of a naturally expanding group. One or two of the larger crocuses such as the cultivated forms of *Crocus vernus* will survive in thick grass, as will the summer snowflake, *Leucojum aestivum*, which tolerates or even prefers wet soils.

The smaller and choicer bulbs will need to be planted in thinner grass if they are to do more than survive. The alpine meadows at Wisley and at the Savill Garden, Windsor, are good examples of what can be done on acid soil, and rather similar examples can be seen on chalky soil at Highdown near Worthing and in several places in Cambridge. A further refinement is the 'Meadow Garden' described by Chrisopher Lloyd in his *Well Tempered Garden*, where bulbs form only part of the floral display and a collection of more or less wild flowers is equally important.

In the sandy, acid 'alpine' meadow the earliest bulbs are snowdrops and *Crocus tommasianus*. These are followed by the dwarf narcissus, *N. bulbocodium*, with *N. triandrus* in the drier parts, and *N. cyclamineus* in the wetter parts. *Erythronium* species, particularly the European *E. dens-canis*, look well with blue *Chionodoxa* and scillas. Wild bluebells (*Hyacinthoides non-scriptus*) and *Narcissus poeticus* can be very beautiful in this setting; the earliest lily, *L. pyrenaicum*, rounds off the spring flowers. Autumn starts in early September with *Crocus nudiflorus* and *Colchicum autumnale*, though the white *Crocus vallicola* which would grow well here, if it could be obtained, would flower in August. Other colchicums and crocuses come later; the finest are the beautiful bluish *Crocus speciosus* and the purplish *Colchicum speciosum*.

The neutral or chalky meadow will suit a greater range of bulbs, which flower over a long period. Crocuses and snowdrops do better here than in the acid meadow; the dwarf narcissus do less well. *Scilla bifolia* and *Anemone blanda* can form carpets of blue in place of the yellow of *Narcissus bulbocodium*. Fritillaries, *F. meleagris* and *F. pyrenaica*, will thrive with various *Ornithogalum* species, especially the green-striped *O. nutans*. *Tulipa sylvestris* is unreliable but has become naturalised successfully in several places. Later come the red tulips, forms of *T. gesnerana* and finally *Tulipa sprengeri*, a beautiful intense scarlet; few bulbs contribute towards summer colour; the sombre martagon lily (*L. martagon*) is naturalised in some places, and at Great Dixter, *Iris latifolia* makes a fine show in late June. The irises have made most of their growth by mid-July and will not be weakened by being out. If possible, the lilies should be left until they go yellow.

For the 'Meadow Garden' to work well, the correct cutting regime must be carefully followed and no nitrogenous fertiliser should be allowed near the grass. The first cutting of the grass is not before July and hay is made with the grass before it is cleared away. It is important that the grass is not left to rot on the surface or the more delicate plants will be smothered and only the coarse grasses such as cock's foot (*Dactylis glomerata*) will survive. For the next two months the grass is kept short, again removing any which has been cut. By September careful watch is kept for the emerging flowers of the autumn crocus and the colchicums so that they are not decapitated by the mower. A final cut can generally be fitted in in late October or November after the autumn-flowering bulbs have faded and before any leaves have emerged. The meadow is then ready again for the first snowdrops of spring.

Planting of most of the bulbs will be done in the autumn as soon as they are received, and if the soil is heavy or slug-ridden, it is beneficial to surround the bulbs with fine, sharp grit or coarse sand to give them a good start. Again, it is important to place them as informally as possible and to make sure that they are well scattered so that they have room to spread.

(ii) Bulbs in Lawns

Few bulbs are suitable for growing in lawns because their leaves need to be left in early summer to go yellow while the lawn needs to be kept mown. Only the earliest flowering are suitable, e.g. crocuses, snowdrops and early scillas, as their leaves will die down in May. Even then the places where they have been will be brown for a week or two. They are slightly more satisfactory under deciduous trees where the grass will grow less vigorously anyway as soon as the trees begin to come into leaf.

(iii) The Caucasian Herb Field

Many of the most satisfactory garden bulbs in wet climates come from the mountains of northern Turkey and the Caucasus. They grow there in places where the ground is covered with deep snow in winter and by large leafy herbaceous plants in summer, in clearings in the forest, either in the open or in the shade of lofty trees. The bulbs flower in the brief spring before the leafy herbs grow up to shade them. As the herbs are very deep rooted, and the bulbs can exploit the top 15 cm (6 ins) or so of soil the two can co-exist in harmony. I have attempted to recreate this habitat in my garden in southern England. Wild ivy has established itself as a low groundcover; it survives beneath the large herbs and makes a good foil for the bulbs in spring. Snowdrops are found in this habitat in nature and have done especially well as have spring snowflakes, *Leucojum vernum*. Another success has been *Iris histrioides*, and *I. winogradowii* and their hybrids should do equally well. *Scilla bifolia*, *Anemone blanda* and *Eranthis* have also done well, and *Fritillaria latifolia* is surviving. Lilies grow up with the herbs and both *L. martagon* and *L. szovitzianum* should feel at home here. The white-veined leaves of *Arum italicum* look well among the ivy.

There are many wild herbaceous plants which are appropriate in this setting. Most common in the forests of northen Turkey are *Telekia speciosa*, whose broad basal leaves suppress any lesser weeds, and the closely related *Elecampanes* (*Inula* spp.);

other frequent ones are *Campunala lactiflora*, *Geranium psilostemon*, and the yellow-flowered *Salvia glutinosa*; *Gentiana asclepiadea*, *Aconitum* spp., *Mulgedium* spp., and *Veratrum lobelianum*. In sunnier sites paeonies, *Ferula*, *Gypsophila paniculata*, *Alchemilla mollis* and *Scabiosa caucasica* will have the same effect. The beautiful *Symphytum caucasicum* with its blue flowers has proved rather rampant and is unsatisfactory because it is already leafy when the bulbs are in flower, and the native English Queen Anne's lace, *Anthriscus sylvestris*, is best avoided for the same reason. The ideal plants for the purpose are compact, deep-rooted, emerging late in spring and shading out any weeds with large leaves. They provide interest and colour in an area which would otherwise be bare or have to be kept cut during the summer.

The same effect can be achieved using plants from other areas of the world. Hostas are very suitable and provide good summer cover for erythroniums as well as snowdrops and *Eranthis*, especially in shadier places. Deciduous *Agapanthus* will associate with dwarf tulips or anemones, in the sun. *Rheum palmatum* and *Osmunda* are good by the waterside, and one of the most charming sights at Wisley is *Narcissus cyclamineus* where it has naturalised itself in an old clump of *Osmunda*. In another place *Leucojum vernum* has done the same within a few inches of the water. Other bog garden plants and moisture-loving bulbs can be combined to similar effect.

Once this feature has been established it needs the minimum of maintenance in contrast to the true herbaceous border. The dead flower stems of the herbaceous plants can be cut in mid-winter, and the bulbs will benefit from a general fertiliser or bone meal applied in late autumn. Fertility is no danger here as it is in the meadow. Weeds are tolerated because they are generally swamped; any which appear can be spot-treated with weedkiller.

(iv) Bulbs in Woodland

Woodland gardens also differ in character depending on whether they are on acid or alkaline soil; a different range of bulbs grows successfully in each.

Acid woodland tends to be peaty and moist throughout the summer and the bulbs which thrive here are from North America or the Far East. The wild garden at Wisley or the woodlands at the Savill garden or at Knightshayes are examples, each with its own specialities. *Erythronium* species grow well, the pink *E. revolutum* being the most beautiful of the commoner species; *E. americanum* a small yellow one, is naturalised at Wisley. Trilliums are happy in this situation, though I know of nowhere where they carpet the woods as they do in America. *T. grandiflorum* and *T. sessile* are the best to try to establish. Later come arisaemas from Japan and China, which are becoming more widely grown. The pink-flowered *A. candidissimum* is especially beautiful at Knightshayes. I believe it is unusually susceptible not to winter cold, but to summer drought, and that may have prevented it from becoming commoner in gardens. It emerges and flowers in late June. About this time, some of the American lilies flower. *L. pardalinum* and its hybrid 'Shuksan' are among the easiest as is *L. superbum*. They have large turk's cap flowers in various shades of yellow or orange. *L. canadense*, though common in north-eastern North America, has proved very unwilling to succeed in Europe. It is most beautiful with elegant, flared, hanging bells.

The giant (2.5-m or 8-ft) *Cardiocrinum giganteum* is easy to grow in any moist woodland. Its bulbs are monocarpic. A splendid show can be had by growing them to flowering size (or buying them) and then planting them out; however, the following year there will be few, if any, spikes. A more natural and long-lasting effect can be had by raising a large number from seed (which is a slow but easy business). The first will flower in about the sixth year, but thereafter there will be a good number of spikes every year. The seed heads should be removed before they begin to develop and side bulbs formed around the dying bulb will themselves flower in two or three years without disturbance.

Ground cover in the acid woodland will consist either of small herbaceous plants or of a mulch of leafmould. A beautiful effect may be had by cultivating moss, either the pale *Leucobryum glaucum* or the bright green *Mnium hornum*. These may be encouraged and the weeds killed by paraquat which has the convenient property of killing all green flowering plants but leaving mosses unharmed. Bulbs will also be undamaged if they are underground but any green leaf on which the paraquat falls will be killed.

(v) Calcareous Woodland

Most gardens contain some large trees which have either bare soil or poor, thin grass underneath for much of the summer. In autumn, after the leaves have fallen, the grass appears healthier for a time as the tree roots become less active. This is an ecological niche favoured by many bulbs which begin growing when the soil becomes moist in autumn and go dormant as it dries out when the leaves expand in early summer. Other non-bulbous plants which can grow in this habitat are good companions for the bulbs, e.g. primroses, violets and other woodland flowers, and ivy, which can form effective ground-cover.

Trees vary in the amount of shade they produce and bulbs vary in the amount of shade they can tolerate. The most shade-tolerant are the *Cyclamen*. *C. neapolitanum* looks and grows especially well if planted around the base of an old oak or beech. It will also grow well under conifers where the slanting rays of the winter sun can reach the leaves. The other species which make their leaves in autumn, e.g. *C. cilicium*, *C. coum*, *C. pseudibericum*, etc., are equally shade-tolerant.

The very early flowering scillas, *sibirica* and *bifolia*, snow-drops and winter aconites (*Eranthis*), will also do well directly under deciduous trees, as will *Corydalis solida*, chionodoxas and *Anemone blanda*. Their leaves will all have had plenty of time to expand before the trees come into leaf. The native English bluebell (*Hyacinthoides non-scriptus*) and wood anemone (*A. nemorosa*) and its cultivars flower somewhat later and will tolerate quite dense cover. They do best, however, in open woodland where they get dappled sun, or in coppices where the tree cover is removed about every ten years. Most fritillaries require more sun but *F. meleagris* will survive in open woods, even among bluebells, and *F. pontica*, a green-flowered species from Greece, is also worth trying. Lilies can also be naturalised in clearings; *L. martagon* has been a fine sight among the trees at the back of St. John's College, Cambridge, for many generations and there are photographs of *L. monadelphum* growing in thousands near Broadway in Worcestershire. This lily with its large, yellow, delicately spotted flowers is long-lived but difficult to establish; in the wild it grows both in woods and in open meadows.

Bulbs in Formal Gardens

(i) Bedding

Many people's idea of bulbs will be of perfect blocks of identical hyacinths or serried ranks of bright tulips above a sea of forget-me-nots or wallflowers. Bulbs are eminently suitable as bedding plants. They can be guaranteed to flower and, as most varieties are all of one clone (the progeny of a single bulb), they will all flower at the same height and on the same day when they are planted in similar conditions. Tulips and hyacinths are the traditional favourites although modern *Narcissus* are coming into favour. Lilies were often used in more affluent times, but are now seldom planted in large numbers. Beautiful displays can be seen in many parks, notably in Regent's Park in London and at the Keukenhof in Holland. It is tulips and hyacinths which make up most of the colour in the bulb fields.

For the best results the soil in the beds should be rich and well drained without lumps of fresh manure which might encourage the bulbs to rot and without slugs or snails which make unsightly holes in the leaves or eat through the stems at ground level. It is worthwhile buying good bulbs in the first place, especially of the *Narcissus* which are the most sensitive to drying. If they are carefully looked after, the bulbs can be used for many years. When the time comes to replace the spring bedding with summer bedding, the bulbs should be lifted carefully, keeping some soil around the roots and planted in boxes to dry off naturally. Hyacinths and tulips may then be cleaned and stored until autumn in a cool, airy shed. *Narcissus* are better replanted in a place where they can be left undisturbed till needed again.

Different combinations of spring bedding plants and bulbs can be had to suit any taste, or bulbs alone can be used. In general, the effect of two colours only is, I believe, more elegant. A cool and distinctive effect is made by the white, lily-flowered tulip, White Triumphator, underplanted with tall, blue forget-me-nots. An early-flowering red tulip such as the dwarf *T. praestans* 'Fusilier' could also be planted in this scheme; it will flower three weeks earlier than the lily-flowered type. Wallflowers also make a suitable background; again, keeping to one or two colours looks more sophisticated, if less bright. Dwarf Kaufmanniana and greigei tulips can be grown with the compact *Myosotis* for an earlier and shorter effect, and bedding daisies (*Bellis*) and pansies or violas are also suitable. A blue background can also be created with grape hyacinths (*Muscari*), or *Anemone blanda*.

For summer bedding, lilies and alliums have great impact. They will need planting in autumn, so they must either be grown in pots and then carefully planted out without disturbing the roots, or planted among the spring bedding and left undisturbed. The finest and easiest are probably *Lilium regale* and *Allium christophii* with its shining starry, purple flowers;

they are shown off best by the grey foliage of *Helichrysum petiolatum* or *Artemisia* 'Powys'. Dutch and English irises or gladioli can be used in a similar way. In this scheme another plant will be required for colour in late summer, possibly a fuschia cultivar or one of the many heliotropes or verbenas which can grow up above the grey background.

Many bulbous plants are suitable for tropical bedding schemes. The plants must be kept inside away from frost in winter and then planted out in early summer – say, in late May in southern England – in a warm situation in very rich, moist soil.

Hedychium species do well and give an exotic effect with their large leaves. *H. gardnerianum* should do well but the white scented *H. coronarium* does not get enough heat in England to flower and I think that lack of heat was the cause of my failure with *Gloriosa*. *Gladiolus callianthus* has been more successful and flowers over several weeks, and *Eucomis* and *Galtonia* would be good in climates in which they cannot be left outside in winter. All these and other summer-growing bulbs do better in the warmer summers of central Europe or North America. They mostly require much feeding and water whilst in growth and can safely be stored in a cool, dry, dark place in winter.

(ii) Bulbs in Herbaceous Borders

Bulbs can be rather a nuisance in herbaceous borders; most of them do not want to be disturbed in winter, and the gaps between the clumps of herbaceous plants cannot be forked over for fear of spiking the bulbs. Again, most bulbs do not like the top dressing of manure which is beneficial to the border.

One or two clumps of the larger bulbs are probably worthwhile as long as they are kept compact and clearly marked. Crown imperials (*Fritillaria imperialis*) are appropriate in this setting, and clumps of the modern large daffodil or narcissus hybrids will do well. The latter can be lifted in winter without spoiling their flowering prospects. *Eremurus* make a fine background in summer but their young shoots need protection against late frosts. They are best planted with the centre of the crowns in a pile of sharp grit to ward off excess moisture and slugs. Finally, many of the Liliaceae or Iridaceae with fleshy roots are eminently suitable as they behave as herbaceous perennials, e.g. the deciduous *Agapanthus* cultivars, *Iris spuria* or *Iris sibirica* in wetter soils.

Figure 6.1
Galtonia viridiflora

20·6·78   5 cms   29·6·78   2 cms

(iii) Bulbs in Mixed Borders

The mixed border, one which contains trees, shrubs and perennials combined together, provides a more suitable home for bulbs than the purely herbaceous border. By its very nature the mixed border cannot be gone over as thoroughly as the herbaceous, so the bulbs are less of a nuisance.

For early spring, dwarf bulbs can be naturalised and they will look well with hellebores and other early flowers. *Scilla*, *Chionodoxa*, *Anemone blanda* and *A. hortensis* are all suitable, and they will be followed by almost every bulb which will grow outside, up to and including the colchicums. Numerous combinations of shrubs and bulbs can be tried but a particularly beautiful one is *Corylopsis pauciflora* carpeted with blue *Chionodoxa* or *Anemone blanda*. Borders under sunny walls are

133

most useful and it is here that most South African bulbs have to be grown in England if they are to flower freely: *Nerine bowdenii*, the belladonna lily (*Brunsvigia rosea*), watsonias, *Eucomis*, *Dahlia* species, and anything which requires more warmth than can be had in the open garden.

If both winter-growing (mediterranean) and summer-growing bulbs are grown, they should be kept apart so that the former can be left dry and dormant, while the latter are watered and fed. This is an important distinction for those fortunate enough to garden in mediterranean climates. Areas of winter-growing bulbs should be left dry in summer and protected from the sprinklers which keep the lawns green because many, if watered in summer, are liable to rot.

Bulbs in Rock Gardens

The rock garden is essentially a place where small plants can be grown in well-drained soil and, as such, it is suitable for all dwarf bulbs. Only the ones which flower in mid-winter or require some frost protection or have to be kept dry in summer are better grown in the alpine house or bulb frame.

The essential soil requirements of bulbs are the same as for most alpines. They need very gritty fertile soil, with a high percentage of leafmould or peat. It is often said that bulbs are not happy growing up through mats of alpines such as *Aubretia* but they would grow in these places in nature and many look better here than growing out of bare soil. I think the danger is probably slugs which lurk under the leafy mats and eat the succulent shoots of the bulbs before they emerge. Alpines from the mountains by the Mediterranean which can survive drying out in summer are especially suitable companions for bulbs. Origanums are typical examples, being restricted to a dense rootstock during winter, but requiring room to spread in summer.

Bulbs in Peat Banks

The peat bank or peat wall is essentially an adjunct to the woodland garden where choice, moisture-loving plants can be grown in semi-shade, or at least on a north-facing slope.

It is the best place to grow the more choosy and difficult bulbs from the Himalayas, China, Japan and humid North America. Good examples of peat banks can be seen at Wisley, at Edinburgh Botanic Gardens, and at Kew, and the whole concept of the peat garden is well described by Alfred Evans in *The Peat Garden and its Plants* (Dent, 1974). Here the smaller trilliums such as *T. cernuum*, *T. rivale*, and the rarer yellow and white forms of *T. erectum* can be cherished as can the erythroniums such as *E. hendersonii* and *E. tuolumnense*, the clintonias, *Fritillaria camschatcensis* and other Americans. This is the place for the high alpine lilies such as *L. macklinae* and *L. formosanum* var *pricei*, the nomocharis, the arisaemas and the weird *Paris polyphylla*. Many mediterranean bulbs will also do well here, especially snowdrops and fritillaries. *F. acmopetala*, in nature a strictly mediterranean plant, grows well, and this is an ideal habitat for the beautiful pale-green *F. pallidiflora* from the mountains of southern Siberia. If pleiones are to be attempted outside they can occupy a vertical crevice between the peat blocks where they may be protected from rain by a sheet of glass in winter.

A peat bank is easy to construct if enough of the right materials are to hand. You will need peat blocks, preferably the more fibrous ones from the top of the bog, sharp lime-free grit, and leafmould or peat; good sandy loam will complete the soil mix. The site should be chosen to face north, and it should not be overhung by trees unless the canopy is very high and open. Terraces can be built up with retaining walls made of peat blocks, or blocks can be set irregularly into the surface to support a slope. The main planting will be of dwarf rhododendrons and other small peat-loving shrubs; the bulbs will associate well with these and with the primulas, gentians and other small herbaceous plants. Generally speaking, the bulbs will do best in the drier and better-drained spots such as near the tops of the walls and in crevices between the blocks.

The dwarf rhododendrons and other shrubs will make good supports for some of the tuberous climbers. *Tropaeolum tuberosum* will grow well here; in the south of England it can prove difficult to grow satisfactorily, in Scotland it can easily become a weed. Tuberous *Codonopsis* such as *C. vinciflora* and *Aconitum volubile* require a similar site, and the shrubs will also protect the young shoots of the lilies from late frosts.

The Bulb Frame

The bulb frame has been developed in order to grow bulbs from mediterranean climates in the summer-wet climate of northern Europe. It is essentially a raised bed of stony soil which can be covered with a frame to keep out all the rain in summer and to give some protection against very low temperatures in late winter and spring.

For many of the bulbs from the drier parts of the Middle East, Central Asia and California a bulb frame is almost essential. The Juno (subgenus *Scorpiris*) and Oncocyclus irises, many fritillaries, tulips and crocuses need summer drought to ripen their bulbs. They soon rot in a wet English summer. Many others such as reticulata irises, *Calochortus*, the rest of the fritillaries, most cyclamen, most of the easier crocuses, *Tecophilaea cyanocrocus*, *Gentiana olivieri* and many anemones may not need a bulb frame, but do better in one, and their delicate flowers are protected from early spring rain and snow. Many, also, seem to do better planted out than if they are grown in pots; their roots then have room to develop freely and they are not likely to dry off prematurely.

A bulb frame is easy to make. The actual frame should let in as much air as possible. Dutch lights can be used if they are raised well above the surface and have sufficient overlap to prevent drips blowing into the frame in summer. A similar and very effective covering can be made with corrugated perspex. The old 'pluie' frames are good; they are no longer made but as they are more or less indestructible, they may be found second-hand or rejected – the ones with the side extensions designed for tomatoes are ideal. The modern equivalent are 'Access' frames and again, those with high sides are best. The sides are vertical so can be left open or partly open most of the time; rain can be admitted by sliding the top glass. But a word of warning! They are not nearly as strong as the iron 'pluie' frames and a few days before I wrote this mine collapsed under the weight of snow, squashing all the early-flowering irises, crocuses and romuleas and the emerging fritillaries with lumps of wet snow and broken glass. If snow is threatening, the side glasses should all be closed for maximum rigidity and a heavy covering of snow should not be allowed to build up on the roof of the frame.

The sides of the frame can be made either of brick, of concrete or breeze blocks, or simplest of all, of old railway sleepers. The minimum of foundations will be necessary. The walls can be any height from 30 cm (1 ft) upwards so that the soil in which the plants are growing is raised above the surrounding level. If the surface is at about waist height, small bulbs can be seen better. It is wise to cover the base of the frame with fine wire mesh to keep out moles and field mice in Europe, and gophers in America. Though moles do not eat plants, they can cause havoc if they get among the carefully labelled bulbs.

A good layer of drainage material should cover the base of the growing area. It can be old rubble, broken bricks or coarse gravel. About 10 cm (4 ins) will be sufficient, but it may be deeper as it is the cheapest material with which to fill up unwanted spaces. A layer of coarse peat, old mushroom compost or fibrous turf should be laid on the drainage material to prevent the compost being washed into it and either clogging it up or being wasted.

On top of this goes the compost in which the bulb's roots will feed. It should consist of sterilised loam, peat or leafmould, coarse sand and grit in roughly equal parts for bulbs such as fritillaries and crocus which do better in a rather rich soil. Double the amount of grit is probably advisable for oncocyclus irises and the Juno group and other plants which require really excellent drainage. The addition of crushed limestone or powdered dolomite is beneficial to all bulbs but especially the difficult irises. For a small area John Innes Potting compost No. 3 can be used instead of the loam; it is 7 parts loam anyway to 5 of other ingredients and has a general fertiliser added. If ordinary loam is used, a general fertiliser should be added in the recommended quantity. For a large frame the dark red-brown soil from the bonfire can be used instead of loam: in many ways it resembles the mediterranean terra rossa soils and bulbs seem to thrive in it.

Between 20 and 30 cm (8 and 12 ins) of this mixture is ample for the bulbs to root in and if a frame is being planted this can be put in first. The bulbs themselves should be planted in a layer of coarse silver sand on top of the root mixture, with sand both below and above the bulb. E.A. Bowles, a great grower of rare bulbs, recommends this for crocuses, and Christabel Beck used it for fritillaries. I have found it beneficial in promoting good root growth by encouraging many small roots to form at the base of the bulbs and it also helps to discourage any slugs which may find their way into the frame. Above the sand 5 to 8 cm (2 to 3 ins) of very gritty compost is used to keep the moisture in the area around the bulbs. Only the largest bulbs such as crown imperials, lilies or crinums need planting any deeper than this and they are usually not grown in a bulb frame anyway. The surface layer should consist of about 6 cm (about 2 ins) of coarse grit. Limestone or sandstone is better than crushed shingle on which the moisture tends to condense.

137

Labelling

Each group of bulbs should be carefully labelled. Various methods for keeping adjacent groups apart can be used. Slates or tiles can be sunk between the groups and care taken that adjacent species are not so similar that they become muddled. The plastic lattice pots made for aquatics can be used: the bulb roots can go through the lattice but the bulbs themselves cannot get muddled. The labels can be securely fixed to the pots; aluminium Hartley labels are best for this purpose – if a supplier can be found. These plastic pots are also useful for odd small bulbs planted out in the garden. The plants are then less likely to be lost or dug up by mistake.

Watering

The watering regime of the bulb frame should follow the pattern of natural watering of the bulbs in the wild. For most this will mean watering first in late September or early October. Californian bulbs can be left a month or so later so that they do not make too much leaf growth before the cold of winter sets in. One or two really thorough waterings or a few weeks of natural rain in autumn should be sufficient, and from then until spring the soil should be kept just moist. It is very important that the bulbs do not dry out and it is also important that they are not very wet or the more sensitive ones may rot. The surface grit should be kept as dry as possible and, except in very foggy or frosty weather, the sides of the frame should be left open to admit as much air as possible. More water can be given again in warm dry spells from February onwards or when the bulbs start to grow and flower. At this stage in nature they would be receiving melting snow or heavy spring rains. Watering can continue generously until May, or until the plants are past flowering or the leaves begin to go yellow. It should then cease altogether until late September. The summer-flowering Californian bulbs flower in nature after their leaves have died – *Calochortus* and *Brodiaea* are found growing out of dead grass – and so with them watering can cease before or while they are in flower: the condition of the leaves rather than the flowering stem will be the indicator.

Feeding

Most bulbs do much better in a rich fertile soil. The finest snowdrops I have ever seen were growing in almost pure sheep manure in a place in central Turkey where the sheep sheltered in summer under a small north-facing cliff. *Crocus vallicola* and *Colchicum speciosum* were growing best and biggest where the cow manure was thrown out of the sheds onto the hillside.

In the garden, feeding wants to be rather more circumspect because of the danger of moulds, especially botrytis, on soft, sappy leaves. The best fertilisers are those which are high in potash and phosphates and rather low in nitrogen, such as are recommended for fruiting tomatoes, chrysanthemums or roses. These will produce strong, healthy growth, not too lush, and plenty of good flowers. The fertiliser may be applied either as granules sprinkled on the surface or as liquid in the watering. 'Growmore' is a recommended brand for the former. For the latter, I have used 'Tomorite' with good results, mixed at the recommended strength at more or less weekly intervals which usually means at every watering. One or two feeds with 'Liquinure' or a higher nitrogen formulation would probably be beneficial in early spring, especially to young plants which have not yet reached flowering size. Similarly, foliar feeds can be used on specific plants which require a 'boost'.

Spraying

Some spraying programme will be necessary if a lot of bulbs are grown close together. Aphids make themselves a real nuisance by deforming the leaves and flowers and especially by spreading virus. A systemic insecticide should be used reglarly, that is, about every three weeks or at least at the first sign of any infestation. Special care should be taken to spray any plants which are suspected of having virus if the gardener is too soft-hearted to burn them on suspicion. Similarly, a watch must be kept for moulds and any infected plants should be removed or sprayed with benlate, captan or a suitable fungicide.

Most of the plants grown in the bulb frame require as much sun as they can get in northern Europe and the site chosen for the frame should receive as much sun as possible, especially in winter and spring. However, in sunnier climates it may be beneficial to provide some shade in summer to prevent delicate bulbs such as fritillaries from being killed by desiccation. This happened in some places, even in England, in the hot summer of 1976.

The Shady Bulb Frame

A raised bed in shade or one which is shaded by trees in summer is really an adjunct to the peat bed where more delicate plants can be looked after more carefully. The soil should be leafy and well drained, kept moist in summer and rather dry in winter. This is the place to grow dwarf Japanese bulbs such as the very difficult *Fritillaria japonica* and *F. amabilis*, small anemones, arisaemas, and the dwarf trilliums and claytonias. It will also be suitable for asiatic bulbs such as special cyclamen and snowdrops which do not like the harsh, dry summers of the sunny bulb frame.

The Mediterranean House

This is the most sophisticted way to grow mediterranean bulbs and also the most comfortable as they can be enjoyed to the full on cold winter days. The house should be as large and airy as possible and the beds should be built inside in a similar way to a bulb frame although they need not be built up so high because they are more insulated from outside conditions. Ventilation is very important and as much air as possible should be admitted at all times except in very cold or damp weather. The watering regime will depend on the type of bulbs grown; part of the house may be kept for winter-growing bulbs and part for summer-growing bulbs and it is important that these two types be kept separate. The warm, dry conditions in the house are especially good for red spider and aphids, and a constant watch must be kept for them: the red spider is best controlled by the use of a predator while aphids must be sprayed or watered with systemic insecticide, trying, at the same time, to avoid killing the red spider predators! Ants must also be destroyed. They do not do much direct damage to bulbs but they spread aphids, especially root aphids, and can thus cause much harm.

Bulbs from warmer mediterranean climates, such as South Africa, will do especially well, as will those that need the extra warmth of the mediterranean house. The tenderer species may be grown with the addition of only marginal heat, such as from a fan heater set to come on at 0 °C (32 °F) to keep out the frost. Bulbs from regions hot and wet in summer will often flower better than in the open garden, even though they are not strictly tender. *Lycoris squamigera* is an example of this group, a shy flowerer in the open garden, but flowering profusely in a totally unheated mediterranean house.

I.B. Barton describes some of the successes and failures of his mediterranean house in an article in the Alpine Garden Society's *Bulletin* for 1981. Among the plants he mentions is

Tropaeolum tricolorum, which seems to do much better planted out than kept in a pot in the mediterranean house.

Bulbs in Pots

If bulbs are to be exhibited at flower shows or brought into the house, they must be grown in pots. Pot culture is also used widely at Kew, Wisley, Cambridge Botanical Garden and other gardens where the plants are brought into an alpine house for exhibition to the public and then returned to frames after they have flowered.

The planting, feeding and watering regimes are the same as for the bulb frame: indeed, at Wisley, the bulbs used in the alpine house are grown in the plastic lattice pots recommended for the bulb frame and then dug up and slipped into ordinary plastic pots as they come into flower.

Feeding is even more important to pot-grown bulbs as they have more restricted root systems and any nutrients are quickly leached out by waterings in which the water runs through the pot. At the same time, the soil in pots, especially clay pots, dries out more quickly than soil in a raised bed. Such drying must be avoided at all costs when the plant is in active growth. Most small bulbs, notably crocuses, reticulata irises and fritillaries, have annual roots which are very delicate and in some cases unable to branch if the growing tip is killed. If these roots are damaged by drying, no new ones can be formed that year, and the plant is greatly weakened as a result; it thinks that summer has come and immediately goes dormant until the autumn. The same goes for many South African bulbs such as lachenalias which require ample water with no drying out until after they have flowered. When they have had sufficient water, the difference in, and the quality of, the flowers is remarkable. Because of this, all these bulbs will do better if the pots are plunged in sand.

Repotting can be done every year, but this is not necessary if feeding is properly carried out. If the bulbs are encased in silver sand, the surface soil can easily be removed and replaced with fresh, fertile soil. Some large bulbs, such as nerines, are said to flower better when pot-bound, and they should be left undisturbed for several years. A high potash feed will probably encourage flowering, as will a top dressing of still warm bonfire ash; smoke has been shown to induce flowering in several of these southern hemisphere bulbs (Tompsett, 1983).

Bulbs in Tubs

Many bulbs grow well in large containers such as tubs or half-barrels which can be kept under cover in winter and put out into the garden in spring. This was a common way of growing the evergreen *Agapanthus* which is not frost-hardy. Many other summer-growing bulbs such as lilies respond well to this type of cultivation. In California, Roger Macfarlane tells me that he has found half-barrels ideal for growing fritillaries and other small bulbs, both native ones and those from the old-world Mediterranean. They are raised well above soil level so that they do not receive water in the summer even when the garden around them is irrigated, and they are large enough so that the bulbs do not become too desiccated in hot weather.

A rather rich and heavy soil is best for tubs as small bulbs are in more danger from desiccation than from waterlogging. Summer-growing bulbs cultivated in mediterranean climates need opposite treatment: watering in summer and protection from winter wet.

Many bulbs which will grow in the open ground in temperate, humid climates, e.g. western Europe, grow as well or better in tubs. Lilies are a prime example. In gardens with heavy soil and poor drainage, lilies will grow better in large pots or tubs. They can be stood out in summer and brought under cover and kept almost dry in winter in a shed or unheated greenhouse. In spring the young shoots should be carefully protected from late frosts which damage the buds, and a special watch should be kept for aphids which spread virus. Regular feeding is especially important, as with all pot-grown bulbs, and the tubs will require watering in dry weather. As many lilies grow in pockets of soil on cliffs, they grow very well in these conditions. *L. auratum* and *speciosum* hybrids and trumpet types do especially well in tubs; American lilies from moister conditions are less suitable.

Forcing Bulbs for Christmas Flowering

Hyacinths are the most popular bulbs for flowering at Christmas; Paper White Narcissus and Soleil d'Or are also easy to grow. Small bulbs such as crocus and *Iris reticulata* need rather different treatment and are covered separately below.

Hyacinths come into the shops in September and should be bought as soon as possible and planted immediately, at least before 21 September if they are to be in flower for Christmas. It is important to buy bulbs which have been specially 'prepared'. They are usually planted in special bulb fibre which consists of coarse peat with shell and charcoal added, in bowls without drainage holes. It is very important that the fibre should be well moistened before the bulbs are planted and that it should not be allowed to dry out: it should be just wet enough that water drips from between the fingers when it is squeezed hard. The bulbs should be planted with their tops just above the surface, and when they are watered they should not be wetted or the buds will rot.

After planting the bulb bowls should be put in a cool dark place (10 °C or 50 °F) for at least two months while the roots develop. By this time the shoots should be about 7 cm (almost 3 ins) long and the bulbs can be brought into the light in a warmer place such as a shady windowsill: they should then flower in about four weeks. A watch should be kept on them to make sure that they do not dry out or all curve one way towards the light. If the cool dark growing period has been too short, the stems will not elongate properly and the flowers will be hidden down among the leaves. Roman hyacinths are the most dainty and the easiest to bring to flowering at Christmas, but now they are hard to find and have been superseded by the coarser 'multiflora' type. The ordinary large hyacinths differ mainly in colour but the pink 'Rosalie' is one of the earliest and is more graceful than most.

The Paper White Narcissus and 'Soleil d'Or' are very easy to grow. They are planted in fibre or in gravel in which the water level is kept just below the base of the bulbs which should be about half-hidden. They need a sunny windowsill from the start and flower in about five weeks from planting. It is important to buy the largest possible bulbs, even if they are more expensive, as they produce so many more flowers. The container used should be as small as the bulbs will go into without touching.

Narcissus such as 'Ice Follies' and 'Cragford' can also be forced but they need a cool rooting period as is described for hyacinths, and the same goes for tulips. They are probably better if they are not forced for Christmas but brought into the warm in late January or February. All these bulbs may be planted into the garden but seldom do well at least for the next season or two. Dwarf spring flowering bulbs are charming in the house and are better if left outside, if possible in a frame, until they come into bud. They can then be brought inside to flower and put out again immediately the flowers have faded to grow on for next year. *Iris reticulata*, *histrioides* 'Major' and *danfordiae* will happily flower in January indoors, and crocuses will do the same. It is important that they have a long enough cool period and, if they are to be forced, they should be planted and watered by the end of September.

Amaryllis are also very popular for room decoration. Large

bulbs will produce two or three stems each with about four huge flowers. They are grown mostly in Florida, outdoors, or in greenhouses in Holland. The bulbs should be planted as soon as they are received, in a rich soil containing loam, and some peat or leafmould and coarse sand, similar to John Innes compost No. 3. The roots must be handled carefully and any broken ones cut back. They are planted so that the soil comes over the widest part of the bulb. They should be kept as warm as possible (15–20 °C/59–68 °F), and watered sparingly until new growth is apparent. The flower spikes grow very quickly and will flower in three or four weeks from the planting of the bulbs.

CHAPTER 7

Cultivation of Tender Bulbs

Most of the bulbs originating in the summer-humid areas of the southern hemisphere and the tropics need to be grown inside in Europe and North America and given protection from frost. In the southern hemisphere, and in areas warmer than zone 7 in the United States, many of them can be grown happily outside if they are kept dry at the required season.

The most important factors to be considered when tropical bulbs are grown in pots are feeding, the dry season and light.

Because their root growth is restricted to the pot, the bulbs are likely to suffer from lack of nutrients after one growth period if not sooner. Each time a pot is watered, and the water runs through, there is a certain degree of leaching of nutrients and it is important that these are replaced regularly, either by a yearly top dressing or by regular liquid feeds. High-potash feeds such as 'Tomorite' are suitable, and a weekly dose or a dose with every other watering is not too much if the bulbs are growing well. Most bulbs in tropical climates grow in heavy soils so an ordinary potting compost is adequate – one which is freedraining but does not dry out very quickly. Many bulbs flower better after a fire and the addition of bonfire ash and burnt soil to the compost seems to be beneficial to most tropical bulbs. In soil-less composts bulbs should be repotted every year and particular attention must be paid to feeding.

Nearly all bulbs have a distinct resting period and should be kept dry during this time. If in doubt, the length and timing of the rest period for each species can be found by looking at the duration of the dry season in its natural habitat, described in Chapter 4. Some will rot if watered through the dry period, others continue to grow feebly and will probably not flower. During the growing period most need copious watering.

Nearly all tender bulbs in nature grow in open places and receive full light during their growing period. For summer-growing bulbs grown in the northern hemisphere this causes no

Tender Bulbs in Pots

145

Figure 7.1
*Hymenocallis
calathina*

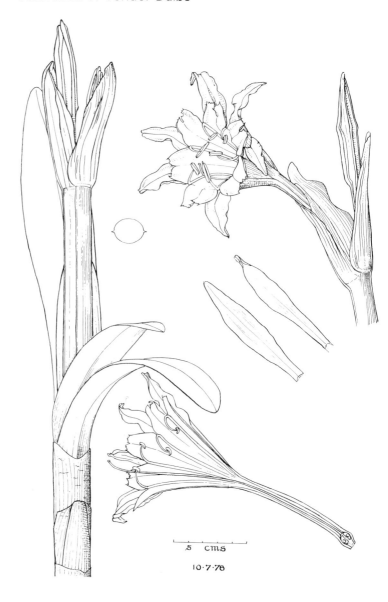

.5 cms

10·7·78

trouble, but winter-growing and flowering bulbs from South
Africa and South America need all the light they can get in the
dull autumns and winters of western Europe. They are best
kept outside in full sun until there is a danger of frost and
thereafter kept in as much light as possible.

Two common bulbs of contrasting types provide good
examples. The first, the glory lily, *Gloriosa superba*, is a
summer-growing bulb with a strange, finger-like tuber and

146

climbing stems with beautiful frilled flowers of red, yellow or orange. It is common in east Africa and in India, where it grows in bushy and grassy places. The tubers should be planted horizontally in large pots in spring and watered and fed well once growth has started. The temperature should be 18 °C (64 °F) or over. After flowering and growth are finished and the foliage begins to go yellow, watering is ceased, and the pots are kept warm and dry throughout the winter.

Other commonly grown bulbs of this type are *Cannas*, *Eucomis*, *Zantedeschia*, *Ismene* and *Gladiolus callianthus*. In warmer climates than southern England, or in warm summers, many of them will do well outside. Other genera with similar growth cycles are commonly grown outside, e.g. most hybrid gladioli, *Galtonia*, *Tigridia pavonina*. They are planted out in spring and then brought inside and kept dry in autumn. A second group of tropical summer-flowering bulbs are inhabitants of forests and mossy rocks and require some shade in summer. Gloxinias, tuberous begonias and *Achimenes* all come from South America. They need a warm humid atmosphere and moist peaty soil with good light but not direct sun. They should be kept quite dry in winter. The few bulbs which come from tropical forests need some water, though much less in winter as the plants are evergreen and only semi-dormant; they need shade and water in summer. The beautiful white *Eucharis amazonica* is an example of this group, and there are some crinums, gingers, amaryllis and clivias with similar requirements.

The second contrasting type are lachenalias which are typical tender winter-growing bulbs from South Africa. Most species have tubular long-lasting drooping flowers on erect stems, and basal leaves; they are thus adapted to pollination by sun birds. The two most commonly cultivated species are *L. pendula* with red flowers tipped with green and *L. tricolor* with yellow and orange flowers and spotted leaves and stems.

The bulbs will show signs of growth in August, even before they are watered, and they should then be repotted or top-dressed with fresh soil and put outside to get autumn rain. They must have as much sun as possible but have to be brought in before there is any danger of frost. The leaves develop immediately, the flowers follow in December, January and February. At all times when in growth lachenalias must have plenty of water; if they dry out, the buds are likely to abort. After flowering, watering should continue until the leaves begin to die down; then the bulbs must be kept dry until autumn. One problem with these, and with other Cape winter-flowering bulbs such as freesias, is to give the bulbs sufficient light during the dull days of winter. If they are kept too dark, the stems grow soft and collapse and the leaves become lush, floppy and pallid. Other common bulbs requiring the same treatment as lachenalias are the colourful sparaxis, ixias, tritonias and freesias, all Iridaceae, and *Veltheimia bracteata* in the Liliaceae. Many other genera of South African bulbs grow through the winter and flower in autumn before the leaves emerge. Nerine is the most commonly grown of these. *N. sarniensis* should be watered first when the leaves or flowers appear and watering and feeding should continue until early summer when the leaves die down. The hardy species, e.g. *N. bowdenii* from high in the Drakensberg, flowers in autumn but the leaves do not emerge until spring and most of the growth is made in the summer.

Tender Bulbs in a Mediterranean House

The mediterranean bulb house in which hardy bulbs are planted out more or less permanently has been described in Chapter 6 (see page 140). By adding winter heat to keep out all frost and by watering in summer instead of in winter, the same type of house could be used for summer-growing bulbs, although if the two types are grown in the same house, they should be kept in separate areas. There will be no conflict of interest as far as atmospheric moisture is concerned in winter but in summer, the humidity required to keep down red spider may be injurious to some of the moisture-sensitive mediterranean species.

A bulb house of this type would be best for growing many *Watsonia* species in cold climates (colder than zone 7), species of *Agapanthus*, many *Amaryllis*, *Brunsvigia*, gladioli, crinums, nerines, hedychiums and others not suitable for pot culture.

Figure 7.2
*Hymenocallis
fragrans*

5   cins

13 · 12 · 80

CHAPTER 8

Propagation of Bulbs

In general, bulbs are very easy to propagate. Most of them increase well if they are happy and there are various ways in which those that do not divide freely may be induced to do so. Bulbs are also easily grown from seed, although with most it is a slow business and several years of care may be needed before flowering size is reached.

Seed

The main advantage of propagation by seed is that the seedlings are always healthy to begin with. The main disadvantage is that they take so long to reach flowering size. Virus diseases are always transmitted by vegetative propagation but only very rarely by seed, so seed-raised bulbs have the advantage in that they start healthily and are not debilitated or disfigured by viral symptoms.

Viability

Seeds of most bulbous plants are adapted to withstand a dry season so they tend to keep their viability for a few years without special treatments. They will, however, germinate better if sown fresh, and some of the large, fleshy seeds of the Amaryllidaceae and Liliaceae must be sown as soon as they are ripe; seeds of winter-growing bulbs should be sown in early autumn, usually without artificial heat, while those of summer-growing bulbs should be started in heat in the spring.

Sowing Hardy Species

Seeds can be sown in pots, pans or in carefully marked areas in a frame. They should generally be about 2.5 cm (1 in) below ground level and will do best if they are placed in a seam of coarse silver sand. Those which grow slowly, such as fritillaries and tulips, can be sown thickly, so that each is almost touching its neighbour, without ill effect. Below them should be a normal seed compost and, if they are to be grown in pots, some glass wool at the base of the pot above the drainage material. This acts as a barrier to worms and slugs coming upwards and to the tiny bulbs which usually end up near the bottom of the pot. Above the sand layer should be a shallow layer of soil and a topping of small shingle (3 to 5 mm or less than ^{1}s in in diameter) to conserve moisture in the sand layer. The pots should be plunged but left outside to get rain and frost. Any seedlings which appear in autumn, such as some *Calochortus*, should be protected but most are better left open until spring and will not emerge until then as they require to have undergone a cool period of several weeks before they will germinate.

The first leaves are thin and grass-like and should be kept green as long as possible: they are better if slightly shaded and protected from too much drying, even in summer. Alternatively, the seed may be 'sown' in polythene bags in autumn in moistened sand, peat, vermiculite or a mixture of these, and kept in a cool, shady place where they can get some frost or in the bottom of an ordinary refrigerator. After mid-winter they must be carefully watched and planted in the normal way as soon as germination occurs. Sowing in polythene bags has the advantage that the seeds can be watched and that only those which have germinated are using valuable space, pots and compost. If germination is slow, the seedlings are immediately in fresh compost and not in a moss-covered, sour potful of stale soil.

Seeds which germinate in spring after autumn sowing, or those which germinate immediately on sowing, and often push up the seed coat on top of the first leaf, are said to show epigeal germination (see Figure 8.1 (left), p. 153). Fritillaries, tulips, crocuses and many *Lilium* species have this type of germination.

Other lilies, e.g. *L. auratum*, and many other plants show what is known as hypogeal germination (see Figure 8.1 (right), p. 153). In this the seed germinates underground but the leaf does not appear above ground until some months later; then it is not the thin cotyledon, but a broader true leaf. If hypogeal seeds are planted normally they will not appear above ground until the second spring. Their appearance can be speeded up by sowing them in moist peat or a peat/sand mixture in a polythene bag, and keeping them at a warm temperature, around 20 °C (68 °F), until they are seen to have germinated and formed a tiny bulb: then they are transferred to the bottom of the refrigerator for a minimum of eight weeks before being sown normally and grown on. Seed of many American lilies germinates in autumn and grows very slowly through the winter before emerging in spring. In some cases these show hypogeal, and in other cases epigeal germination. (See Derek Fox, 'The Propagation of Lilies' in *The Plantsman*).

Some seeds, for instance, irises of the Oncocyclus group, can be very slow to germinate: this is probably because they contain a germination inhibitor which needs to be leached out before germination. Experiments to remove this artificially have not been very successful – there may also be inbuilt dormancy. Seeds of these should be planted as soon as ripe and exposed to all rain until germination is seen. The whole pot can then be planted without disturbing it into a bulb frame where the young plants can grow on and further seeds can germinate over a period of several years.

Vegetative
Propagation

(i) Splitting

Most bulbs will increase naturally if they are growing happily. Some split into two and the halves can be replanted separately. Others form small offsets at the side, e.g. daffodils and most amaryllis (*Hippeastrum*), which can be detached and replanted so that they make flowering-sized bulbs the sooner. The best time to divide most bulbs is when they are dormant but some, such as snowdrops and spring snowflakes (*Galanthus* and *Leucojum vernum*), are best divided and replanted just after flowering, and lilies and daffodils will move well if they are replanted at this stage. The great advantage is that they can be found without difficulty and the lilies will make new basal roots before winter.

(ii) Bulbils and Stolons

Many bulbs, notably fritillaries, crocuses, lilies, bulbous *Iris* and *Muscari* make numerous small bulbils on the outside of the bulb. Others produce a small bulb on the end of the stolon. The size of the bulbil varies but they are often very small and will not grow into adult bulbs unless they are removed from the parent and from the crowd of their neighbours. They will

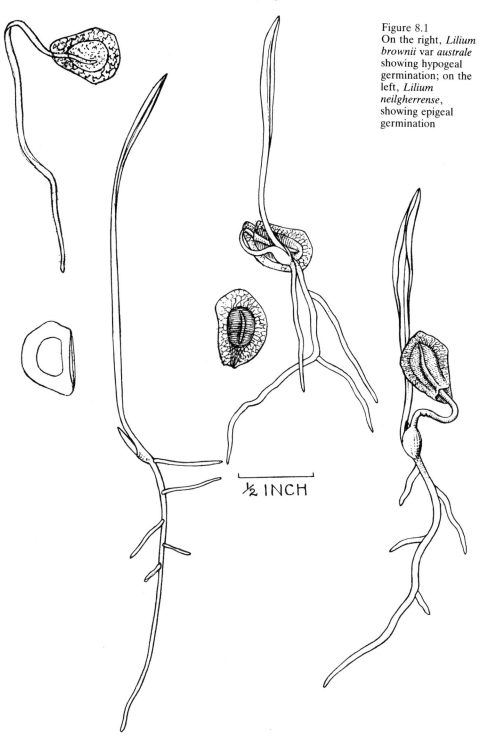

Figure 8.1
On the right, *Lilium brownii* var *australe* showing hypogeal germination; on the left, *Lilium neilgherrense*, showing epigeal germination

½ INCH

continue to put up their grass-like leaves year after year while they are overcrowded.

Bulbs with these young round them should be dug up and the large bulbs separated and replanted and the small young bulbs planted as if they were one-year-old seedlings. They should be well spread out so that they are encouraged to increase in size.

In some instances bulbs continue to divide and produce bulbils but never flower; *Fritillaria thunbergii* often does this. There is no easy way to induce flowering in these but deep planting has been suggested as a remedy, and high-potash (K) fertiliser should encourage production of flower buds.

(iii) Cutting

Bulbs which are slow to increase naturally may be divided by cutting across the base of the bulb. This method has been widely used in the commercial production of hyacinths and amaryllis. The bulb is left in one piece but the cuts go through the basal plate into the scales so that the bud at the centre of the bulb is killed; a small piece of stone may be put into each cut to hold it open. The number of cuts made depends on the size of the bulb but two or three or even four cross-cuts, making four, six or eight radial segments, are usual. Sometimes the bulb is cut up completely and the segments planted separately: each can be almost guaranteed to make one or more new bulbs.

The bulb should then be kept in a warm place such as indoors in a polythene bag with barely moist peat while the bulbils form. If possible, the bulbs should be stood upside down so that the bulbils grow straight. When the bulbils are formed, the whole bulb should be planted again upside down, and grown for a year. By the end of this time, the young bulbs are large enough to detach and be grown on.

(iv) Scaling and Twin-scales

Individual scales of multi-scaled bulbs such as lilies will easily make new plants if they are detached and planted separately. This is the standard way of increasing lily cultivars. Other bulbs may be cut up to make similar scale-like pieces, which may also produce bulbils at their base and so produce new plants.

Few-scaled bulbs, such as fritillaries, can be broken up and each scale planted separately. The inner will probably flower as well as if it had not been touched, the outer will make a flowering-sized bulb next year. The larger bulbs of species such as *F. persica* and *F. imperialis* can be cut into as many as 150 pieces which are then treated in the same way as lily-bulb scales (see below).

'Normal' bulbs, such as amaryllis, can be cross-cut into segments, about 16 in the case of a large bulb, and then each segment can be divided so that each piece has two or three segments of scale, joined by a piece of the basal plate. This is known as twin-scaling. The success rate varies here; in amaryllis it is between a third and three-quarters.

The best time for scaling lilies and for cutting bulbs is when their food reserves are at a maximum, during their dormant stage before new root growth has been started. In most hardy bulbs in the northern hemisphere this will be in late August or early September.

The scales, twin scales or pieces of bulb should be soaked in benlate at 4 gm per litre, or 2 per cent thiram, for about 30 minutes, allowed to dry and then either planted in boxes or flats in an open peaty compost, or put in polythene bags with moist vermiculite or sphagnum peat. The best results with lilies have been produced by a warm period (20–25 °C/68–77 °F) for two months, followed by a cooler period (17 °C/62.6 °F) for four weeks, and then kept cool until spring when the scales, with bulbils attached, are planted. Hardier bulbs, such as fritillaries, should be kept at the lower temperature (20 °C or 68 °F) for two months and then planted and kept cool until the leaves appear in early spring.

Twin-scaling should, theoretically, be suitable for increasing all bulbs with concentric scales and a basal plate. It is commonly used to increase amaryllis commercially. Bulbs such as tulips, *Narcissus* and *Galanthus* usually increase naturally sufficiently quickly but should respond to similar treatment. Twin-scaling is regularly used to propagate virus-free stock of narcissus cultivars. One bulb can produce 100 or more twin-scales, depending on its size. Incubation is at 23 °C (73.4 °F) in a mixture of moist peat and vermiculite, after which the scales with bulbils attached are planted. Some will remain dormant the first year, but 80 per cent will be growing after two years. The earliest may be expected to flower in the third year after propagation.

Cuttings

Most bulbous plants cannot be propagated by cuttings of aerial stems. Lilies are exceptional, as the stem with stem roots can be severed from its bulb after flowering and grown on independently. It then often makes bulbs near ground level which can be detached and grown on, after the stem has died in the autumn.

Many dicotyledonous tuberous plants can be propagated by stem cuttings, and will have formed tubers before they go dormant. Begonias, dahlias and gloxinias can all be propagated by this method. Often only one, two or three shoots are required for the ideal specimen, and the surplus shoots can be used as cuttings. Leaf cuttings, e.g. of *Gloxinia*, will also make new plants.

Meristem culture and the production of virus-free bulbs

Meristem culture is a relatively new method of propagation, ideal for the production of huge numbers of individuals of a commercially valuable cultivar. Its use is usually combined with the production of virus-free stock, as the techniques and equipment used for the two are similar.

The growing point, or meristem, of the bulb is dissected out under sterile conditions and placed in a test tube or flask in a nutrient solution or on nutrient-enriched agar. There is a tendency for viruses to be slow to invade meristematic tissue, so some of the meristems are likely to be virus-free. The meristematic cells continue to divide on the agar and can be tested for virus by examining the cells under an electron microscope. Those meristems found to be virus-free are grown on and further subdivided, so that thousands of separate meristems can be produced from a single individual. When plants are required, leaf and root formation are induced by the appropriate hormone treatment. The plantlets are grown on the agar until large enough to handle, and are then transferred from the agar to the soil, a tricky operation as they are very delicate and susceptible to infection.

CHAPTER 9

Pests and Diseases of Bulbs

The pests and diseases which attack bulbs are so numerous that they could fill a complete book or, at least, booklet! One does indeed already exist, that is, the ADAS (Agricultural Development & Advisory Service) advisory booklet, *HPDI Diseases of Bulbs*, published by HMSO in 1979. This contains beautiful colour pictures of diseases, and instructions on their control on a commercial scale. A new book for the amateur, *Collins Guide to the Pests, Diseases and Disorders of Garden Plants* by Stefan Buczaski and Keith Harris (1981), gives details of some of the commoner diseases, and is the best available source on ways to control pests. It is thoroughly to be recommended.

In this chapter I shall describe only those pests and diseases that I have found to be troublesome in southern England or noticed while collecting bulbs in the wild. Growers in other countries can consult their local agricultural advisory services, though the range of diseases, at least, is likely to be similar for a particular bulb.

Slugs

Pests

Slugs are much more common on some soils, and in some places in the garden, than others. They prefer rich, heavy soils, with high organic content, and generally dislike sands and well-drained soils which dry out in summer. If you do not suffer from slugs, you are lucky! If you do, they are almost certainly the worst pest as far as bulbs are concerned. Some species are supposed to live mainly on dead vegetation, but most are particularly fond of the lush smooth leaves and juicy underground parts of bulbous plants. The small black ones with either white or yellow bellies, so-called keeled slugs (*Milax* spp.), are particular devils as they spend much of their life below ground, living on roots and bulbs.

Small holes in bulbs, sometimes with the whole centre eaten away, are the commonest symptoms of slug damage. Stems are also eaten off at ground level and collapse, and, with lilies especially, the stem roots are grazed off and the plant fails to grow properly.

Tulips and fritillaries, as well as lilies, are all badly affected by slugs; daffodils and snowdrops seem to be less susceptible. Control methods are seldom effective for long. Baiting with the long-lasting blue mini-pellets such as 'Draza' kills a certain number; watering with liquid 'Slugit' is probably partially effective on underground slugs, though its results are not very apparent. Watering the soil with a mixture of salt and potassium permanganate (NaCl and $K_2Mn_2O_8$) is recommended by the Henry Doubleday Association; the solution, $^1\!2$ teaspoon permanganate and $^1\!2$ teaspoon of salt in 9 litres (2 gallons) of water, is too weak to damage the plants, and the slugs are supposed to be driven to the surface where they can be picked up and killed by droping them in a jar of salt. A nightly search with a torch will also produce a good kill, especially on warm wet nights in spring. Alternatively, a slug 'pub', a shallow saucer-like container sunk in the ground and filled with beer, will attract them . . . they fall in and drown; the 'pub' should be replenished every three days.

The most effective method of slug control is probably to add large quantities of sharp fine grit or coarse sand to the soil, and to surround the bulbs with this grit when they are planted. The grit also has the beneficial effect of improving drainage. This method was found most effective with lilies at the Rosewarne Experimental Horticulture Station in Cornwall, England, and the results are described and illustrated in *Lilies and other Liliaceae* (1976).

Aphids

Aphids damage plants directly by sucking the sap and causing deformation and stunted growth. They can be controlled best with systemic insecticides, of which there are many proprietary brands. A close watch should be kept for aphids, especially on the undersides of leaves which show any curling, and spraying should be done as soon as they appear.

Aphids also do great damage by spreading virus; this is described further below.

Red Spider

Red spider (*Tetranychus*) is a minute sucking mite which lives on plant leaves. It is universal in greenhouses, and can breed very quickly in hot, dry conditions; it is not usually a problem outdoors but can appear in a sunny, dry bulb frame in summer. Symptoms of red spider damage are yellowing and pale spotting of the leaves, reduction of growth and, finally, a fine web covering the leaf base. It can be especially damaging to delicate-leaved climbers such as *Gloriosa* and *Canarina*, and thin, smooth-leaved watsonias, tritonias and other tropical Iridaceae. Fleshy-leaved bulbs are not usually attacked.

Sprays are, in general, not very effective. Control is best achieved either by keeping the humidity very high or, if high humidity is undesirable or ineffective, by the introduction of the parasite, *Phytoseilius persimilis*, a native of Chile. This can be obtained by members of the R.H.S. from Wisley. Any general spraying with pesticides must, of course, cease after the predator is introduced, but a spray a week or so before it is introduced is beneficial in cutting down initial members of the pest.

Figure 9.1
*Eurycles
amboinensis*

3 cm
I INCH

IB·7·77

159

Pests and Diseases

Vine Weevils

The adults and subterranean grubs of the vine weevil (*Otiorhynchus sulcatus*) can do great damage to bulbs grown in pots, and other weevils can be active in the garden.

The adults are beetle-like, with a long snout, and are matt-black. They feed on leaves and flowers at night, forming rounded holes along the leaf edges. If disturbed, they fall to the ground and lie still, perfectly camouflaged as crumbs of earth. The adults are mostly female, and each can lay up to 1,000 eggs in the soil. Cyclamen are especially commonly attacked, but I have found weevil grubs in pots of lilies, gloxinias, tuberous begonias as well as many other non-bulbous greenhouse plants: *Primula* and echeverias are favourites.

The white fat grubs live just under the soil surface, eating roots near the base of the plant, the cortex at the stem base or the tuber, and finally burrowing into the bulb or stem and eating into the pith.

Control is not easy. Any sign of damage by adults should be followed by a nightly search; white paper laid under the plant makes finding them easy. The first sign of damage by grubs is often the flagging or death of the plant. Potting soil should be sterilised before use, and any old soil which might harbour grubs should be burnt. Granules of HCH soil insecticide can be spread on susceptible plants near an infestation and any plants which show signs of distress immediately repotted. HCH can also be incorporated into the potting compost of susceptible plants.

Lily Beetle

The lily beetle (*Lilioceris lilii*) is another weevil-like beetle which has become a serious pest of lilies in southern England in recent years. It is native of southern Europe where it feeds on fritillaries as well as lilies. The adults are a beautiful bright red, and feed voraciously on the leaves of lilies; the grubs are a revolting dirty yellow, short and fat and covered in their own black excrement to put off their predators. They feed both on leaves and young capsules. I have seen whole clumps of lilies, both at Wisley and at the Savill Garden, reduced to ragged stems by these pests. Whenever lilies are grown a watch should be kept for them. The adults and grubs can be removed by hand or sprayed with Malathion where the infestation is severe.

Narcissus Flies

The larvae of some species of fly are common pests of *Narcissus*. The large narcissus fly (*Merodon equestris*) is a damaging primary parasite; the small narcissus flies (*Emerus* spp.) are mainly secondary parasites and infest dying bulbs or ones which have been damaged by some other disease.

Apart from *Narcissus*, *Sternbergia*, *Hyacinthus* and *Galanthus* may be affected, and I have found similar grubs in *Iris persica* in Turkey. The small narcissus flies can attack many bulbs and tubers, including cyclamen. Infected bulbs fail to flower and either fail to emerge or are very stunted. The bulbs feel soft and if cut open, reveal one large *Merodon* or several small *Emerus* grubs inside. The whole centre of the bulb will have been eaten away.

The adults of *Merodon* are like small bees. They emerge in May and June and lay their eggs around the base of dying narcissus leaves or in the holes left after the bulbs have died down. They always seem to lay their eggs on plants in full sun, so that bulbs growing in shade are not affected, and where field-grown plants are in danger, they can be shaded with muslin during the susceptible period.

The holes left by the dying leaves are favourite sites for the flies to lay their eggs and they may be filled with loose soil as soon as the leaves begin to go yellow.

In commercial operations, narcissus fly is controlled by hot water treatment (c. 45 °C (113 °F) for three hours). Nematodes are also controlled by HWT and, with the addition of formalin or benomyl, some fungus diseases as well.

Amaryllis Caterpillar (*Brithys pancratii*)

The larvae of this moth are black and white striped, and eat into the leaves and flowers of many Amaryllidaceae, finally reaching and killing the bulb. This pest is found mainly in southern Africa and, as far as I know, has not been recorded in the British Isles or Europe, but it is as well to be aware of it in case it appears. Control is probably best effected with a systemic insecticide.

Cutworms

Cutworms are the larvae of various noctuid moths, notably the turnip moth (*Agrotis segetum*) and the yellow underwing

161

(*Triphaena pronuba*). These eat the roots, leaves and flowers of many bulbs but seem to be especially fond of cyclamen. They hide in the ground by day and can be very hard to find, but they can often be caught at night by torch light. E.A. Bowles recommends catching them 'by making a hole with one's finger in the soil, close by the evidences of damage, and plugging the top of it with a lettuce leaf or a juicy little Brussels sprout. It is never long before the caterpillar finds the bait and avails itself of the provided bedchamber below it, and the inquiring finger detects a plump little body at the bottom of the hole.' Though they can be found all over the garden, they seem particularly partial to the loose, dry soil of a bulb frame.

Mice and Moles

Mice can be great pests and once they have developed a taste for a particular bulb, will soon destroy a whole colony. They seem especially fond of crocuses but I have also had fritillaries and romuleas eaten. The more slimy bulbs such as snowdrops and daffodils seem to be avoided. Traps baited with apple will often catch the offenders, but a good mousing cat which will like the warm frame, is the best form of protection.

Moles do not eat bulbs but do great damage by burrowing at root level, especially below anything recently planted or something which is being watered in dry weather. The roots may be broken or simply starved of moisture by the tunnels below. Bulbs may also be pushed along the tunnels and so come up in unexpected places, sometimes where they will be smothered.

Trapping of moles is usually only temporarily successful as they soon recolonise from fields or woods nearby, so precious bulbs are best protected by wire netting put in the ground or by being planted in the plastic lattice pots recommended for bulb frames. The bulb frame itself should always have wire netting underneath to protect it against both moles and mice.

Other Animals

In countries outside Europe other burrowing animals may be a nuisance. In California gophers burrow like moles and eat bulbs, too. In the Middle East mole rats do the same thing, making stores of large numbers of bulbs for the winter. In Africa baboons and wart hogs may dig up bulbs (babianas were so called because baboons were fond of them). Pheasants are said to be very fond of both fritillaries and crocuses, but I have seen them feeding in the garden without doing any damage.

Bird Damage

In some years, especially in dry springs, sparrows, and probably tits and chaffinches, may be a great nuisance, tearing up the flowers of crocuses and dwarf early narcissus, as well as those of primroses. The only good way of protecting them is to spread fine black cotton above the flowers. A few strands should be almost invisible and enough to keep these birds away.

Virus

Virus disease seldom kills the plant outright but debilitates it and makes it more susceptible to other diseases. In addition, its symptoms spoil the appearance of the plants, usually producing yellow-streaked unhealthy-looking leaves, and breaks of colour on the flowers.

Many of the commercial strains of bulbs are infected with virus; these cultivars are sufficiently tolerant of it to be successfully propagated and sold while they are infected; most stocks of the *Iris reticulata* group in particular, appear to be infected. Nowadays, by the use of laboratory micro-propagation techniques, virus-free stocks can be obtained and they show greatly increased vigour. The lily 'Enchantment' was one of the first to be produced virus-free on a large scale, and as the methods become routine so they will become cheaper and more virus-free stocks will be available.

In gardens where only common bulbs are grown, virus will seldom be a problem, but as soon as the gardener wants to grow rarer, more expensive bulbs, some precautions to prevent its spread will be worth-while. Lilies and Oncocyclus irises are especially susceptible to virus; fritillaries seem to be resistant or at least not to show very obvious symptoms.

Most viruses are spread by aphids, so a regular spraying programme is important to prevent infection from taking place. It is most important to spray those plants which are suspected of being infected, as it is aphids flying from these to unaffected plants which spread the disease; once the aphid's stylus has penetrated the plant's cell, infection may have occurred. Any plants obviously affected should be destroyed. Spread of virus may also be lessened by spraying the plants with an oil emulsion which prevents the aphids from inserting their styluses.

For the amateur, the only way of producing virus-free stock of a plant is to raise it from seed. Of course, most cultivars will not come true, but for wild species and for such plants as *Iris reticulata* and many lilies, the seedlings are probably as good as the parents. Viruses are not usually transmitted by seed in bulbous plants, but in some annuals, e.g. chickweed (*Stellaria media*), viruses are transmitted through the seed and so can act as a reservoir and source of infection for common viruses such as cucumber mosaic virus.

The identification of plant viruses requires specialist knowledge and equipment. Some are specific to one genus, some can infect plants of many different families. It is best to regard all viruses as dangerous and try to harden one's heart and destroy any infected plants that appear in the garden.

Rots (*Botrytis, Rhizoctonia, Sclerotium*)

The worst diseases of bulbs are the various fungi which attack the leaves and bulbs, either killing or disfiguring them.

The various species of botrytis are probably the most damaging, especially in damp climates. Bulbs vary greatly in their susceptibility to botrytis but it probably causes more bulbs to be lost to cultivation than any other factor.

Tulips, fritillaries and Juno and Oncocyclus irises often rot at the base, either as they emerge or after the leaves have developed. The fungus will be found at around ground level, probably making grey powdery spores which can infect other plants nearby. Tulip fire, *B. tulipae*, is one of the commonest fungi and it can cause great losses in places where many tulips are grown, spreading quickly from a single source in wet weather. Juno irises, such as *I. persica*, are especially badly affected by fungus; the rot begins in the mushy remains of the dead flower and spreads down into the bulb. I managed to keep some for about ten years by putting captan powder (benlate would probably do as well) on the base of the fading flower and on the bracts, but they finally succumbed. Very deep planting is recommended to prevent infection by botrytis of tulips, and is worth trying in susceptible species of other genera.

Summer-growing bulbs such as lilies are also liable to be infected by botrytis, especially in warm, wet weather (10–16 °C/

50–65 °F). The disease begins with spots on the leaves, and soon kills whole leaves, and, if unchecked, all the leaves and flowers.

Control of botrytis has recently (since 1970) become much easier with the introduction of benlate, a systemic fungicide. It can be used either as a powder, a drench or a spray. Bulbs should be soaked in benlate before planting or shaken in a bag with benlate powder. The leaves of lilies and other susceptible plants should be sprayed at the first sign of any attack or even at the onset of warm, humid weather. Diseased plants should also be removed from the neighbourhood of other susceptible ones immediately they are spotted: if common, they should be burnt; if precious, they should be treated with a spray and a drench of benlate and kept in isolation to see if they can be rescued.

Other diseases such as *Rhizoctonia* and *Sclerotium* affect bulbs and are spread in the soil. When a diseased bulb is dug up (it will often have failed to appear above ground), the earth will be found to be sticking to it. In this case, infected bulbs will be dead and should be burnt, and the earth surrounding it, which may have fungal spores or resting bodies in it, should be removed and burnt on the bonfire. These diseases can be controlled by soaking the bulbs in benlate before planting, and by making sure that no diseased bulbs are planted; the rounded, hard, black nesting bodies of the fungus can be seen attached to the tunics of the bulbs, and any infected bulbs should be thrown away.

Basal rot is a very common disease of lilies. They fail to come up or go yellow, and on inspection all the scales are found to be loose, and the basal plate has rotted away. The disease is caused by *Fusarium oxysporum*, f. *lilii*. It is more prevalent where soil temperatures are high, and some lilies are more susceptible than others; in North America, Bellingham hybrids, *L. canadense*, *superbum* and *henryi*, and the Aurelian and trumpet hybrid lilies seem to be especially resistant. If there is any sign of the disease in one part of the garden, lilies should not be planted there for some years or the soil should be sterilised. Lilies should be potted in sterilised soil, and new bulbs should be soaked in benlate or dusted with quintozene before planting. Similar bulb rot can be caused by waterlogging of the soil, and all lilies, even the bog lovers, should be planted in well-drained soil. When the bulb has rotted, the scales can be used for propagation. The basal part should be cut off and any other signs of diseased tissue removed, and the scales should be well soaked or dusted before planting, as described on page 154.

Where benlate is used a lot, and especially where it is used on

165

a commercial scale, there is a danger of the appearance of mutations of botrytis and other fungi resistant to it. It is probably wise to spray at least some of the time with an alternative. Bordeaux mixture will control diseases of the leaves; dichlofluanid will be suitable for soaking or as a dip.

Other Bulb
Troubles

The commonest trouble, especially of pot-grown bulbs, is abortion of the flowers. The buds are there but they go white and do not develop. This is often caused by the growing bulb having dried out at some time during the winter, or having been watered or planted too late, so that the roots are incapable of supporting fully developed flowers. Bulbs should not be allowed to dry out while they are in active growth. If they do, growth will cease as the plant tries to go dormant as quickly as possible before the onset of summer and drought. Similarly, summer-growing bulbs should be kept well watered while they are in growth.

Late frosts are a common cause of a similar problem in lilies, especially those which emerge early, such as *L. regale*. The shoots may appear to be almost undamaged but the young buds will have been killed. Whenever possible, young shoots should be protected from morning sun after cold nights, and, if possible, from frost. Species which emerge early should be planted under or on the western side of shrubs which can protect them. Lavenders or rosemary, for instance, form suitable shelter for *Lilium regale*. As a last resort, a slate can be propped up on the eastern side of the lily shoots to keep the early sun off them. This method is often used in China although I have not, myself, tested its efficacy.

Bulb Genera, Notes and Sources

ACHIMENES PERS. (Gesneriaceae)
About 50 species mainly in South America. Bulbs elongated with overlapping scales, usually subterranean. Flowers tubular with an expanded corolla, usually bluish or small and red. Literature: Moore, H.E., 'Some cultivated Gesneriaceae and hybrids', *Gentes Herbarum*, **8**(5): 375–403 (1954).

ACONITUM L. (Ranunculaceae)
About 300 species in the northern hemisphere of which many have tuberous roots, and others, e.g. *A. volubile*, single tubers and climbing stems. Literature: Shteinberg, E.I. in *Fl. U.S.S.R.*, **7**: 183–236 (1937).

AGAPANTHUS L' Her. (Liliaceae)
Ten species and ten subspecies in southern Africa. Literature: Leighton, F.M., *Journ. S. Afr. Bot. Supp.*, Vol. IV (1965).

ALBUCA L. (Liliaceae)
About 50 species in southern Africa.

ALLIUM L. (Liliaceae)
About 500 species throughout the northern hemisphere. Literature: Munz, P.A. and Keck, D.D., *A California Flora*: 1368–78 (1959) (38 spp.); Stearn, W.T., '*Allium* and *Milula* in the central and eastern Himalaya', *Bull. Brit. Mus. (N.H.) Botany*, **2**(6): 161–91 (1960); Stearn, W.T., in *Flora Europaea*, **5**: 49–69 (1980) (110 spp.); Vvedensky, A.I., *Consp. Fl. Asiae Mediae*, **2**: 39–89 (1971) 191 species; Wendelbo, P.W. in *Flora Iranica*, **76**: 3–100 (1971); Wendelbo, P. et al. in *Lily Year Book, R.H.S. 1967*, pp. 86–100 (1966).

ALOE L. (Liliaceae)
About 275 species in Africa and Asia, of which the majority are shrubby and succulent. Most are bird-pollinated. One or two species have poorly developed bulbs, e.g. *A. myriacantha* from the mountains of East Africa and *A. kniphofioides* from the E.

Transvaal. Literature: Reynolds, G.W., *The Aloes of Africa*, 4th edn Balkema, 1982, (c. 150 spp.)

ALOPHIA Herb. (Iridaceae)
About 5 species in south-eastern USA through Mexico to South America. Rootstock bulbous. Literature: Goldblatt, P., *Brittonia* **27**: 380–2 (1975).

ALRAWIA (Wendelbo) K. Persson and Wendelbo (Liliaceae)
Two species in Iran and northern Iraq. Close to *Hyacinthella*. Literature: Persson, K. and Wendelbo, P., '*Alrawia*, a new genus of Liliaceae-Scilloideae', *Bot. Not.*, **132**: 201–6 (1979).

ALSTROEMERIA L. (Alstroemeriaceae)
About 50 species in South America, mainly in Chile. Most species have tuberous rootstocks and upper petals beautifully marked. Literatuure: Anderson, E.B., *Alstroemerias. Daffodil Year Book*, p. 57 (1967).

AMANA Honda (Liliaceae)
About 3 species in China and Japan. Literature: Ohwi, J., *Flora of Japan* (translation), Washington, 1965.

AMARYLLIS L. (Amaryllidaceae) = HIPPEASTRUM
Seventy-six species from Mexico and the West Indies to Argentina and Chile. One species in west central Africa (cf. Cactaceae). Most species are summer-growing with large bulbs, native in the Amazon basin. Flowers vary from red, through green and tessellated to white. Two species (*H. calyptrata* and *H. arboricola*) are epiphytic and have little or no rest period. The South African 'Amaryllis beeladonna' should correctly be called *Brunsvigia rosea* (q.v.), see Tjaden, W.L., *Plant Life*, 1981. Literature: Traub, H.P., *The Amaryllis Manual*, Macmillan, 1958. Also many articles in *Plant Life*, notably 'Exploring for Amaryllids in S. America 1969–70', *Plant Life*: 8–17 (1972).

ANDROCYMBIUM Willd. (Liliaceae)
About 35 species in Africa, mainly in the south, and one in Spain and in the Canary Islands.

ANEMONE L. (Ranunculaceae)
About 150 species worldwide. Tuberous species are found in the Mediterranean areas of the northern hemisphere: woodland species with thin fleshy rhizomes are found throughout Europe,

Asia and North America. Literature: Toubøl, U., 'Clonal variation in *Anemone nemorosa*', *The Plantsman*, **3**, Pt 3: 167 (1981)

ANOIGANTHUS = CYRTANTHUS (q.v.)

APONOGETON L. fil. (Aponogetonaceae)
About 45 species in Africa and Asia. Most species are water plants, but many have tuberous rootstocks, including *A. distachyon*. Literature: Bruggen, H.W.E. van, 'Revision of the genus Aponogeton. . .', *Blumea*, 16: 243–63 (1968); 16: 264–5 (1968); 17: 121–37 (1969); 18: 457–86 (1970); *Bull. Jard. Bot. Nat. Belg.*, **43**(1–2): 193–233 (1973).

ARISAEMA Mart. (Araceae)
About 150 species mainly in the Himalaya, China and Japan. Many have weird flowers with long, slender appendages, and may be pollinated by snails. Literature: Lancaster, R., 'Arisaemas in the wild', *The Garden*, **108**(1): 36–7 (1983); Mayo, S.J., 'A survey of cultivated species of Arisaema', *The Plantsman*, **3** (4): 193–209 (1982).

ARISARUM Miller (Araceae)
Three species, in the Mediterranean region. Literature: Engler, A., *Das Pflanzenreich* IV 23F: 144–9 (1920).

ARGYROPSIS Herbert (Amaryllidaceae)
One species. *A. candida* often called *Zephyranthes candida* q.v.), from Argentina and Uruguay.

ARUM L. (Araceae)
About 15 species, mainly in Europe and the Mediterranean region. Literature: *Arum* in *Flora Europaea*, **5**: 269–71 (1980); *Arum* in Flora of Turkey (forthcoming); Prime, C.T., *Lords and Ladies*, Collins, 1960.

ASPHODELINE Rchb. (Liliaceae)
About 15 species in Europe and western Asia.

ASPHODELUS L. (Liliaceae)
About 10 species in the Mediterranean region from Spain to the Himalayas. Literature: Richardson, I.B.K. and Smythies, B.E., in *Flora Europaea*, **5**: 17 (1980) 5 species.

BABIANA Ker-Gawl. (Iridaceae)
About 80 species mainly in South Africa, with one in Socotra. Literature: Lewis, G.J., 'The genus *Babiana*', *Journ. S.Afr. Bot. Suppl.*, Vol. 3: 1–149 (1959).

BEGONIA L. (Begoniaceae)
About 900 species mostly tropical, but *B. evansiana*, one of the tuberous species, is almost hardy (zone 7). The winter-flowering *B. socotrana* has true bulbs. The large-flowered tuberous species have been bred from South American species. Literature: Bedson, F.J., *Successful Begonia Culture*, Collingridge, 1954; Haegeman, J., *Tuberous Begonias: origin and development*, J. Cramer, 1979.

BELAMCANDA DC. (Iridaceae)
One species in China, Japan and north-east Asia. Literature: Mathew, Brian, *The Iris*, p. 186, Batsford, 1981.

BELLEVALIA Lapeyr. (Liliaceae)
About 50 species in the Mediterranean region eastwards to Afghanistan, and Soviet central Asia. Literature: Freitag, H. and Wendelbo, P., 'The genus *Bellevalia* in Afghanistan', *Israel J. Bot.*, 19: 220–4 (1970); Heywood, V.H., *Bellevalia* in *Flora Europaea*, **5**: 44–5 (1980); Persson, K. and Wendelbo, P., '*Bellevalia hyacinthoides*, a new name for *Strangweia spicata*' *Bot. Not.*, 132: 65–70 (1979).

BIARUM Schott (Araceae)
About 15 species in southern Europe and south-west Asia. Literature: Prime, C.T. and Webb, D.A., *Biarum* in *Flora Europaea*, **5**: 271 (1980). See also *Flora of Turkey*, **8** (forthcoming).

BLOOMERIA Kell (Liliaceaea)
Two species in California. Literature: Bloomeria in Munz, P.A. and Keck D.D., *A California Flora*: 1379–85 (1968); Hoover, xx., *Plant Life* (Herbertia) 11:21 (1955).

BONGARDIA C.A. Mey. (Berberidaceae)
One species in the eastern Mediterranean area, to Pakistan. Literature: Rix, Martyn, 'The Herbaceous Berberidaceae', *The Plantsman*, **4**(1): 2–4 (1982).

BOWIEA Harv. ex Hook. fil. (Liliaceae)
One species, *B. volubilis*, in southern Africa, with a much-

branched, twining inflorescence. Literature: Jessop, J.P., *Journ. S.Afr. Bot.*, **43**:4;: 313–14 (1977).

BREVOORTIA see DICHELOSTEMMA.

BRODIAEA Sm. (Liliaceae)
About 10 species in western North America. Literature: Munz, P.A. and Keck, D.D., *A California Flora*: 1379–85 (1968). See also TRITELEIA and DICHELOSTEMMA.

BRUNSVIGIA Heist (Amaryllidaceae)
About 18 species in Africa from Tanzania to the Cape. This genus now includes the Cape belladonna *B. rosea*.

BULBINE Willd. (Liliaceae)
About 50 species in southern Africa, most with tuberous roots.

BULBINELLA Kunth (Liliaceae)
About 15 species in southern Africa and Australasia, with fibrous roots.

BOOPHONE Herbert (Amaryllidaceae)
About 5 species in southern Africa.

BULBOCODIUM L. (Liliaceae)
Two species in Europe and western Asia. Like Merendera, but with a single trifid style. Literature: Valentine, D.H. in *Flora Europaea*, **5**:25 (1980).

CALOCHORTUS Pursh (Liliaceae)
About 60 species in western North America from British Columbia to Mexico. Literature: Elliott, J. 'Calochortus – a survey', *The Plantsman*, **2** (4): 196–213 (1981); Munz, P.A. and Keck D.D., *A California Flora*: 1344–54 and supplement 174 (1968). Farwig, S. and Girard, V. 'Neglected Calochortuses' *Pac. Hort.* Spring 1981: 19–28 (1981).

CALOSCORDUM Herbert (Liliaceae)
One species, *C. neriniflorum*, from China, Mongolia and eastern Siberia. Literature: Rix, M. and Phillips, R., *The Bulb Book*, p. 145(i) Pan (1981).

CAMASSIA Lindl. (Liliaceae)
About 5 species in North America, 1 in South America. Literature: Munz, P.A. and Keck, D.D., *A California Flora*: 1344–54 (1968).

CANNA L. (Cannaceae)
About 55 species in Tropical Asia and America. Literature:
Kranzlin, F. in Engler, *Pflanzenreich*, 56 (iv. 47): 1–77 (1912).

CARDIOCRINUM Endl. (Liliaceae)
Three species in the Himalaya to China and Japan. Literature:
Synge, P.M., *Lilies*, Batsford, 1980.

CHIONODOXA Boiss. (Liliaceae)
About 6 species in Crete and south-west Turkey. Literature:
Richardson, I.B.K. in *Flora Europaea*, **5**:44 (1980). See also
Flora of Turkey, **8** (forthcoming) and Speta, F. in *Naturk.
Jahrb. Stadt Linz*, 21: 19 (1976).

× CHIONOSCILLA
Hybrids between *Chionodoxa* and *Scilla bifolia*.

CLAYTONIA L. (Portulacaceae)
About 18 species in North America, a few of which have corms
or thick fleshy rootstocks. Literature: Davis, R.J. 'The North
American perennial species of *Claytonia*', *Brittonia*, 18: 285–
300 (1967).

CLIVIA Lindl. (Amaryllidaceae)
Four species in South Africa. Literature: Eliovson, S., *Wild
Flowers of Southern Africa*, 6th edn, pp. 84–5 (1980).

CODONOPSIS Wall. (Campanulaceae)
About 40 species from central Asia to China. Several species
are climbers with tuberous roots. Literature: Knox Finlay, M.,
'On *Codonopsis* which grow at Keillour', *Journ. R.H.S.* Vol.
97: 82–7 (1972).

COLCHICUM L. (Liliaceae)
About 70 species in Europe and Asia, mostly in the eastern
Mediterranean area. Literature: Brickell, C.D. in *Flora Euro-
paea*, **5**: 21-5 (1980). See also *Flora of Turkey*, **8** (forthcoming).

CORYDALIS DC (Fumariaceae)
About 300 species in the northern hemisphere; many species
from southern Europe and south-west and central Asia are
tuberous. Literature: Davis, P.H. and Cullen, J., *Corydalis* in
Flora of Turkey, **1**: 238–42 (1965); Pazij, V.K. in Vvedensky,
A.I., *Consp. Fl. Asiae Mediae*, **4**: 17–28 (1974) (in Russian);
Wendelbo, P. in *Flora Iranica*, **10**: 1–32 (1974).

CRINUM L. (Amaryllidaceae)
About 130 species throughout the Tropics. Plants often aquatic or growing in marshes. Literature: Nordal, I., 'Revision of the East African taxa of the genus *Crinum . . .*', *Norw. J. Bot.*, **24**(3): 179–94 (1977); Verdoon I.C., '*Crinum* in Southern Africa', *Bothalia*, **11** (1 and 2): 27–52 (1973).

CROCOSMIA Planchon (Iridaceae)
About 6 species in southern Africa, now again kept distinct from *Tritonia* (q.v.). Literature: Goldblatt P., *Iridaceae* in Dyer, R.A., *The genera of S. African Flowing Plants*, Vol. 2 (Pretoria, 1976).

CROCUS L. (Iridaceae)
There are 80 species and 36 subspecies from Europe eastwards to central Asia and western China. Literature: Mathew, Brian, *The Crocus*, Batsford, 1982.

CYCLAMEN L. (Primulaceae)
About 15 species in Europe and the Mediterranean area eastwards to Iran. Literature: Nightingale, Gay, *Growing Cyclamen*, Croom Helm, 1982.

CYRTANTHUS Aiton (Amaryllidaceae)
About 50 species from Tanzania to South Africa.

DAHLIA L. (Compositae)
About 20 species in Mexico and central America, and many thousands of cultivars.

DELPHINIUM L. (Ranunculaceae)
About 250 species, some of which, in south-west Asia, have tuberous rootstocks which become dry and dormant in summer. Cf. *Gentiana* (q.v.). Other species, e.g. in California, have clusters of tuberous roots. Literature: Davis, P.H., *Flora of Turkey*, **1**: 108–117 (1965); Munz, P.A. and Keck, D.D., *A California Flora*: 81–91 (1968).

DICENTRA Bernh. (Fumariaceae)
About 20 species in North America and Asia. *D. uniflora* and related species from western North America have tubers. Literature: Munz, P.A. and Keck, D.D., *A California Flora*: 202–3 (1968).

DICHELOSTEMMA Heller (Liliaceae)
About 6 species in western North America. Literature: Hoover R.F., 'The genus *Dichelostemma*', *Bull. Torr. Bot. Club*, 24: 463–76 (1940).

DIERAMA C. Koch (Iridaceae)
About 25, or according to some authorities only 3 or 4, species in eastern and southern Africa.

DIPCADI Medicus (Liliaceae)
About 50 species from the Canaries and North Africa to India. One species, *D. serotinum*, in south-western Europe. Literature: Deb, D.B. and Dasgupta, S., 'Revision of the genus *Dipcadi . . .* in India and adjoining regions', *J. Bombay Nat. Hist. Soc.*, **75**(1): 50–70 (1978); Maire, R., *Flore de l'Afrique du Nord*, **5** (1958).

DIPIDAX Laws ex Salisb. (Liliaceae)
Two species in South Africa, the commonest, *D. triquetra*, usually growing in vleis and flowering as it emerges from the water.

DODECATHEON L. (Primulaceae)
About 14 species in North America, mostly in wet places, but some species from dry habitats have bulbils or fleshy roots. Literature: Munz, P.A. and Keck, D.D., *A California Flora*: 400–3 (1968).

DRACUNCULUS Miller (Araceae)
Three species in Europe and the Canary Is. Literature: Henderson, Andrew, 'More on Dragon Plants', *The Garden* **107**(12): 498–9 (1982).

DRIMIA Jacq. ex Willd. (Liliaceae) including *Urginea* Steinh. About 120 species in Asia and Africa, 3 species in Europe. *D. haworthoides* has a strange bulb of many separate scales, which sits on the soil surface. Literature: Jessop, J.P. 'The taxonomy of *Drimia* and certain allied genera', *J.S. Afr. Bot.*, **43**(4): 265–319 (1977); Stearn, W.T., 'Mediterranean and Indian species of *Drimia*', *Ann. Mus. Goul.*, 4: 199–210 (1978).

EMINIUM Schott (Araceae)
About 5 species in south-west and central Asia. Literature: Pazij, V.K. in Vvedensky, A.I. *Consp. Flor. Asiae Mediae*, **2**: 7–8 (1971). See also *Flora of Turkey*, **8** (forthcoming).

ERANTHIS Salisb. (Ranunculacae)
About 7 species from Europe and Asia to Japan. Literature:
Schipcz, O. in *Fl. U.S.S.R.*, **7**: 60 (1937).

EREMOSTACHYS Bunge (Labiatae)
About 60 species mainly in central Asia. *Salvia*-like plants with
tuberous roots.

EREMURUS Bieb. (Liliaceae)
About 50 species from Europe eastwards, mostly in central
Asia. Literature: Vvedensky, A.I. and Kovalevskaja, S.S. in
Consp. Fl. Asiae Mediae, **2**: 14–27 (1971); Wendelbo, P.,
Eremurus in *Flora Iranica*, **151**: 6–24 (1982).

ERYTHRONIUM L. (Liliaceae)
About 25 species in North America, northern Asia and Europe.
Leaves lanceolate to ovate, often spotted or blotched. Litera-
ture: Applegate, E.I., 'The genus *Erythronium* . . . the western
North American species', *Madrono*, 3: 58–113 (1935).

EUCHARIS see URCEOLINA.

EUCOMIS L'Her. (Liliaceae)
About 10 species, mostly in south Africa, and several subspecies.

EURYCLES Salisb. (Amaryllidaceae)
3 species in Malaysia and north-eastern Australia. Literature:
Herklots, G.A.C., '*Eurycles* and *Vagaria*', *The Plantsman*,
3(4):220–9 (1982).

EUSTEPHIA Cav. (Amaryllidaceae)
About 8 species in Peru, Argentina and Bolivia. Literature:
Vargas, C., *Plant Life 1967*: 47–8 (1967).

FERRARIA Burm. ex Miller (Iridaceae)
About 10 species in southern Africa, often with brownish
mottled, starry flowers. Literature: de Vos, M.P., 'The African
genus *Ferraria*', *Journ. S. Afr. Bot.*, **45**(3): 295–375 (1979).

FREESIA Klatt (Iridaceae)
11 species from southern Africa. Multicoloured hybrids and
double-flowered cultivars have been made. Literature:
Goemans, R.A., 'The History of the modern Freesia' in
Birckell, Cutler, and Gregory, *Petaloid Monocotyledons*, pp.

161–170 (1980). Goldblatt, P., 'Systematics of *Freesia* Klatt', *Journ. S. Afr. Bot.*, **48**(1): 39–91 (1982).

FRITILLARIA L. (Liliaceae)
About 100 species throughout the northern hemisphere except eastern North America. Literature: Chen and Hsia, K.-C. in *Acta Phytotax. Sin.* **15**(2): 31-46 (1977) (20 spp. in Chinese); Macfarlane, R.M., 'North American *Fritillaria*, A preliminary account', *Lilies 1975 and other Liliaceae*: 53–66 (1975). Rix, E.M. in *Flora Europaea*, **5**: 31–4 (1980); '*Fritillaria* in Iran', *Iran Journ. Bot.*, **1**(2): 75–95 (1977). Turrill, W.B. and Sealy, J.R., *Hook. Ic.* **39**(1 and 2) (1980). See also *Flora of Turkey*, **8** (forthcoming).

GAGEA Salisb. (Liliaceae)
About 100 species in Europe and Asia, with the majority in central Asia. Literature: Richardson I.B.K. in *Flora Europaea*, **5**: 26–8 (1980); Vvedensky, A.I., *Consp. Fl. Asiae Mediae*, **2**: 27–39 (1971). See also *Flora of Turkey*, **8** (forthcoming).

GALANTHUS L. (Amaryllidaceae)
About 12 species in southern Europe and the Mediterranean region, eastwards to Iran. Literature: Artiushenko, Z.T., *R.H.S. Daffodil Year Book. 1967*, pp. 62–82 (1967); Webb, D.A. in *Flora Europaea*, **5**: 77–8 (1980); Yeo, P. F., 'The hybrid origin of some cultivated snowdrops', *Baileya*, **19**(4): 157–62 (1975). See also *Flora of Turkey*, **8** (forthcoming).

GALAXIA Thunb. (Iridaceae)
Twelve species in the Cape Province of South Africa and Namaqualand. Ovary subterranean at flowering. Literature: Goldblatt, P., 'The biology and systematics of Galaxia', *Journ. S. Afr. Bot.* **45**(4): 385–423 (1979).

GALTONIA Decne (Liliaceae)
Three species in South Africa.

GENTIANA L. (Gentianaceae)
About 400 species throughout the world, mostly in the mountains. One species, *G. olivieri*, from Turkey to Central Asia has a thick rootstock which becomes dry and dormant in summer. Literature: Pritchard, N.M. in *Flora of Turkey*, **6**: 185–6 (1978).

GERANIUM L. (Geraniaceae)
About 400 species worldwide, some of which have tuberous roots, notably the *G. tuberosum* group from eastern Europe to central Asia. Literature: Davis, P.H., *Flora of Turkey*, **2**: 62–6 (1967).

GETHYLLIS L. (Amaryllidaceae) (Including *Klingia.*)
About 21 species, 2 in South Africa. Crocus-like plants with subterranean ovary and flowers in early summer with the leaves. Literature: Obermayer, A.A. in *Bothalia*, **13**(1 and 2) (1980).

GLADIOLUS L. (Iridaceae)
About 300 species, mainly in South Africa. Literature: Hamilton, A.P. 'The European Gladioli', *Glad. Annual. 1976*, pp. 35–9 (1976); Lewis, G.J., Obermeyer, A.A. and Barnard, T.T., 'A revision of the South African species of *Gladiolus*', *Journ. S. Afr. Bot. Suppl.*, **10** (1972).

GLORIOSA L. (Liliaceae)
About 5 species in Africa and India. Literature: Field, D.V. in *Lilies 1973 and other Liliaceae*: 93–5 (1972).

GYMNOSPERMIUM Spach. (Berberidaceae)
About 6 species from eastern Europe to northern China. Literature: Rix, E.M., 'The Herbaceous Berberidaceae', *The Plantsman*, **4**(1): 6–8 (1982).

GYNANDRIRIS Parl. (Iridaceae)
About 20 species mainly in South Africa, but with 1 species, *G. Sisyrinchium*, widely distributed in Europe and south-west Asia. Close to *Moraea*.

HABRANTHUS Herb. (Amaryllidaceae)
About 23 species in central and South America. Literature: Herklots, G. in *The Plantsman*, **2**(2): 90–100 (1980).

HAEMANTHUS L. (Amaryllidaceae)
Nine species and species complexes. Bulbous species with one or more flat leaves arising direct from the bulb. Flowers in dense umbels with white, pink or red bracts. Mainly in South Africa. Literature: Friis, I. and Nordal, I., 'Studies on the genus *Haemanthus* 3', *Norw. J. Bot.*, **23**(2): 63–77 (1976); 'Division into *Haemanthus* and *Scadoxus, 1 and 2*', *Norw. J. Bot.*, 19(xx): 187–222 (1972).

HAYLOCKIA Herbert (Amaryllidaceae)
About 4 species in Bolivia and Uruguay. Ovary subterranean: flowers after the leaves have died. Literature: Cardenes, M. in *Plant Life 1973*: 41–5 (1973).

HEDYCHIUM Koenig (Zingiberaceae)
About 50 species in Tropical Asia and Madagascar. Literature: Schilling, T., 'A survey of cultivated Himalayan and Sino-Himalayan *Hedychium* species', *The Plantsman*, **4**(3): 129–49 (1982).

HERMODACTYLUS Salisbury (Iridaceae)
One species, *H. tuberosus*, in the Mediterranean region. Literature: Mathew, Brian, *The Iris*, p. 183, Batsford, 1981.

HERBERTIA see TRIFURCIA Herb.

HIPPEASTRUM see AMARYLLIS.

HOMERIA Vent. (Iridaceae)
About 37 species in southern Africa. Literature: Goldblatt, P. in *Journ. S. Afr. Bot.*, **39**(2): 133–40 (1973).

HOMOGLOSSUM Salisb. (Iridaceae)
About 20 species in southern Africa. Distinguished from *Gladiolus* only by the shape of the perianth. Literature: de Vos, M.P., 'The South African species of *Homoglossum*', *Journ. S. Afr. Bot.*, **42**(4): 301–59 (1976) (in Afrikaans).

HYACINTHELLA Schur. (Liliaceae)
Sixteen species in south-east Europe and south-west Asia. Dwarf plants like grape hyacinths, often with leaves. Literature: Persson, K. and Wendelbo, P., 'Taxonomy and cytology of the genus Hyacinthella . . . with special reference to the species in S.W. Asia', *I. Candollea*, 36: 513–41 (1981); *II Candollea*, 37: 157–75 (1982).

HYACINTHOIDES Medicus (Liliaceae)
About 3 species in western Europe. The English bluebell, *H. non-scripta*, belongs here. Literature: Heywood, V.H. in *Flora Europaea*, **5**: 43–4 (1980).

HYACINTHUS L. (Liliaceae)
Three species in the eastern Mediterranean and central Asia, if *Hyacinthella* (q.v.) is excluded. *H. orientalis* is the common

hyacinth. Literature: Bentzer, B. et al. 'Cytology and morphology of the genus *Hyacinthus* s.str.' *Bot. Not.*, 127: 297–301 (1974).

HYMENOCALLIS Salisb. (Amaryllidaceae)
About 70 species in central and South America. Flowers white or yellow, often with a large corona and narrow petals. Literature: W.S. Flory, *Plant Life 1978*: 47–59; 'Distribution, chromosome numbers and types of various species and taxa of *Hymenocallis*', *Nucleus*, **19**(3): 204–27 (1976).

HYPOXIS L. (Hypoxidaceae)
About 100 species, mainly in southern Africa. Flowers small, yellow and starry.

IRIS L. (Iridaceae)
About 300 species throughout the northern hemisphere. Literature: Mathew, Brian, *The Iris*, Batsford, 1981.

IXIA L. (Iridaceae)
About 60 species in South Africa. Mostly tall, slender plants with spikes of starry flowers, growing in winter. *I. viridiflora* has glaucous blue-green flowers with black centres. Other species are very colourful, notably the hybrids of *I. maculata*. Literature: Lewis, G.J., *Journ. S. Afr. Bot.*, 28: 45–195 (1962).

IXIOLIRION Fisch. (Amaryllidaceae)
Three species in central Asia westwards to Turkey. Literature: Pazy, V.K., *Ixiolirion* in Vvedensky, A.I., *Consp. Fl. Asiae Mediae*, **2**: 119–20 (1971); Wendelbo, P., *Ixiolirion* in *Flora Iranica*, **67**: 2–3 (1970).

KOROLKOWIA see FRITILLARIA.

LACHENALIA Jacq. (Liliaceae)
About 60 species, mostly in the winter-rainfall area of South Africa and in Namaqualand. Flowers usually tubular and hanging in shades of red, yellow, blue or green. Leaves in a basal rosette, often marked. Useful for winter flowering. Literature: Barker, W.F., 'Ten new species of *Lachenalia* (Liliaceae)', *Journ. S. Afr. Bot.* **44**(4): 391–418 (1978); **45**(2): 193–219 (1979).

LAPEIROUSIA Tourn. (Iridaceae)
About 50 species in southern Africa. Literature: Goldblatt, P.

in *Contr. Bolus Herb.*, 4: 1–108 (1972).

LEONTICE L. (Berberidaceae)
Four species and subspecies in south-east Europe, western and central Asia. Literature: Rix, E.M., 'The Herbaceous Berberidaceae', *The Plantsman*, **4**(1): 4–6 (1982).

LEUCOCORYNE Lindl. (Liliaceae)
About 6 species in South America. Literature: Zöllner, O., *Anales de Museo de Nat. Hist. de Valparaiso*, **5** (1972).

LEUCOJUM L. (Amaryllidaceae)
Eleven species in Europe and North Africa eastwards to Iran. Literature: Stern, F.C., *Snowdrops and Snowflakes*, Royal Horticultural Society, 1956; Webb, D.A. in *Flora Europaea*, **5**: 76–7 (1980).

LEUCOCRINUM Nutt. (Liliaceae)
One species, *L. montanum*, in California and Oregon to Nebraska and New Mexico. Literature: Munz, P.A. and Keck, D.D., *A California Flora*: 1330 (1968).

LEWISIA Pursh (Portulacaceae)
About 18 species in western North America. Several species have fleshy roots or corms. Literature: Munz, P.A. and Keck, D.D., *A California Flora*: 296–9 (1968).

LILIUM L. (Liliaceae)
About 80 species throughout the northern hemisphere, south to the Philippines. Literature: Synge, P.M., *Lilies*, Batsford, 1980.

LITTONIA Hook. (Liliaceae)
One species, *L. modesta*, in southern Africa. Literature: Eliovson, S., *Wild Flowers of Southern Africa*, p. 125 (1980).

LLOYDIA Salisb. ex Rchb. (Liliaceae)
About 20 species in Eurasia. One species, *L. serotina*, from Wales to Central Asia, the rest in the Himalaya.

LYCORIS Herbert (Amaryllidaceae)
About 18 species in eastern Asia from Japan to Burma. Literature: Adams, P. '*Lycoris* – Surprise Lilies', *Pac. Hort.*, **37**(3): 23–9 (1976).

LYSICHITUM Schott (Araceae)
Two species, *L. americanum* in western North America and *L. camtschatcense* in north-eastern Asia.

MASSONIA Thunb. (Liliaceae)
About 8 species in South Africa. Broad, fleshy leaves lie flat on the ground with a stemless tuft of flowers between them. Literature: Jessop, J.P., 'The taxonomy of *Massonia* and allied genera', *Journ. S. Afr. Bot.*, **42**(4): 401–37 (1976).

MERENDERA Ramond (Liliaceae)
About 10 species in Europe and western Asia east to Afghanistan. Similar to *Colchicum*, but with free petals not united into a tube. Literature: Valdes, B. in *Flora Europaea*, **5**: 25 (1980). See also *Flora of Turkey*, **8** (forthcoming).

MUSCARI Miller (Liliaceae).
About 60 species in Europe and west Asia. Literature: Davis P.H. and Stuart D.C. in *Flora Europaea*, **5**: 46–9 (1980). See also *Flora of Turkey*, **8** (forthcoming).

MORAEA L. (Iridaceae)
About 100 species in southern Africa, many very similar to *Iris*. Literature: Barnard, T.T., 'Peacock Moraeas', *Journ. R.H.S.*, 75: 323–26 (1950); Goldblatt, P., 'The genus *Moraea* in the winter rainfall region of southern Africa', *Ann. Miss. Bot. Gard.*, 63: 1–23 (1976) and 657–786 (1977); Goldblatt, P., 'Systematics of *Moraea* . . . in Tropical Africa', *Ann. Miss. Bot. Gard.*, **64**(2): 243–95 (1978).

NARCISSUS L. (Amaryllidaceae)
About 40 species in Europe and North Africa, and many hundred hybrids and cultivars. Literature: Maire, R. in *Flore de l'Afrique du Nord*, **5**: xxx (1958); Webb, D.A. in *Flora Europaea*, **5**: 78–84 (1980).

NECTAROSCORDUM Lindl. (Liliaceae)
Three species in the Mediterranean area eastwards to Iran. Literature: Stearn, W.T. in *Flora Europaea*, **5**: 69 (1980); Wendelbo, P.W. in *Flora Iranica*, **76**: 1–3 (1971). See also *Flora of Turkey*, **8** (forthcoming).

NEMASTYLIS Nutt. (Iridaceae)
Five species in Mexico and south-east USA. Literature: Goldblatt, P. in *Brittonia*, 27: 375–80 (1975).

Appendix I

NERINE Herbert (Amaryllidaceae)
About 30 species in South Africa, 1 in Zimbabwe, and numerous cultivars. Literature: Traub, H.P., 'A review of the genus *Nerine*', *Plant Life*, 23, addendum 1–32 (1967).

NOMOCHARIS Franch. (Liliaceae)
About 10 species in the Himalaya. Literature: Synge, P.M., *Lilies*, Batsford, 1980.

NOTHOLIRION Wall. ex Boiss. (Liliaceae)
About 5 species in the Himalaya and one in Iran. Literature: Synge, P.M., *Lilies*, Batsford, 1980.

NOTHOSCORDUM Kunth (Liliaceae)
About 35 species in South America, 1 of which, *N. inodorum*, is widely naturalised elsewhere. Close to *Allium*, but without smell.

NYMPHAEA L. (Nymphaeaceae)
About 40 species, some of which have corms which can survive drought. Literature: Conard, H.S., 'The Waterlilies; a monograph of the genus *Nymphaea*', *Carnegie Inst. Washington Publ.*, 4: 1–279 (1905); Swindells, P., *Waterlilies*, Croom Helm, 1983.

ORNITHOGALUM L. (Liliaceae)
About 150 species in Europe, south-west Asia and Africa. Literature: Obermayer, A.A., 'A Revision of the South African species of *Ornithogalum*', *Bothalia*, **12**(3): 323–76 (1978); Zahariadi, C. in *Flora Europaea*, **5**: 35–40 (1980).

OSTROWSKIA Regel (Campanulaceae)
One species, *O. magnfica*, in central Asia.

OXALIS L. (Oxalidaceae)
About 800 species worldwide, of which about 500 are in South Africa. Most have bulbs. Literature: Kunth, R. in *Das Pflanzenreich*, **iv**, (130): 43–389 (1930).

PANCRATIUM L. (Amaryllidaceae)
About 20 species from the Canaries and the Mediterranean to Tropical Asia and South Africa.

PARDANTHOPSIS (Hance) Lenz (Iridaceae)
One species, *P. dichotoma* (*Iris dichotoma* Pallas), in Mongolia

182

and north-east Asia. Literature: Mathew, Brian, *The Iris*, Batsford. 1981.

PARIS L. (Liliaceae)
About 20 species from Europe to China.

PELARGONIUM L'Her. (Geraniaceae)
About 250 species from Turkey and Iraq to South Africa, where many are tuberous. Literature: van der Walt, J.J.A., *Pelargoniums of Southern Africa*, Vol. 1 (1977), and Vorster, P.J., Vol. 2 (1981).

PHAEDRANASSA Herbert (Amaryllidaceae)
About 8 species in the Andes from Peru to Costa Rica.

PHYCELLA Lindl. (Amaryllidaceae)
About 7 species in Peru, Chile, Argentina and Uruguay.

PLACEA Miers ex Lindl. (Amaryllidaceae)
About 6 species in Chile.

PLEIONE D. Don (Orchidaceae)
Sixteen species in the Himalaya and China. Literature: Cribb, P.J., Tang C.Z. and Butterfield, I., 'The genus *Pleione*', *Bot. Mag.*, 184, n.s. tt. 860–71 (1983).

POLIANTHES L. (Agavaceae)
About 12 species in Mexico and central America.

POLYXENA Kunth (Liliaceae)
Two species in South Africa. Literature: Mathew, Brian, 'Polyxena', *The Plantsman*, **4**(3): 179-81 (1982).

PRIMULA L. (Primulaceae)
About 500 species, mainly in Asia. One species from central Asia, *P. fedtschenkoi* Regel, has a tuft of tuberous roots which become dormant in summer. Literature: Rix, M. and Phillips, R., *The Bulb Book*, p. 63, Pan, 1981.

PUSCHKINIA Adams (Liliaceae)
One or two species in south-west Asia. Literature: Rix, E.M. and Phillips, R., *The Bulb Book*, pp. 42-3, Pan, 1981. See also *Flora of Turkey*, **8** (forthcoming).

Appendix I

PYROLIRION Herbert (Amaryllidaceae)
Five to ten species in Peru and Bolivia. Literature: Herklots, G.A.C. in *The Plantsman*, **4**(3): 171–8 (1982).

RANUNCULUS L. (Ranunculaceae)
About 400 species, mainly in the northern hemisphere; many cultivated species have tuberous roots, notably *R. asiaticus* and the celandine, *R. ficaria*. Literature: Davis, P.H., *Flora of Turkey*, **1**: 146–95 (1965).

RHODOHYPOXIS Nel (Hypoxidaceae).
About 6 species in South Africa. Literature: Hilliard, O.M. and Burtt, B.L., *Notes Roy. Bot. Gard. Edinb.*, **36**(1): 43–76 (1978).

RHODOPHIALA Pres. (Amaryllidaceae)
About 35 species in Chile and Argentina, 1 species in Brazil.

RIGIDELLA Lindl. (Iridaceae)
About 4 species in Mexico, Guatemala and Peru. Literature: Cruden, R.W., *Brittonia*, **23**(2): 217 (1971).

ROMULEA Maratti (Iridaceae)
About 90 species in South Africa and the Mediterranean region. Literature: Marais, W. in *Flora Europaea*, **5**: 99–100 (1980). See also *Flora of Turkey*, **8** (forthcoming); de Vos, M.P., 'The genus *Romulea*', *Journ. S. Afr. Bot. Suppl.*, Vol. 9 (1900).

ROSCOEA Royle (Zingiberaceae)
About 15 species in the Himalaya and China.

SANDERSONIA Hook. (Liliaceae)
One species, *S. aurantiaca*, in Natal. Literature: Eliovson, S., *Wild Flowers of Southern Africa*, p. 137 (1980).

SAUROMATUM Schott. (Araceae)
About 6 species from Tropical Africa to Malaysia.

SCADOXUS Raf. (Amaryllidaceae)
Nine species and three subspecies from Ethiopia to the Cape. Literature: as for *Haemanthus*.

SCHIZOSTYLIS Backh. & Harv. (Iridaceae)
Two species in southern Africa, and a few garden varieties.

Literature: Drewe, Beatrice, '*Schizostylis coccinea* "Tambara" ', *Journ. R.H.S.*, **96**(7): 314–15 (1971).

SCILLA L. (Liliaceae)
About 100 species in Europe, western and central Asia and Africa. Literature: Jessop, J.P., 'Studies in the bulbous Liliaceae: 1. *Scilla*', *Journ. S. Afr. Bot.*, **36**(4): 233–66 (1970); McNeill, J. in *Flora Europaea*, **5**: 41–3 (1980); Speta, F., 'The spring-flowering *Scilla* species from the eastern Mediterranean region', *Naturk. Jahrb. Stadt. Linz* 25: 19–198 (1980).

SINNINGIA Nees (Gesneriaceae)
About 20 species in Brazil. Literature: as *Achimenes*.

SPARAXIS Ker-Gawl. (Iridaceae)
About 6 species in the Cape region of south Africa. Literature: Goldblatt, P. in *Journ. S. Afr. Bot.*, **35**: 219–52 (1969).

SPHENOSTIGMA Baker (Iridaceae)
About 16 species in North, Central and South America. Literature: Goldblatt, P. in *Brittonia*, 27: 374–5 (1975).

SPILOXENE Salisb. (Hypoxidaceae)
About 20 species in South Africa.

SPREKELIA Heist (Amaryllidaceae)
Two species in Mexico and South America. Literature: Hannibal, L.S., *Journ. R.H.S.*, **93**(8): 334–6 (1968).

STENOMESSON Herbert (Amaryllidaceae)
About 26 species in Ecuador, Peru, Bolivia and northern Chile.

STERNBERGIA Waldst. & Kit. (Amaryllidaceae)
Five species in the eastern Mediterranean area. Literature: Mathew, Brian in *The Plantsman*, **4**(4): 193–219 (1983).

SYNNOTIA Sweet (Iridaceae)
About 5 species in South Africa. Literature: Lewis, G.J., *Ann. S. Afr. Mus.*, 40: 137–51 (1956).

SYRINGODEA D. Don (Iridaceae)
Eight species in South Africa. Literature: de Vos, M.P., *Journ. S. Afr. Bot.*, **40**(3): 207–54 (1974).

TECOPHILAEA Bertol. ex Colla (Tecophilaeaceae)
Two species in Chile. Literature: Rix, M. and Phillips, R., *The Bulb Book*, p. 47, Pan, 1981.

TAPEINANTHUS Herbert, now included in *Narcissus*.

TIGRIDIA Juss. (Iridaceae)
About 12 species in Mexico and Central America. Literature: Molseed, J.W., Univ. of California publ. Bot. 54 (1970).

TRIFURCIA Herbert. (Iridaceae), (includes *Herbertia* Sweet)
About 5 species in south-eastern USA and South America. Literature: Goldblatt, P. in *Brittonia*, 27: 382–5 (1975).

TRILLIUM L. (Liliaceae)
About 30 species, mostly in North America, but with about 4 in east Asia; many varieties. Literature: Ahles, H.E., '*Trillium* L. in Eastern N. America', *Lilies 1974 and other Liliaceae*: 56–64 (1974); Roderick, Wayne, '*Trillium* in California', op. cit., pp. 67–70; Szczawinski, A.F. and Taylor, T.M.C., 'Trilliums of Western N. America', op. cit., pp. 64–7.

TRITELEIA Dougl. ex Lindl. (Liliaceae)
About 15 species in western North America. Literature: Munz, P.A. and Keck D.D., *A California Flora*: 1379–83 (1968) under *Brodiaea*.

TRITONIA Ker-Gawl. (Iridaceae)
About 30 species in southern Africa, especially the Cape. Literature: de Vos, M.P., 'The African genus *Tritonia*. Pt. 1', *Journ. S. Afr. Bot.*, **48**(1): 105–63 (1982).

TRITONIOPSIS L. Bolus (Iridaceae)
14 species in South Africa. Literature: Lewis, G.J., 'The genus *Tritoniopsis*', *Journ. S. Afr. Bot.*, 25: 319–55 (1959).

TROPAEOLUM L. (Tropeaolaceae)
About 90 species in South America, many of which are tuberous.

TULBAGHIA L. (Liliaceae)
About 21 species in southern Africa. Literature: Burbidge, R.B., 'A revision of the genus *Tulbaghia* (Liliaceae)', *Notes Roy. Bot. Gard. Edinb.*, **36**(1): 77–103 (1978).

TULIPA L. (Liliaceae)
About 100 species, mainly in central Asia, and thousands of
cultivars. Literature: Botschantseva, Z.P., *Tulips*, trans. and
ed. by H.Q. Varekamp (Balkema, 1982). See also *Flora of
Turkey*, **8** (forthcoming) and Hoog, M.H., 'On the Origin of
Tulipa', *Lilies and other Liliaceae 1973*: 47–64 (1972).

UNGERNIA Bunge (Amaryllidaceae)
About 8 species in central Asia and Iran. Literature: Artiushenko, Z.T., *Plant Life 1970*: 173 (1970).

URCEOLINA Reicht. (Amaryllidaceae)
About 29 species in Peru and Costa Rica. Literature: Ravenna,
P.F., *Plant Life*, 38: 48–48 (1982).

URGINEA, now included in DRIMIA (q.v.)

VAGARIA Herbert (Amaryllidaceae)
Three species in North Africa, one in Syria and Israel.
Literature: Herklots, G.A.C., '*Eurycles* and *Vagaria* (Amaryl-
lidaceae)', *The Plantsman*, **3**(4): 225–9 (1982).

VALLOTA, now included in CYRTANTHUS (q.v.)

VELTHEIMIA Jacq. (Liliaceae)
Two species in South Africa. Literature: Marais, W., 'The
correct names for Veltheimias', *Journ. R.H.S.*, **97**(11): 483–4
(1972).

WACHENDORFIA Burm. (Haemodoraceae)
About 20 species in southern Africa.

WALLERIA J. Kirk. (Tecophilaeaceae)
Three species in central Africa. Literature: Carter, Susan in
Kew Bull., 16: 185–90 (1962–3).

WATSONIA Mill. (Iridaceae)
About 40 species in South Africa. Literature: Snijman, D.A.,
'The genus *Watsonia*', *Veld & Flora*, **64**(3): 93 (1978).

WORSLEYA Traub (Amaryllidaceae)
One species, *W. rayneri* in Brazil, growing on cliff ledges.
Flowers blue; the large seeds are said to be carried upwards by
parrots. Often included in *Amaryllis*. Literature: Blossfeld, H.,
Plant Life, 22: 15 (1966); [*JRHS*, Jan. 1950].

WURMBEA Thunb. (Liliaceae)
About 8 species in southern Africa and Western Australia. Literature: Nordenstam, B., 'The genus Wurmbea in Africa, except the Cape region', *Notes Roy. Bot. Gard. Edinb.*, **36**(2): 211–33 (1978).

ZANTEDESCHIA Sprengel (Araceae)
Six species and two subspecies in southern Africa. Literature: Letty, C. in *Bothalia*, **11**(1 and 2): 5–26 (1973).

ZEPHYRANTHES Herbert (Amaryllidaceae)
About 65 species from Texas to south America. Literature: Herklots, G.A.C., 'Windflowers: *Zephyranthes* and *Habranthus*', *The Plantsman*, **2**(1): 8–19 (1980).

ZIGADENUS Michx. (Liliaceae)
18 species in North America and northern Asia, west to the Urals. Literature: Munz, P.A. and Keck, D.D., *A California Flora*: 1333–5 (1959).

Suppliers and Societies

Name and Address	Specialities	Commercial Bulb Suppliers in Britain and the Republic of Ireland
Mrs J. Abel-Smith, Orchard House, Letty Green, Nr Hertford, Herts. Tel. Hatfield 61274 or 61	Daffodils.	
Amand Garden Centre 17 Beethoven Street, London, W1O 4LG. Tel. 01–969 9797	*Gladiolus, Tulipa.*	
Appledore's Answer, Court Lodge, Appledore, Kent. Tel. 023–383–391	Daffodils. *Tulipa.*	
Avon Bulbs, Bathford, Bath, Avon, BA1 8ED.	Miniature bulbs. Uncommon and rare species.	
Aylett Nurseries Ltd, North Orbital Road, London Colney, St. Albans, Herts, AL2 1DH Tel. 0727–22255	*Dahlia.*	
Mrs Helen Ballard, Old Country, Mathon, Malvern, Hereford & Worcs.	*Galanthus. Leucojum. Lilium.*	
Ballydorn Bulb Farm, Killinchy, Co. Down, N. Ireland. Tel. 0238–541250	Daffodils.	
Begonias from Belgium, 24 Hazelwood Road, Northampton, NN1 1LN. Tel. 0604–38014	*Begonia.*	

Blackmore and Langdon,
Stanton Nursery, Pensford, Bristol,
Avon, BS18 4JL.
Tel. 027–589–2300

Begonia. Freesia. Cyclamen (greenhouse). *Gloxinia. Nerine.*

Blom, Walter & Sons Ltd,
Leavesden, Watford, Herts.
Tel. 092–73–72071

Anemone. Crocus. Dwarf *Narcissus. Freesia. Gladiolus. Lilium. Tulipa.*

S.W. Bond,
Thuya Cottage Alpine Nursery,
Petersfield Road, Whitehill, Bordon,
Hants, GU35 9AH
Tel. 042–03–2739

Cyclamen (hardy).

Bressingham Gardens,
Diss, Norfolk, IP22 2AB.
Tel. 037–988–464

Crocosmia.

Broadleigh Gardens,
Barr House, Bishop's Hull, Taunton,
Somerset.
Tel. 0823–86231

Dwarf bulbs, especially *Anemone. Colchicum. Crocus. Cyclamen* (hardy). *Fritillaria. Galanthus. Gladiolus. Iris. Muscari. Narcissus.*

Bullwood Nursery,
54 Woodlands Road, Hockley, Essex,
SS5 4PY.

Lilium and other Liliaceae.

Thomas Butcher Ltd,
60 Wickham Road, Shirley, Croydon,
Surrey.
Tel. 654–3720

Lilium and tender bulbs.

Butterfield's Nursery,
Harvest Hill, Bourne End, Bucks,
SL8 5JJ.
Tel. 062–85–25455

Dahlia. Pleione.

Carncairn Daffodils Ltd,
Carncairn Lodge, Broughshane,
Co. Antrim, N. Ireland.
Tel. 0266–861216

Daffodils.

P.J. & J.W. Christian,
Pentre Cottages, Minera, Wrexham,
Clwyd, Wales.
Tel. 051733–9889

Allium.
Colchicum.
Crocus.
Fritillaria.
Galanthus.
Lewisia. Lilium.
Trillium.

Cornish Bulb Company,
13a Church Street, Falmouth,
Cornwall, TR11 3DR.
Tel. 0326–74284

Agapanthus.
Daffodils.
Hemerocallis.
Nerine.

Cramphorn Ltd,
Specialist Gladiolus Dept, Chelmsford
Garden Centre, Cuton Mill,
Chelmsford, Essex, CM2 6PD.
Tel. 0245–466466

Gladiolus.

Daisy Hill Nurseries,
Hospital Road, Newry, Co. Down,
N. Ireland.
Tel. 0693–2474

Crocosmia.

P. de Jager & Sons Ltd,
The Nurseries, Marden, Kent,
TN12 9BP.
Wallace & Barr are also at this address.

Daffodils.
Hyacinthus.
Gladiolus. Tulipa.
Lilium.

Dickson, Brown & Tait Ltd,
Attenbury's Lane, Timperley,
Altrincham, Cheshire, WA14 5QL.
Tel. 061973–2214

Eranthis.
Chionodoxa.
Hyacinthus.
Tulipa. Scilla.
Lily-of-the-valley.
Fritillaria.

Dunshelt Nurseries,
Ladybank Road, Dunshelt,
Auchtermuchty, KY14 7HG.
Tel. 03372–274

Dahlia.

Edrom Nurseries,   *Anemone.*
Coldingham, Eyemouth, Berwickshire,
TD14 5TZ.
Tel. 03903–386

Fibrex Nurseries Ltd,   *Arum. Begonia.*
Harvey Road, Evesham,
Hereford & Worcs.
Tel. 0386–6190

A. Goatcher & Son,   *Agapanthus.*
The Nurseries, Rock Road, Washington,   *Crocosmia.*
Nr Pulborough, West Sussex, RH20 3BJ.   *Nerine.*
Tel. 0903–892626

Greenbank Nursery,   *Galanthus. Iris.*
Sedburgh, Cumbria, LA10 5AG.   *Trillium.*

Home Meadows Nursery,   *Dahlia.*
Martlesham, Woodbridge, Suffolk,
IP12 4RD.

Mr V.H. Humphrey,   *Iris.*
8 Howbeck Road, Arnold, Nottingham,
NG5 8AD.
Tel. 0602–260510

Hydon Nurseries,   *Agapanthus.*
Clock Barn Lane, Hydon Heath,
Nr Godalming, Surrey, GU8 4AZ.
Tel. 048632–252

W.E.Th. Ingwersen, Ltd,   *Colchicum.*
Birch Farm Nursery, Gravetye,   *Crocus.* Dwarf
East Grinstead, Sussex.   *Narcissus.*
Tel. 0342–810236

M. Jefferson-Brown,   Daffodils.
Lakeside, The Gaines, Whitbourne,
Hereford & Worcs.

Kelway's Nurseries,   *Gladiolus. Iris.*
Langport, Somerset, TA10 9SL.   *Lilium. Narcissus.*
Tel. 0458–250521   Dwarf *Narcissus.*
                               Tulipa.

John Lea,   Daffodils.
Dunley Hall, Stourport-on-Severn,
Hereford & Worcs.
Tel. 02993–2040

Martens Hall Farm,
Longworth, Abingdon, Oxon,
OX13 5EP.
Tel. 0865–820376

Hardy bulbs,
especially
Colchicum.

Nerine Nurseries,
Welland, Malvern, Hereford & Worcs,
WR13 6LN.
Tel. 06846–2350

Nerine.

Rathowen Daffodils,
Knowehead, Dergmoney, Omagh,
Co. Tyrone, N. Ireland.
Tel. 0662–2931 or 0662–2192

Daffodils.

Tamar Valley Daffodils,
Marsh Farm, Landulph, Saltash,
Cornwall, PL12 6NG.
Tel.

Daffodils
(ministry-
inspected) for
garden display and
exhibition.

Van Tubergen,
304a Upper Richmond Road West,
London, SW14.
Tel. 01–878–0462

Anemone. Iris.
Dwarf *Narcissus.*

J. Wessels,
Windmill Nurseries & Bulb Co.,
Meadow Heights, Upton, Huntingdon,
Cambs, PE17 5YF.
Tel. 0480–890646

Iris. Lilium.

Where to Obtain Bulbs

Agapanthus

A. Goatcher & Son Cornish Bulb Company
Hydon Nurseries

Allium

P.J. & J.W. Christian

Anemone

Walter Blom & Sons Ltd Broadleigh Gardens
Edrom Nurseries Van Tubergen

Arum

Fibrex Nurseries Ltd

Begonia

Begonias from Belgium   Blackmore and Langdon
Fibrex Nurseries Ltd

Colchicum

Broadleigh Gardens
 P.J. & J.W. Christian   W.E.Th. Ingwersen Ltd
Martens Hall Farm

Crocosmia

Bressingham Gardens   A. Goatcher & Son
Daisy Hill Nurseries

Crocus

Walter Blom & Sons Ltd   Broadleigh Gardens
P.J. & J.W. Christian   W.E.Th. Ingwersen Ltd

Cyclamen

S.W. Bond   Broadleigh Gardens   P.J. & J.W. Christian

Dahlia

Aylett Nurseries Ltd   Butterfield's Nursery
Dunshelt Nurseries

Erythronium

P.J. &J.W. Christian

Freesia

Blackmore and Langdon   Walter Blom & Sons Ltd

Fritillaria

Broadleigh Gardens   P.J. & J.W. Christian

Gelanthus

Mrs Helen Ballard   Broadleigh Gardens   Greenbank Nursery

Gladiolus

Amand Garden Centre   Walter Blom & Sons Ltd
Broadleigh Gardens   Cramphorn Ltd

Gloxinia

Blackmore and Langdon

Iris

Broadleigh Gardens   Greenbank Nursery
Mr V.H. Humprey   Kelway's Nurseries

Lilium

Walter Blom & Sons Ltd   Bullwood Nursery
Thomas Butcher Ltd   P.J. & J.W. Christian
Kelway's Nurseries   Wallace & Barr

Muscari

Broadleigh Gardens

Narcissus

Mrs J. Abel-Smith   Ballydorn Bulb Farm
Carncairn Daffodils Ltd   Cornish Bulb Company
John Lea   Rathowen Daffodils   Tamar Valley Daffodils
Wallace & Barr

Narcissus (dwarf)

Walter Blom & Sons Ltd   Broadleigh Gardens
W.E.Th. Ingwersen Ltd   Van Tubergen   Wallace & Barr

Nerine

Blackmore and Langdon   A. Goatcher & Son
Nerine Nurseries

Pleione

Butterfield's Nursery

Trillium

P.J. & J.W. Christian   Greenbank Nursery

Tulipa

Amand Garden Centre   Walter Blom & Sons Ltd
Wallace & Barr

Britain

Societies and
Associations

British Gladiolus Society (Mrs M. Rowley),
10 Sandbach Road, Thurlwood, Rode Heath, Cheshire.

British Iris Society (Mr G.E. Cassidy),
67 Bushwood Road, Kew, Surrey, TW9 3BG.

Bulb Information Desk,
Stubbings House, Henley Road, Maidenhead, Berks,
SL6 6QL.

Cyclamen Society (Dr M.P. Summers),
7 Montreal Road, Ilford, Essex, IG1 4SH.

Daffodil Society (Mr D.J. Pearce),
1 Dorset Cottages, Birch Road, Copford, Colchester, Essex.

RHS Lily Group (Mrs A. Dadd),
21 Embrook Road, Wokingham, Berks.

National Begonia Society (Mr E. Catterall),
3 Gladstone Road, Dorridge, Solihull, W. Midlands.

National Dahlia Society (Mr B. Damp),
26 Burns Road, Lillington, Leamington Spa, Warwickshire.

Overseas

American Begonia Society (Elisabeth Sayers),
369 Ridge Vista Avenue, San Josa, CA 95127.

American Daffodil Society (W.O. Ticknor),
Daffodil Corner, Tyner, North Carolina 27980.

American Iris Society (James Burch),
717 Pratt Avenue, N.E. Box 10003 Huntsville, AL 35801.

Auckland Lily Society (Mrs D. Gross),
34 Maungakiekie Avenue, Greenlane, Auckland 5, New
Zealand.

Australian Lilium Society (Mr J.H. Young),
24 Halwyn Street, West Preston, Victoria 3072, Australia.

The Danish Iris and Lily Society (Mr A.H. Sorensen),
Nedermarken 51, 8850 Bjerringbro, Denmark.

Iris Society of Australia (Miss P.D. Hobbs),
8 Brassey Avenue, Rosanna 3084, Victoria, Australia.

National Daffodil Society of New Zealand (Mr F.W. Taylor),
P.O. Box 30–661, Lower Hutt, New Zealand.

Nederlandse Dahlia Vereniging,
P.O. Box 50, Hillegom, Holland.

New Zealand Lily Society (Mr J. Gover),
P.O. Box 1394, Christchurch, New Zealand.

South African Lily Society,
7 Beatty Road, University Estate, Cape Town 8000, South
Africa.

Bibliography

Introduction

Arditti, J., *Orchid Biology — reviews and perspectives II: 309-36*, Cornell University Press, 1982
Cook, C.D.K. *et al.*, *Waterplants of the World*, Junk, 1974
Mathew, Brian, *Dwarf Bulbs*, Batsford, 1973
——, *Larger Bulbs*, Batsford, 1978
Rix, Martyn and Phillips, Roger, *The Bulb Book*, Pan, 1981
Thomas, G.S., *Perennial Garden Plants*, revised edn Dent, 1983
Tjaden, W., 'Amaryllis belladonna Linn., an up-to-date summary', *Plant Life*, 37: 21-6 (1981)
Weathers, J., *The Bulb Book*, John Murray, 1911
Willis, J.C. revised Airy Shaw, H.K., *A Dictionary of the Flowering Plants and Ferns*, Cambridge University Press, 1966

Chapter 1

Baranova, M.V., 'Ecologo-morphological peculiarities of the underground organs of . . . the genus *Fritillaria*', *Botaniskeskij Jurnal*, 66(10):1369-87 (1981)
Herklots, G.A.C., *Vegetables in South-east Asia*, George Allen & Unwin, 1972
Marloth, Rudolph, *The Flora of South Africa*, Cape Town, 1912-32
Raunkiaer, C., *The Life Forms of Plants*, Oxford University Press, 1934
Rees, A.R., *The Growth of Bulbs*, Academic Press, 1972
Stebbins, G. Ledyard, *Flowering Plants, Evolution above the Species Level*, E. Arnold, 1974

Chapter 2

Agnew, A.D.Q., *Upland Kenya Wildflowers*, Oxford, 1974

Burtt, B.L., *Israel Journ. Bot.*, 19:77-90 (1970)

Eliovson, Sima, *Wild Flowers of Southern Africa*, Macmillan, 1980

Faegri, K. and Van der Pijl, L., *The Principles of Pollination Ecology*, Pergamon Press, 1966

Mathew, Brian, *The Iris*, Batsford, 1982

Prime, C.T., *Lords and Ladies*, Collins, 1960

Proctor, M. and Yeo, P., *The Pollination of Flowers*, Collins, 1973

Rix, E.M. and Rast, Dora, 'Nectar sugars and subgeneric classification in *Fritillaria*', *Biochem. Syst. & Ecol.*, 2:207-9 (1975)

Smithers, P., '*Lilium sulphureum*', *Lilies and Related Plants* (in press)

Wendelbo, P., *Tulips and Irises of Iran*, Tehran, 1977

Chapter 3

Van der Pijl, L., *Principles of Dispersal in Higher Plants*, Berlin, 1969

Chapter 4

Adamson, R.S., *The Vegetation of South Africa*, London, 1938

Adamson, R.S. and Salter, T.M., *Flora of the Cape Peninsula*, Cape Town and Johannesburg, 1950

Barclay, C., '*Chionodoxa* . . .', *Journ. RHS*, XCV: 20 (1970)

Boucher, C., 'A Provisional checklist of the Flowering plants and Ferns of the Cape Hangklip Area', *Journ. S. Afr. Bot.*, 43:57-81 (1977)

Bramwell, D. and Z.I., *Wild Flowers of the Canary Islands*, London, 1974

Davis, P.H., *Flora of Turkey*, Edinburgh, 1965 et seq.

Eliovson, Sima, *Wild Flowers of Southern Africa*, 6th edn, 1980

——, *Namaqualand in Flower*, 1978

Erikson, George, A., Marchant, N. and Morcombe, *Flowers and Plants of Western Australia*, Perth, 1980

Eyre, S.R., *Vegetation and Soils, a World Picture*, E. Arnold, 1963

Fernald, M.L., *Gray's Manual of Botany*, New York, 1950

Hithcock, C.L., Cronquist, A. *et al.*, *Vascular Plants of the Pacific Northwest*, Seattle, 1955-69

Hutchinson, John, *A Botanist in Southern Africa*, London, 1946

Bibliography

Kearney, T.H. and Peebles, R.H., *Arizona Flora*, Berkeley and Los Angeles, 1951

Maire, R., *Flore de l'Afrique du Nord*, vol. 4 et seq. (1957-)

Moore, L.B. and Edgar, E., *Flora of New Zealand II*, 1970

Moriarty, Audrey, *Wild Flowers of Malawi*, Purnell, 1975

Munz, P.A. and Keck, D.D., *A California Flora*, University of California Press, 1959

Ohwi, J., *Flora of Japan*, Washington, 1965

Polunin, Oleg, *Flowers of Greece and the Balkans, A Field Guide*, Oxford University Press, 1980

Polunin, O. and Huxley, A., *Flowers of the Mediterranean*, Chatto & Windus, 1965

Polunin, O. and Smithies, B.E., *Flowers of Southwest Europe, A Field Guide*, Oxford University Press, 1973

Ravenna, Pierfelice, 'Contributions to South American Amaryllidaceae I-IX', *Plant Life*, 24-38 (1968-82)

Rix, Martyn, 'Some Fritillaries and their Habitats', *Lilies 1978-9 and other Liliaceae*, 89-94 (1978)

Stebbins, G.L., *Variation and Evolution in Plants*, Columbia University Press, 1950

Stocken, C.M., *Andalucian Flowers and Countryside*, Thurleston, Devon, 1969

Storer, T.I. and Usinger, R.L., *Sierra Nevada Natural History*, University of California Press, 1963

Tutin *et al.* (eds.), *Flora Europaea*, notably vol. 5, Cambridge University Press, 1980

Veitch, J.E., *Hortus Veitchii*, Chelsea, 1906

Walter, H., Harnickell, E. and Mueller-Dombois, D., *Klimadiagram . . .*, Gustav Fischer Verlag, Stuttgart, 1975

Watson, J.M., 'Andes 1971 and 1972', *Bull. Alpine Gard. Soc.*, 42-5, in 15 parts (1974-7)

Webb, D.A., 'Flora Europaea — a Retrospect', *Taxon* 27(1):3-14 (1978)

Wilson, E.H., *The Lilies of Eastern Asia*, London, 1925

Chapter 5

Abbe, E., *The Plants of Vergil's Georgics*, New York, 1965

Allan, Mea, *E.A. Bowles and his Garden at Middleton House*, London, 1973

Anon, 'Dr Otto Stapf FRS', *Kew Bull. 1933*, 369-90 (1933)

Blunt, Wilfrid, *The Art of Botanical Illustration*, Collins, 1950

——, *Tulips and Tulipomania*, Basilisk Press, 1977

Boissier, E., *Flora Orientalis*, vol. I, Geneva, 1867

Bretschneider, E., *A History of Botanical Discoveries in China*, London, 1898

Coates, Alice, *The Quest for Plants*, London, 1969

Cotton, A.D., 'John Gilbert Baker', *Lily Year Book 1937*, 3-4 (1937)

Davis, P.H., '*Mediterranean and Turkish Itineraries*, *Notes R.B.G. Edinburgh*, 21 et seq. (1955-)

Derrick, C.F., 'Edward Whittall', *Bull. Alp. Gard. Soc.*, 43:240-1 (1975)

Desmond, Ray, *Dictionary of British and Irish Botanists and Horticulturists . . .*, London, 1977

Douglas, David, 'On . . . Calochortus', *Trans. Hort. Soc.*, VII:275-80 (1830)

Elwes, H.J., *Memoirs of Travel, Sport and Natural History*, London, 1930

Furse, Paul, 'Iran and Afghanistan 1964', *Journ. Roy. Hort. Soc.*, XC:462-75 and 504-9 (1965)

——, 'Afghanistan 1966', *Journ. Roy. Hort. Soc.*, XCIII (1968)

Hadfield, M., *A History of British Gardening*, London, 1979

Haw, S., 'Fritillaries in China', *Bull. Alp. Gard. Soc.* (1982)

Herbert, W., *Amaryllidaceae*, 1837, reprinted 1966

——, *Trans. Hort. Soc.*, III:187-96 (1820) and IV:43-7 (1822)

——, *A Dictionary of National Biography*, 26:234

Hunger, F.W.T., *Charles de L'Escluse*, 's-Gravenhage, 1927

Krelage, E.H., *Drie Eeuwen Bloembollenexport*, 's-Gravenhage, 1946

Le Lievre, A., *Miss Willmott of Warley Place*, London, 1980

Maclean, Fitzroy, *A Person from England*, London, 1938

Mahurin, Ken, Letter to editor re Purdy, *Pacific Hort.*, 54-6 (Fall 1981)

Mathew, B. and Baytop, A., *The Bulbs of Turkey* (in press)

Rix, Martyn, *The Art of the Botanist*, Lutterworth, 1981

Synge, H., 'Endangered Monocotyledons in Europe and S.W. Asia' in C.D. Brickell, D.F. Cutler and M. Gregory (eds.), *Petaloid Monocotyledons*, Academic Press, 1980

Takhtajan, Armen, *Rare and Vanishing Plants of the U.S.S.R., to be Protected*, Leningrad, 1981

Van Tubergen, C.G., *New Tuberous and Bulbous-rooted Plants Introduced by C.G. van Tubergen Ltd*, Haarlem, 1947

Chapter 6

Alkema, H.Y., 'Method for Rapid Vegetative Propagation of Fritillaria', *Lilies 1976*, 55-9 (1976)

Barton, I.B., 'The "Med." House', *Bull. Alpine Gard. Soc.*, 49:309-19 (1981)

Bowles, E.A., *A Handbook of Crocus and Colchicum for Gardeners*, 2nd edn, London, 1952

Evans, A., *The Peat Garden and its Plants*, Dent, 1974

Flint, G.J., 'Narcissus propagation using the chipping technique', *Daffodils* (in press)

Fox, D.B., 'The Propagation of Lilies', *The Plantsman*, 4(1):16-29 (1982)

Lloyd, C., *The Well-tempered Garden*, Collins, 1970

Ministry of Agriculture, 'Bulb Production', *Bulletin no. 62* (1964)

Tompsett, Andrew, '*Chincherinchee*', *Lilies and Related Plants* (in press)

Tompsett, A.A. and Eaton, H.J., 'Lily bulb production investigations at Rosewarne . . . Cornwall', *Lilies 1978-9*, 9-16 (1979)

Chapter 9

Buczaski, S. and Harris, K., *Collins Guide to the Pests, Diseases and Disorders of Garden Plants*, Collins, 1981

Eaton, H.J. and Tompsett, A.A. 'Avoiding Slug Damage to Lily Bulbs', *Lilies 1976*, 63-5 (1976)

Halstead, A.J., 'The Lily Beetle', *Lilies and Related Plants* (in press)

Henry Doubleday Research Association, *Newsletter 89*, Summer 1982

Ministry of Agriculture, *HPDI Diseases of Bulbs*, ADAS, 1979

Index

Achimenes 8, 147, 167
Aconitum volubile 9, 28, 135, 167
Aegean 57-8
Agapanthus 142, 148, 167
Aitchison, Surgeon-Major 106
Albury, Sydney 116
Algiers 68
Allen, James 109
Allium 15, 55, 63, 67, 74, 167; *akaka*
    65, 114; *aucheri* 104; *beesianum*
    17; *christophii* 110, 131; *evansiae*
    27; *insubricum* 17; *narcissiflorum*
    17; *paradoxum* 63
Alma Ata 66
Alophia lahue 78
Alrawia bellii 16, 168
Alstroemeria 28, 101, 168
Amanus mountains 61
Amaryllis 22, 77, 78, 101, 117, 143, 155,
    168; *advena* Fig. 5.6; *belladonna* 4;
    calyptrata 36, 86, Fig. 4.10; *candida*
    111; *evansiae* 27; *psitaccina* 36;
    rayneri 88; *solandrifolia* 22, Fig.
    2.5
Amaryllis caterpillar 161
Amorphophallus 91; *campanulatus*
    91; *titanum* 34
Anamur 61
Anatolia 63
Androcymbium 168; *europeum* 55;
    graminifolium 68; *psammophilum*
    68
Anemone 168; *blanda* 9, 57, 58, 126,
    127, 130, 133; *coronaria* 19, 55;
    heldreichii 104; *hortensis* 133;
    nemorosa 130; *pavonina* 19;
    tuberosa 75
Ankara 64
Ant dispersal of seeds 41
Anthericum 81; *torreyi* 75
Antholyza ringens 38
Antirrhinum 29
Ants 140
Aphids 139, 140, 142, 158, 163
Arbutus menziesii 72
Arisaema 47, 49, 169; *candidissimum*
    107, 129; *vulgare* 34
Arisarum proboscoideum 34, 55, 169
Aristolochia clematitis 34
Arthropodium candidum 46
Arum 41, 169; *creticum* 59, 111;
    italicum 127; *maculatum* 33;
    pictum 53; *pictum* Album 111
Arum flower-type 33

Ashkabad 66
Atacama desert 77
Attica 57
Aubriet 97
Aucher-Eloy, P.M.R. 104
Australia 84

'Badlands' 65
Baker, J.G. 109
Balansa, B. 104
Balearic Islands 53
Balkans, the 55
Balls, E.K. 114-15
Banks, Sir Joseph 97
Barneoudia major 78
Basal rot 165
Bauer, Francis 97
Bees, honey, as pollinators 25
Beirut 61
Belamcanda 29, 170
Bellevalia 39, 170; *longipes* 40;
    webbiana 55
Bertero, M.D. 101
Biarum davisii 59, 115, 170
Bird damage 163
Bird dispersal of seeds 41
Birds, as pollinators 22, 27, 28, 34-8,
    72, 74
Biskra 68
Black Sea coast, the 62
Blomfeld, Harry 111
Bloomeria crocea 72, 170
Blowflies, as pollinators 17, 34
Bluebell *see Hyacinthoides non-*
    scripta
Bogota 86
Boissier, Edmund 102
Bokhara 105, 110
Bomarea 28; *kalbreyrei* 42
Boophane disticha 99
Botrytis 80, 164-5
Bowles, E.A. 114
Brodiaea 74, 101, 138, 171; *coronaria*
    72; *douglasii* 71; *elegans* 72;
    hyacinthina 72, 73; *ida-maia* 72;
    laxa 72, 73; *lutea* 73; *minor* 72;
    minutiflora 73; *peduncularis* 73;
    pulchella 72, 73; *stellaris* 71;
    volubilis 120
Brunsvigia rosea 4, 22, 81, 134, 171
Buenos Aires 88
Bulb collecting 93
Bulb collecting today 118
Bulb frame, the 135

Index

Bulb frame, the shady 139
Bulbs: as bedding plants 131; in
    formal gardens 130; in herbaceous
    borders 132; in lawns 127; in
    mixed borders 133; in peat banks
    134; in pots 141; in rock gardens
    134; in tubs 142; in woodland 128;
    naturalised in grass 125; structure
    of 5
Bumble bees 16
Busbecq, Ogier Ghiselin de 93

Cabo de Gata 53
Calcareous woodland 129
California 69
Calochortus 85, 118, 138, 151, 171;
    albus 73, 101; *amoenus* 73;
    caeruleus 74; *clavatus* 73; *kennedyi*
    19, 75; *leichtlinii* 74; *luteus* 17, 72,
    101; *macrocarpus* 75, 101; *nuttallii*
    75, 101; *obispoensis* 73; *pulchellus*
    17, 39, 73, 101; *splendens* 72, 101;
    superbus 72, 73; *tolmei* 72;
    uniflorus 71; *venustus* 72, 73, 101;
    vestae 72; *weedii* 73
Calydorea speciosa 78
Camassia quamash 72, 101, 118, 171
Canarina: abyssinica 69; *canariensis*
    69; *eminii* 69
Canary Islands 68
Cape Peninsula 81
Cape Town 78
Cardiocrinum 172; *cordatum* 29, 98;
    giganteum 7, 29, 129
Casablanca 68
Caspian coast, the 62
Caucasus, the 62, 110, 112
Caucasian herb field, the 127
Ceanothus thyrsiflorus var. *repens* 70
Central Asia 66, 110
Chaparral 73
Chasmanthe 36
Chihuahua 85
Chile 75
China 48
Chionodoxa 60, 172; *albescens* 59;
    cretica 59; *gigantea* 112; *tmoli* 112
×*Chionoscilla allenii* 109
Chlorogalum pomeridianum 72
Claytonia 172; *lanceolata* 74;
    umbellata 74
Clivia caulescens 37, 172; *nobilis* 37
Clusius 94
Codonopsis vinciflora 135, 172
Cokvice 56
Colchicum 20, 41, 55, 119, 172;
    autumnale 44, 126; *autumnale* f.
    album 95; *bivonae* 59; *boissieri* 57;

corsicum 54; *kesselringii* 20, 105;
    kotschyi 104; *luteum* 21, 95;
    macrophyllum 59, 60; *parlatoris*
    57; *sibthorpii* 97; *speciosum* 20, 44,
    63, 119, 126, 139; *variegatum* 59
Colla, L.A. 101
Colocasia antiquorum 91
Conanthera bifolia 26, 78;
    campanulata 78
Conservation of bulbs today 118
Cooperia drummondii 101
Coquimbo 77
Corfu 56
Corms, structure of 8
Cornus nuttallii 72
Corsica 53-4
Corydalis 95, 172; *aitchisonii* 106;
    cava 28; *macrocentra* 28; *rutifolia*
    65; *solida* 57, 65, 130
Costus 91
Crete 59
Crinum 22, 41, 43, 49, 91, 173; *moorei*
    22; *natans* 91
Crocus 20, 41, 55, 102, 108, 116, 120,
    141, 142, 152, 173; *adanensis* 61;
    alatavicus 20, 110; *aleppicus* 119;
    ancyrensis 65; *antalyensis* 60;
    autrani 63; *baytopiorum* 60;
    biflorus 55, 60; *biflorus* subsp.
    adami 65; *biflorus* subsp.
    melantherus 57; *biflorus* subsp.
    pulchricolor 60; *boryi* 57; *boulosii*
    67; *cambessedesii* 53; *cancellatus*
    20, 60, 119; *candidus* 60;
    carpetanus 52; *caspius* 63, 110;
    chrysanthus 58, 60; *clusii* 95;
    corsicus 54; *cvijicii* 56; *dalmaticus*
    56; *danfordiae* 60, 108; *etruscus*
    55; *fleischeri* 60; *gargaricus* 60;
    goulimyi 57; *hadriaticus* 57;
    imperati 55; *karduchorum* 104;
    korolkowii 20; *kosaninii* 56;
    kotschyanus 20, 65, 104; *laevigatus*
    57; *malyi* 56; *medius* 54; *minimus*
    53-4; *nevadensis* 52; *niveus* 57;
    nudiflorus 126; *olivieri* 56;
    olivierii subsp. *balansae* 60;
    pallasii 60, 97; *pelistericus* 56;
    sativus 93; *scardicus* 56; *scharojani*
    20, 63, 110; *sieberi* 56; *sieberi*
    subsp. *atticus* 57; *sieberi* subsp.
    sieberi 59; *speciosus* 20, 63, 110,
    126; *thomasii* 56; *tommasinianus*
    56, 125; *tournefortii* 58, 59, 97;
    vallicola 20, 63, 121-2, 126, 139;
    veluchensis 56; *vernus* 125;
    versicolor 54
Crocus flower 19

Cutworms 161
Cyclamen 12, 41, 98, 173; balearicum
    53; cilicium 130; cilicium var.
    intaminatum 114; coum 61, 63, 130;
    coum subsp. elegans 63; creticum
    59; graecum 12; hederifolium 12;
    libanoticum 119; neapolitanum
    130; parviflorum 63; persicum 59;
    pseudibericum 61, 130;
    purpurascens 12; repandum 57, 59;
    rohlfsianum 67
Cyclamen-type flower 25
Cypella: aquatilis 88; herbertii 88
Cyrtanthus 22, 173; mackenii 22;
    obliquus 22, 36

Dactylorhiza foliosa 1
Dahlia 134, 156, 173; coccinea 85;
    imperialis 85; merkii 85; scapigera
    f. merkii 85
Dalmatian coast 56
Davidia, Pere Armand 106
Davidi involucrata 106
Davis, Peter 115
Delavay, Pierre 107
Delphinium 173; californicum 113;
    cardinale 113; nudicaule 113
Dendrobium nobile 8
Desfontainea 101
Dicentra 74, 173; pauciflora 74;
    uniflora 74
Dichelostemma ida-maia 36, 174
Dierama 17, 84, 174; pendulum 84;
    pulcherrimum 84
Dietes bicolor 32
Dioscorides 97
Dodecatheon meadia 25, 174
Douglas, David 100
Dracunculus canariensis 68, 174;
    vulgaris 34
Drakensberg, the 82
Drimia 91, 174; haworthoides 7

Eliovson, Sima 117
Elwes, H.J. 108
Eminium albertii 105, 174
Epigeal germination 151, Fig. 8.1
Eremostachys 67, 175; speciosa 28
Eremurus 63, 66, 67, 119, 175;
    cristatus 14; furseorum 116;
    lactiflorus 39; olgae 15, 106;
    regelii 14; spectabilis 14
Erythronium 26, 74, 175; americanum
    129; californicum 73, 74; dens-
    canis 44, 126; helenae 73;
    hendersonii 74, 135; montanum
    74; oregonum 46; purpurascens 74;
    revolutum 46, 72, 129;
    tuolumnense 73, 135

Erzurum 64
Escallonia rubra var. macrantha 101
Euboea 58
Eucharis amazonica 147, 175; candida
    Fig. 3.2, 42
Eucomis 81, 147, 175
Euphorbia apios 57
Eurycles 91, 175; amboinensis Fig.
    9.1; cunninghamii Fig. 4.13
Eustephia coccinea 76, Fig. 4.5, 175

Fedtschenko, Alexei 105, 106
Fedtschenko, Boris A. 106
Fedtschenko, Olga 106
Feeding bulbs 138
Fethiye 60
Forcing bulbs for Christmas flowering
    142
Forrest, George 107
Fort Worth 85
France, southern 54
Freesia 81, 175
Fritillaria 21, 49, 55, 118, 141, 142,
    152, 154, 176; acmopetala 61, 104,
    135; acmopetala subsp. wendelboi
    61, 116; affinis 16, 71, 72, 120;
    agrestis 72; alburyana 65, 116;
    alfredae subsp. glaucoviridis 61;
    amabilis 140; armena 39, 65;
    assyriaca 65; aurea 61; biflora 17,
    72; bithynica 60; bucharica 67;
    camschatcensis 7, 17, 46, 118, 135;
    carica 58; collina 63; crassifolia 60;
    crassifolia subsp. hakkarensis 65;
    crassifolia subsp. kurdica 65;
    davidii 106; davisii 57, 115;
    eduardii 105, 110; ehrhartii 58;
    elwesii 61, 108, 115; epirotica 115;
    euboeica 58; forbesii 115; gentneri
    36; gibbosa 106; glauca 74;
    glaucoviridis 114; graeca 17, 57,
    58; graeca subsp. thessala 56;
    gussichae 56; hermonis ssp. amana
    114; imperialis 7, 95, 155;
    involucrata 54; japonica 140;
    kotschyana 63, 104; latifolia 16,
    63, 127; liliacea 7, 71, 118;
    lusitanica 52; macedonica 56;
    maximowiczii 105; meleagris 7, 16,
    41, 44, 126, 130; messanensis 55,
    57, 58; messanensis subsp. gracilis
    56; michailovskyi 65; obliqua 58;
    olivieri 114; pallidiflora 67, 105,
    135; persica 95, 96, 155; pinardi
    60, 65; pluriflora 72; pontica 59,
    130; purdyi 74, 113; pyrenaica 17,
    126; raddeana 67, 110, 116;
    recurva 17, 36, 74; reuteri 104;

Index

rhodia 59; *rhodocanakis* 58; *severtzovii* 67; *sibthorpiana* 97; *striata* 72; *thunbergii* 98, 119, 154; *tubiformis* 54; *tuntasia* 58; *uva-vulpis* 116; *viridea* 73; *whittallii* 61, 112
Fritillaria-type flower 16
Furse, Admiral and Mrs Paul 115

Gagea 66, 67, 176; *bithynica* 60; *graeca* 57
Galanthus 152, 176; *allenii* 109; 'Atkinsii' 109; *elwesii* 95; *fosteri* 111; *ikariae* 63; *nivalis* subsp. *reginae-olgae* 55; *rizehensis* 63
Galtonia viridiflora Fig. 6.1, 176
Gargano 55
Garrya elliptica 101
Gaultheria shallon 71
Gentiana 176; *olivieri* 67, 136; *pyrenaica* 56
Gethyllis 81, 177
Gladiolus 81, 91, 99, 177; *byzantinus* × *cardinalis* 111; *callianthus* 23, Fig. 2.4, 147; *cardinalis* 102; *citrinus* 28; *colvillei* 102; *gandavensis* 102; *natalensis* × *oppositifolius* 102; *orchidiflorus* 28; *papilio* 17, 84; *stellatus* 15, 28; *tristis* 102
Gloriosa 24, 177; *superba* Fig. 2.6, 91, 146
Gourlay, W. Balfour 114-15
Graeber, P.L. 110
Greece 55
Greek mountains 58
Grey-Wilson, Christopher 116
Gundelscheimer, D.A. 97
Gymnospermium alberti 105, 177
Gynandriris sisyrinchium 55, 177
Gypsophila paniculata 40

Habranthus andicola 77, 177
Haemanthus 35, 177; *coccineus* 99, Fig. 5.3
Hall, Sir Daniel 114
Hawkins, John 97
Hawkmoths, as pollinators 22, 23, 24
Hedychium 91, 178; *coronarium* 91; *gardnerianum* 132
Heldreich, Theodore de 104
Helleborus vesicarius 40
Henry, Augustine 107
Herbert, Hon. William 102
Hermodactylus tuberosus 32, 178
Hesperocallis undulata 22, 75
Hewer, Prof. Tom 116

Himalayas 48
Hippeastrum: elwesii 108; *puniceum* 4
Honaz Dag 60
Hover-flies, as pollinators 22
Humming birds, as pollinators 17, 34
Hyacinthella pallens 56, 178
Hyacinthoides non-scripta 16, 43, 44, 130, 178
Hyacinthus 93, 142, 178; *orientalis* 6, 65; 'Rosalie' 143
Hymenocallis 85, 179; *calathina* Fig. 7.1; *fragrans* Fig. 7.2
Hymettus 57
Hypogeal germination 151, Fig. 8.1
Hypoxis 91, 179; *mexicana* 75; *pusilla* 47; *rooperi* Fig. 2.1

Iberian peninsula 51
Insect-pollinated flowers 14
Iphigenia novae-zelandiae 47
Iran, northern 63
Iris 63, 66, 116, 152, 179; *afghanica* 31, 116; *aitchisonii* 106; *attica* 33; *aucheri* 65, 104; *bakeriana* 109; *barnumae* 110; *caucasica* 40, 65,; *cycloglossa* 32, 116; *danfordiae* 29, 31, 65, 108, 111, 143; *drepanophylla* 32; *elegantissima* 31, 65; *foetidissima* 42; *fosteriana* 32; *fulva* 36; *gatesii* 31, 111; *graeberiana* 110; *heweri* 116; *histrio* 61, 110; *histrioides* 127; *histrioides major* 111, 143; *hymenospatha* 116; *juncea* 55; *kolpakowskiana* 31; *kumaonensis* 33; *kuschkensis* 116; *latifolia* 32, 44, 126; *macrosiphon* 33; *magnifica* 33; *missouriensis* 75; *nepalensis* Fig. 1.1; *nicolai* 33; *pallasii* 97; *pamphylica* 32, 61; *paradoxa* 31, 65; *persica* 33, 40, 65; *pinardii* 65; *planifolia* 33, 53; *pseudacorus* 41; *pseudocaucasica* 65; *purdyi* 113; *reticulata* 6, 31, 65, 141, 142, 143, 163, 164; *rosenbachiana* 110; *sari* 65; *serotina* 32; *setosa* 32, 41; *sibirica* 132; *sofarana* 110; *spuria* 132; *stenophylla* 65; *stenophylla* subsp. *allisonii* 61; *susiana* 95; *tingitana* 68; *tubergeniana* 110; *unguicularis* 33; *urmiensis* 110; *vartani* 110; *warleyensis* 109, 110; 'Wedgewood' 6; *wendelboi* 116; *willmottiana* 109; *winogradowii* 127; *xiphium* 6, 95
Isoloma 8
Italy 54

Ixia 81, 179
Ixiolirion pallasii 97, 179

Japan 47-8
Jebel el Akdar 67

Kabul 67
Kaempfer, Engelbert 97
Kaempferia 91
Karroo, the 80, 81
Karst 56
Kesselring, J. 105
Kotschy, Theodore 104
Kronenburg, A. 110

Labelling bulbs 138
Lachenalia 81, 141, 179; *aloides* 36,
   81; *bulbifera* 36, 81; *mutabilis* 16;
   orchioides 16, 81 : *pendula* 147;
   tricolor 147
Lancaster, Roy 49
Lapageria 101
Lapiedra martinesii 53, 68
Las Pas 87
Lebanon 61
Leichtlin, Max 109
Leichtlinia protuberans 109
Leontice leontopetalum 40, 180
Leucocoryne ixiodes Fig. 4.6
Leucocrinum montanum 75, 180
Leucojum aestivum 3, 41, 44, 125,
   180; *autumnale* 55; *fontianum* 68;
   longiflorum 54; *nicaense* 54;
   roseum 54; *trichophyllum* 68;
   vernum 127, 128, 152
Ligozzi, Jacobo 95
Lilium 49, 93, 142, 152, 156, 180;
   arboricola 107; *auratum* 47, 142,
   151; *bolanderi* 36, 73; *brownii* 49;
   brownii var. *australe* Fig. 8.1;
   canadense 45, 129, 165; *candidum*
   (Madonna lily) 7, 22, Fig. 2.3,
   60; *carniolicum* 56; *ciliatum* 115;
   columbianum 71; *concolor* 97;
   davidii 106; *davidii* var.
   willmottiae 109; *formosanum* var.
   pricei 49, 108, 135; *grayi* 36;
   heldreichii 104; *henryi* 107, 165;
   humboldtii 46, 74, 108; *japonicum*
   47; *kelloggii* 72; *lancifolium* 47, 97;
   ledebourii 63; *leucanthum* 107;
   longiflorum 48, 49; *macklinae* 135;
   maritimum 36, 71; *martagon* 24,
   44, 126, 127, 130; *monadelphum*
   44, 63, 130; *nanum* 16;
   neilgherrense 49, Fig. 8.1;
   nepalense Fig. 4.2; *pardalinum* 7,
   46, 72, 74, 129; *pardalinum*
   'Shuksan' 129; *parryi* 46, 74;

parvum 74;
philippinense 49; *pomponium* 54;
   pyrenaicum 24, 44, 126; *regale*
   21, 29, 107, 131; *rubellum* 47;
   rubescens 22, 72, 73; *sherrifiae*
   16, 108; *souliei* 16; *speciosum*
   47, 97, 142; *superbum* 45, 129,
   165; *szovitzianum* 127;
   wallichianum 108;
   washingtonianum 22, 73
Lily beetle 160
Lily flower 21
Limestone 68, 80, 106
Limnanthes douglasii 101
Lobb, William 101
Ludlow, Frank 107
Lusaka 90
Lycoris 49, 180; *aurea* 47, Fig. 4.1;
   sanguinea 47; *squamigera* 140

Madeira 68
Madrid 52
Mahonia aquifolium 101
Mani, the 57
Manissadjian, J.J. 111
Marseilles 54
Masson, Francis 98-9
Massonia 81, 181
Mathew, Brian 116
Maw, George 108
Maximowicz, Carl 105
Meadow garden 125-6
Mediterranean climate 43, 50, 57, 59
Mediterranean house, the 140
Mendosa 87
Merendera pyrenaica 52, 181
Meristem culture 156
Mexico 85
Mexico City 85
Mice 162
Milla biflora 75
Mimicry, in seeds, 42
Mimulus aurantiacus 72
Mohammed II 93
Moles 162
Moraea 81, 91, 181; *spathulata* 84;
   villosa 32
Mountain, W.C. 112-13
Muchuchies 87
Muilla maritima 72
Muscari 15, 152, 181; *armeniacum* 65;
   aucheri 104; *chalusicum* 63, 116;
   comosum 16; *gussoni* 55;
   latifolium 59; *macrocarpum* 95

Nairobi 89
Narcissus 6, 131, 181; *asturiensis* 52;

Index

bulbocodium 68, 126; 'Cragford'
143; *cyclamineus* 126, 128; *elegans*
55; *hedreanthus* 52; *humilis* 53;
'Ice Follies' 143; *longispathus* 52;
marvieri 68; *nobilis* 52; 'Paper
White' 142, 143; *papyraceus* 52;
poeticus 125, 126; *pseudonarcissus*
51, 125; *rupicola* 52, 68; *serotinus*
53, 60; 'Soleil d'Or' 142, 143;
tazetta 94, 95; *triandrus* 52, 126;
viridiflorus 53; *wateri* 68
Narcissus flies 161
Nemastylis tenuis 75, 181
Nerine bowdenii 84, 134, 148, 182;
bowdenii var. *wellsii* 84; *sarniensis*
81, 84, 148
New Zealand 46-7
Nomocharis 46, 182; *basilissa* 107;
farreri 107
North Africa 67
North-eastern America 45
North-western Europe 44
Notholirion 7, 22, 49, 182

Onion-type flower 15
Ornithogalum 15, 81, 182; *nutans* 126
Ostrovskia magnifica 67, 182
Ovary, subterranean 19, 21, Table
2.1, 31, 32
Oxalis 81, 182; *adenophylla* 108;
natans 3; *tuberosum* 88

Pacific north-west 46
Pallas, P.S. 97
Palmyra 61
Pamianthe 88; *cardenasii* 86
Pancratium 85, 91, 182; *canariense* 68;
foetidum 68; *illyricum* 54;
maritimum 23, 95; *trianthum* 68
Papaver rhoeas 19
Paris polyphylla 42, 135, 183
Peloponnese, the 56, 115
Peshawar 67
Petropolis 87
Phaedranassa carmioli Fig. 2.9, 36,
183
Phaeomeria magnifica 91
Pinus ponderosa 73
Pinus radiata 101
Placea arzae 30, 36, 183
Pleione 183; *bulbocodioides* 49;
forrestii 49; *humilis* 49; *pricei* 108
Polunin, Oleg 115
Port Elizabeth 78
Price, W.R. 108
Primula fedtschenkoi 11, 67, 106, 183
Propagation of bulbs 150; by cuttings
155; by seed 150; vegetative 152

Przewalsk 66, 105
Przewalski, N.M. 105
Pseudotsuga menziesii 101
Purdy, Carl 113, 118
Puschkinia 41, 183; *scilloides* 65

Quercus coccifera 120

Ranunculus 184; *acetocellifolius* 52;
asiaticus 11, 19, 59, 67; *ficaria* 11;
kochii 65
Recife 87
Red spider 140, 148, 158
Regel, Albert von 105
Regel, Edward von 105
Rhodes 59
Rhodohypoxis 84, 184
Rhodophiala 184
Ribes sanguineum 101
Rigidella 36, 184
Rock, Joseph 107
Roderick, Wayne 117
Romulea 54, 81, 184; *bulbocodium*
57; *clusiana* 94
Roscoea 29, 184

Saffron 93
Salang Pass 67
Samarkhand 20, 66, 106, 109, 111
S. Antonio 87
San Diego 70
San Francisco 70
Sardinia 53-4
Savannah 43, 80, 90
Saxifraga: *cernua* 8; *erioblasta* 8;
granulata 8
Scadoxus 91, 184; *cinnabarinus* Fig.
3.1; *nutans* Fig. 4.8
Scilla 53, 91, 185; *armena* 65; *bifolia*
14, 57, 126, 127; *cordifolia* 26;
furseorum 116; *hohenackeri* 26;
lilio-hyacinthus 8; *litardierei* 56;
peruviana 15, 55; *sibirica* 17, 65;
verna 15
Scilla-type flower 14
Seed dispersal 39, 42; by ants 41; by
birds 41; by water 40; by wind 39
Seed viability 150
Serpentine rock 57, 60
Sherriff, George 107
Sibthorp, J. 97
Sicily 55
Sierra de Cazorla 52
Sierra de Guaderrama 52
Sierra Nevada 52
Slugs 137, 157
Smith, J.E. 97
Snow patches 65

Index

South Africa 78
Sparaxis tricolor 19, 185
Spiloxene 81, 185; *capensis* 19
Spokane 70
Spraying bulbs 139
Sprekelia formosissima 36, 95, Fig.
    5.1, 185
Stapf, Otto 109
Stenomesson peruvianum 89, Fig.
    4.11, 185; *variegatum* 36, Fig. 2.10
Steppe 39, 63
Sternbergia 185; *candida* 60, 115, 119;
    clusiana 20, 95; *lutea* 55, 57, 67
Styrax officinalis 69
Suleiman the Magnificent 93
Sun-birds, as pollinators 34, 36, 147
Synge, Patrick 115
Syria 61

Tashkent 20
Tauros mountains 61
Tecophilaea cyanocrocus 77, 101, 136,
    186
Temperate climates 44
Tender bulbs in a Mediterranean
    house 148
Tender bulbs in pots 145
'Terra rossa' 56, 57
Thunberg, Carl 98
Tigridia 85, 88, 186; *galanthoides* 17,
    85; *meleagris* 17, Fig. 2.2, 85;
    pavonina 85, Fig. 4.9, 147
Tournefort, J.P. de 97
Trachyandra falcata 82
Treatment of collected bulbs 122
Trillium 41, 44, 45, 186; *cernuum* 135;
    chloropetalum 71, 72; *erectum* 135;
    grandiflorum 41, 43, 129; *ovatum*
    72; *rivale* 41, 135; *sessile* 41, 129;
    tricolorum 141
Tritonia 91, 186; *aurea* 42;
    ×*crocosmiflora* 8; *paniculata* 37
Tropaeolum 186; *azureum* 77, 101;
    polyphyllum 77; *speciosum* 77,
    101; *tricolorum* 77; *tuberosum* 88,
    135
Tropical Africa 89
Tropical Asia 91
Tropical South America 85
Tubers, structure of 9
Tulbaghia 91, 186
Tulipa 6, 21, 63, 66, 67, 187;
    aucheriana 104; *australis* 54, 57;
    clusiana 95; *cretica* 59; *eichleri* 110;
    fosteriana 110; *gesnerana* 95, 126;
    goulimyi 57; *greigi* 105, 110;
    hoogiana 110; *humilis* 65; *juliae* 65;
    kaufmanniana 110; *orphanidea* 60;

praestans 105, 110; *saxatilis* 59;
    sprengeri 111, 126; *sylvestris* 126;
    whittallii 112
Tulip fire 164
Tulip-type flowers 19
Turkish mainland 59
Turkish Mediterranean coast 60
Turk's cap lily 23

Ullucus tuberosa 89
Ulu Dag 60
Ungernia 67, 187
Urginea 81, 187; *maritima* 15, 93;
    noctiflora 68

Vagaria olivieri 68, 187; *parviflora*
    Fig. 4.3
Valdivia 77
Valparaiso 77
Van 64, 65
Vegetative propagation 152; by bulbils
    152; by cutting 154; by scaling
    154-5; by splitting 152; by stolons
    152; by twin-scaling 154-5
Veitch 101
Veldt 43
Veltheimia bracteata 36, 48, 187
Vine weevils 160
Virus 163

Wachendorfia thyrsiflora 15
Wasps, as pollinators 17
Water disposal of seeds 40
Watering bulbs 138
Watson, John 116
Watsonia 81, 148, 187
Wendelbo, Per 116
Whittall, Edward 111
Whiteheadia 81
Willmott, Ellen Ann 108
Wilson, E.H. 107
Wind dispersal of seeds 39
Wind-pollinated flowers 13
Worsleya rayneri Fig. 4.12, 187

Yellowstone Park 70
Yosemite 70
Yucca whipplei 73
Yugoslavia 56

Zantedeschia Fig. 4.7, 147, 188
Zephyranthes 85, 188; *longifolia* 75
Zigadenus 15, 85, 188; *racemosus* 71
Zigana pass 20
Zingiber officinale 91
Zygomorphic flower 27-9, 36